THE NOVELS OF SAMUEL BECKETT

THE NOVELS OF
SAMUEL BECKETT

By

JOHN FLETCHER

Second Edition

1970
CHATTO & WINDUS
LONDON

Published by
Chatto and Windus Ltd
42 William IV Street
London W.C. 2
★
Clarke, Irwin and Co. Ltd
Toronto

SBN 7011 0695 6

First published 1964
Second Edition 1970

Printed in Great Britain by
Lewis Reprints Limited
Port Talbot, Glamorgan

For Beryl

e reducemi a ca per questo calle

CONTENTS

PREFACE

In the meantime the voice continues. . . .

THE UNNAMABLE

THIS book is an attempt to provide a convenient and helpful guide to Samuel Beckett's fiction, by tracing (in three phases) the evolution of the hero in his novels and the development of his style in English and French from the first manuscript *Dream of Fair to Middling Women* to the most recent work *How It Is*.

Since unwieldy apparatus would be out of place in a general work of this kind, quotations are not usually provided with page numbers, footnotes are generally avoided, and the list of criticism is kept to a minimum. On the other hand, the bibliography of Samuel Beckett's novels is as near as possible complete; it should clarify less well-known aspects of his activity. My broad aim has been not to seek any specious explanation of the fiction but simply to assist the interested reader in exploring it for himself. I have consulted the work of several other critics, whom I enumerate in my bibliography, and have also benefited from Mr. Beckett's courtesy and generosity. He was kind enough to lend me the typescripts of two of what he calls *faux départs*, *Dream of Fair to Middling Women* and *Mercier et Camier*, and to permit quotations from them, to translate extracts from the last-named as well as from *Textes pour rien* and *Comment C'est*, and to answer in interview or by letter the biographical and bibliographical questions I put to him. He has not, however, influenced my interpretation in any way and I know he would wish me to insist that it is an entirely personal one, for which I am solely responsible.

Nevertheless, I should like to record my gratitude to him for his assistance, as well as my thanks to Professor V. Dupont of Toulouse University, whose encouragement and help first enabled me to undertake the research studies over which he has kept an interested and benevolent eye ever since. I should also like to thank Mrs. Maria Jolas, Mme. Geneviève Serreau, Mme. Yasushi Tanaka, M. Jérôme Lindon, M. Pierre Coustillas and many other friends and acquaintances for information and help of various

9

kinds. Moreover, the staffs of several libraries have assisted in securing periodicals and furnishing photostats of rare material: in this connection I especially wish to thank Mr. F. Lissauer of London and Miss R. Allen of Princeton. Finally I owe much to my wife; to my mother, for help in typing; and to my brother for valuable comments on parts of the book read in manuscript.

All translations of Beckett's French are his own or done in collaboration as indicated in the bibliography, and other translations from French are my own.

J. F.

Thanks are due to the following authors and publishers for kind permission to reproduce copyright material as indicated:

To Mr. Lawrence Durrell and Messrs. Faber and Faber Ltd. for a quotation from *Justine*; to Mr. T. S. Eliot and Messrs. Faber and Faber Ltd. for quotations from *Ash-Wednesday* and *The Waste Land* in *Collected Poems*; to Mr. Samuel Beckett and Messrs. Chatto and Windus Ltd. for quotations from *More Pricks than Kicks*; to Mr. Beckett and Messrs. John Calder Ltd. for quotations from *Proust, Murphy, Watt, Molloy, Malone Dies, The Unnamable, How It Is, The Vulture, Enueg I* and *Cascando II*; to Mr. Beckett and Les Editions de Minuit, Paris, for quotations in French from *Murphy, Molloy, Malone meurt, L'Innommable, Nouvelles et Textes pour rien*, and *Comment C'est*; to Mr. Beckett and Grove Press, Inc., New York, for quotations from items first published in numbers of the *Evergreen Review*, viz., *From an Abandoned Work* (vol. 1, no.3), *Text for Nothing I* (vol. 3, no. 9), *From an Unabandoned Work* (vol. 4, no. 14), *The End* (vol. 4, no. 15) and *The Expelled* (vol. 6, no. 22); to Messrs. Routledge and Kegan Paul Ltd. for a quotation from *Tractatus Logico-Philosophicus* by L. Wittgenstein, and to Penguin Books Ltd. for quotations from *Plato: The Last Days of Socrates*, translated by H. Tredennick.

Toulouse, New Year 1963

Part One

THE HERO AS CITIZEN

ASSUMPTION
About 1929

DREAM OF FAIR TO MIDDLING WOMEN
About 1932

MORE PRICKS THAN KICKS
Before 1934

MURPHY
Before 1938

Chapter 1

BELACQUA

Ceux d'entre nous dont la loi du développement est purement interne. . . .

M. PROUST

. . . . A very sad animal indeed.

MORE PRICKS THAN KICKS

BORN in 1906 of middle-class Protestant parents at Foxrock near Dublin, Samuel Barclay Beckett went from Portora Royal School, Ulster, to Trinity College, Dublin, in 1923, where A. A. Luce, the co-editor of Berkeley, was his tutor.[1] He read English, French and Italian and his outstanding scholastic ability was soon made evident by a series of examination successes. In 1926 he was elected to a Foundation Scholarship in Modern Languages, and in the B.A. final examination, held late in 1927, was the First Moderator in the First Class in Modern Literature, winning a large gold medal, the prize regularly awarded for exceptional merit. He was by then fully expected to take up an academic career. As a step in this direction, he was awarded a research prize of £50, and later submitted a research essay (on the *Unanimistes*) as the conditions of the grant required.

The degree of Bachelor of Arts was conferred on him in December 1927, soon after the Moderatorship examination, followed by the M.A. degree in December 1931. He spent the first two terms of 1928 teaching at Campbell College, Belfast, before embarking in October 1928 on a two-year *stage* as *lecteur d'anglais* at the Ecole Normale Supérieure in Paris. This post was offered as part of the regular exchange scheme operating between Trinity and the Ecole Normale, and was undertaken by Beckett as a preliminary

---

[1] Mr. Beckett has kindly added for me the following information to the usual *curriculum vitae* given of him: Kindergarten, Miss Ida Elsner's Academy, Stillorgan, Co. Dublin; Prep. School, Earlsfort House School, Dublin (day boy); first trip abroad, Summer 1926, Tours, France; second trip, Summer 1927, Florence.

13

to a professional appointment. This came in September 1930, when he was elected to the newly-created post of Lecturer in . French and assistant to the Professor of Romance Languages at Dublin. His tenure of the Lectureship was due to last in the first instance for three years, but he resigned after only four terms, that is to say in December 1931. Earlier in the same year his excellent study of Proust had been published by Chatto and Windus, but Beckett chose nonetheless at this time to turn his back on a university career. His stay in Paris had not only enabled him to meet Joyce (whom he went to see in 1928, on taking up the *lecteur* post) and become a member of the small circle of people who were admitted into Joyce's friendship, but also to launch himself as a creative writer. The first items he had published were a now well-known essay on *Work in Progress* and a short story, *Assumption*. Both appeared in the June 1929 number of Eugene Jolas' review *Transition*.

Assumption is important to the present study as being Beckett's first piece of fiction. It is not long, and tells simply of an anonymous young man who, through the catalytic agency of a woman's devotion, achieves release into nirvana, and becomes

irretrievably engulfed in the light of eternity, one with the birdless cloudless colourless skies, in infinite fulfilment.

These words were prophetic of much that was to come in Beckett's fiction, from Murphy's retreat into his 'dark' to the Unnamable's exploration of the wastes of his limbo, but at the time they gave rise to little of importance until the appearance in early 1932 (in *Transition*, no. 21) of a prose text entitled *Sedendo et Quiescendo*, which for the first time introduced a young man called Belacqua. This text was in fact an extract from a much longer work, *Dream of Fair to Middling Women*, written in Paris about 1932 and subsequently laid aside in favour of the group of ten short stories which developed out of it, issued in early 1934 by Chatto and Windus under the general title *More Pricks than Kicks*. It was therefore not until that year that the general public was offered the complete saga of the first of all the Beckettian heroes, Belacqua Shuah.

Dream of Fair to Middling Women, the typescript of which has apparently vanished, was written after Beckett's resignation from Trinity, during the period he spent travelling in various countries in Europe before finally making Paris his home. It is a novel consisting of two long chapters, the first of which is set largely in Vienna and Paris, and deals with two women, the Smeraldina-Rima and the Syra-Cusa; the second takes place in Dublin, where the heroine is the Alba. The manuscript then tails off, at the end of an episode which was to become the fourth story (*A Wet Night*) in *More Pricks than Kicks*. Another passage from the manuscript novel became *The Smeraldina's Billet Doux*, the eighth story of the 1934 collection, and we have already noted the excerpt that was published separately as *Sedendo et Quiescendo* in *Transition*.

Thus, Beckett's first novel, left unfinished, served as a depository from which most of the best items were taken for use elsewhere. In itself it is a rambling, discursive story with little unity of purpose or theme ('the only unity in this story', says Beckett, 'is please God, an involuntary unity'), an extended exercise in fiction, and the result is on the one hand repetition (two versions of the same passage occur, for instance, within fifty pages of each other) and on the other occasional obscurity, as in certain passages like *Sedendo et Quiescendo*, which is an impressionistic account, coloured by neologisms and foreign expressions and written in a racy rhythm, of the bustle following on Belacqua's arrival in Vienna to visit his lady-love the Smeraldina-Rima. Those curious to do so may look this episode up in *Transition*, where they will form an adequate impression of the tone and style of the whole.

Together with much experimental material of this sort, several interesting passages were also suppressed when the *Dream* was re-written as *More Pricks than Kicks*. The former alone contains, for instance, a splendid piece of parody, the love-letter from the rugby-playing Jem Higgins (who is mentioned in *A Wet Night*) to the aloof intellectual Alba, and a lively description of the 'Polar Bear' on a shopping expedition in Dublin, as well as several pages of sparkling dialogue. The title of the novel was, however, preserved even after revision: it occurs in a story of the later collection called *What a Misfortune*. Walter Draffin, 'Italianate Irishman', formerly cicisbeo to Mrs. Bridie bboggs, now a bureaucrat in the Land Commission, is the author of a work 'held up in the *limæ labor* stage' for many years but eventually to appear under the title *Dream of Fair to Middling Women*. It is typical of Beckett's sense of humour that he should thus father on an ineffectual character like Walter Draffin one of his own abandoned compositions.

The title, which indeed may seem rather odd, is a parody of Tennyson's *Dream of Fair Women* and Chaucer's *Legend of Good Women*; it is therefore not surprising to find the prologue to Chaucer's poem quoted at the head of Beckett's manuscript (the irony implicit in the original becomes explicit through his replacement of 'and' by 'but'):

> A thousand sythes have I herd men telle,
> That ther is Ioye in heven, and peyne in helle;
> But—

Apart from referring to Chaucer and Tennyson, Beckett may also, in framing his title, have been debunking the novel Henry Williamson first published in 1924, *Dream of Fair Women* (third part of *The Flax of Dream*); it is interesting to note in this connection that Williamson's novel contains a letter written by the mistress of the effete and melancholy hero which, in form at least, resembles the Smeraldina's *Billet Doux*.

The title of *More Pricks than Kicks* is, on the other hand, an obvious (perhaps obscene) play on the words Saul heard on the Damascus Road; and *sedendo et quiescendo anima efficitur prudens* is an Aristotelian dictum said to have been quoted by Belacqua (traditionally a slothful Florentine lute-maker) when Dante reproached him with his idleness: 'it is by sitting and resting that the soul grows wise'; to which Dante is supposed to have answered: 'if it is by resting that one becomes wise, there can be no-one wiser than you'. We notice further that the choice of these titles not only reveals Beckett's taste for allusion but also the influence of his university studies: the works of Chaucer, Tennyson and Dante to which he refers were all on the syllabus of study for the examinations he took at Dublin between 1924 and 1927.

The full name of the hero of these early works is Belacqua Shuah. His surname seems to be taken from *Genesis*: Shuah was the maternal grandfather of the notorious and ill-fated Onan. (One of the sons of Abraham and Keturah was also called Shuah.) Belacqua is of course the Florentine who appears in the fourth

16

canto of Dante's *Purgatorio* as one of the late-repentant, that is one of those who have postponed until the last moment their reconciliation with God. They have avoided hell by doing so, but they are obliged to suffer in Antepurgatory a period of idle waiting equal in time to that of their lives spent on earth, before being allowed to enter Purgatory itself where they will toil up the mountain to atone for their sins. In the canto in question, Virgil has just explained to the weary Dante that he should not think of resting until he has reached the end of the road, when a voice is heard saying in a mocking tone:

> *Forse*
> *che di sedere in pria avrai distretta !*

– 'perhaps before then you'll be glad of a rest'. The two poets notice on their left hand a huge rock in the shadow of which people are lounging. One of them, Belacqua the Florentine, is sitting down, tired out, his head drooping between his knees. He seems to Dante even lazier than if he were brother to sloth herself:

> *più negligente*
> *che se pigrizia fosse sua serocchia –*

and Belacqua, turning his head without raising his eyes much above his thigh, mocks Dante with the words:

> *or va tu su, che se' valente !*

Dante smiles gently at this abruptness of manner and says he is pleased to see that his erstwhile friend has at least escaped damnation. In reply to the poet's questions, Belacqua says he must relive here the period of his earthly life, unless there arise from a heart in a state of grace prayers for his release from this penalty imposed for his procrastination. What the editor Natalino Sapegno calls *l'intelligenza di Belacqua, un po' sofistica e sterile, ma naturalmente viva*, appealed so much to Beckett that Belacqua's name recurs in *Murphy*, *Molloy*, and even in *Comment C'est*. The tradition that he was utterly slothful *in operibus mundi sicut in operibus animae* has been respected by Beckett, whose own Belacqua is 'by nature sinfully indolent, bogged in indolence', living in idleness on an income 'which, however inconsiderable, had a certain air of distinction, *being unearned*'.

*　　*　　*

More Pricks than Kicks has been out of print for many years, and at the time of writing no reprint has as yet been announced.[1] It seems therefore indispensable before proceeding further to give a fairly detailed synopsis of the narrative. After that I shall briefly recount the story of *Dream of Fair to Middling Women* before considering the hero and themes of the two works together.

Dante and the Lobster, the first story in the collection, introduces a youngish Belacqua in Dublin 'stuck in the first of the canti in the moon', trying to unravel the intricacies of *Paradiso*, canto II, where Beatrice refutes Dante's theory about the origin of the spots on the moon. Belacqua, finding this passage 'impenetrable', gives it up as midday strikes, turning his thoughts instead to the preparation of his lunch. This is a most eccentric affair: it entails the burning of two rounds of bread 'black through and through' on the toaster, followed by the spreading of the same with 'a thick paste of Savora, salt and Cayenne'. The resulting 'anguish of pungency' will be sheer delight to him. On his way to the public house where he is to eat his lunch he buys at a small grocer's his daily slab of Gorgonzola cheese to fill the sandwich of peppery toast.

Leaving the public house, he calls at the fishmonger's for a lobster his aunt has ordered, and then goes to the School of Languages for his Italian lesson with the Signorina Adriana Ottolenghi. After the lesson, he takes the lobster home and discovers to his horror, a horror which first baffles and then annoys his down-to-earth aunt, that when lobsters are 'lepping fresh' they are still alive and that they die only in the cooking pot.

In the second story, *Fingal*, Belacqua takes his girl friend Winnie to the Hill of the Wolves outside Dublin, where they gaze upon the Fingal landscape in general and on the Portrane Lunatic Asylum in particular, in which institution Belacqua declares his heart to reside, and Winnie a doctor friend of hers: 'thus she

---

[1] In 1966, in fact, Calder and Boyars issued a limited mimeographed edition 'Hors Commerce for Scholars'.

having a friend, he his heart, in Portrane, they agreed to make for there'. But Belacqua, 'who could on no account resist a bicycle', steals one that a farm-worker has unwisely left in a place where it catches the eye, abandoning his Winnie to her friend Dr. Sholto. Belacqua races full tilt to Mr. Taylor's pub, where he is soon 'drinking and laughing in a way that Mr. Taylor did not like'. Belacqua is indeed really gay only when he has lost his girl friend and won his bicycle; as gay as Molloy is discontented when the woman Lousse takes him into her house and he finds his bicycle gone as a result.

The next story *Ding-Dong* recounts Belacqua's wanderings around his native city and the sorties by which he 'enlivened the last phase of his solipsism before he toed the line and began to relish the world'. On one of these excursions, these 'boomerangs, out and back', whence he usually returns 'transfigured and transformed, very nearly the reverse of the author of the *Imitation's* "glad going out and sad coming in" ', he is approached by a strange woman in a public house who sells him seats in heaven, four for sixpence, despite his doubts and protests; ' "Jesus", she said distinctly, "and his sweet mother preserve yer honour". "Amen", said Belacqua, into his dead porter.'

When the next story (*A Wet Night*) opens, it is Christmas and Belacqua is invited (as is the Alba also) by Miss Caleken Frica to a cocktail party of the intellectuals. He prefers however to get drunk first in a low public house, after which he has a clash with a policeman, enjoys masochistically a self-inflicted wetting in the icy rain, and finally turns up soaked at his hostess's. He stays just long enough to dry himself and feel anguish at the artificiality of it all – ' "Vinegar", moaned Belacqua, "on nitre" ' – when the Alba asks him to see her home. There he enjoys a rest, a bottle, 'some natural tears and in what hair he had left her high-frequency fingers', and re-emerges into a world on which the rain is still falling with 'desolate uniformity'. He collapses with acute stomach-pains on to the pavement and is moved on again by the policeman.

Love and Lethe follows, a comic episode in which a suicide pact, contracted between Belacqua and the spinster Ruby Tough, totally miscarries, bringing the two together not in death but in 'inevitable nuptial' – but Belacqua comforts himself with the words 'of one competent to sing of the matter: *l'Amour et la Mort n'est qu'une mesme chose*'.

In *Walking Out*, the sixth story, Belacqua is – after his own strange fashion – courting Lucy, trying to persuade her to take a cicisbeo after their marriage and thus establish their life together 'on this solid basis of cuckoldry'. She continues to refuse this eccentric request, but is soon afterwards cruelly disabled in an accident (but not before she has realized that Belacqua is a Peeping Tom for whom the sexual activities of others are of far greater interest than his own). As a result of her accident, however, they can marry and live very happily without the question of cicisbeism ever needing to arise: 'he finds in her big eyes better worlds than this, [and] they never allude to the old days when she had hopes of a place in the sun'.

The next story is entitled *What a Misfortune*, an expression which Beckett took from *Candide* and which he has used more than once, both in its original form in Italian (*Che sciagura*, the title of a short text published in 1929) and in its French equivalent *quel malheur* (in *Malone meurt*). Ironically enough, the story thus entitled tells of Belacqua's marriage after Lucy's death to Thelma bboggs, 'a fairly young person with expectations'. The episode is highly comic and written with satirical *fougue*. It is followed by the Smeraldina's passionate if misspelt love-letter, her *Billet Doux*, quoted *verbatim* and *in extenso*, and in the next story, *Yellow*, Belacqua is in a nursing home summoning up his courage before an operation on the tumour on his nape; this episode ends with his dying in a ridiculous manner under the anæsthetic. In *Draff*, the facetiously-named last story, the Smeraldina (who, we are now told for the first time, has been Belacqua's third wife and is now his widow – Thelma née bboggs having perished on her honeymoon), and his best friend Capper ('Hairy') Quin, bury him and then go off to make a new life together: ' "Perhaps after all", murmured the Smeraldina, "this is what darling Bel would wish".' 'So it goes in the world' is the author's wry comment, which ends the book.

It should be remarked that although the ten stories, arranged in chronological order, are not explicitly linked (transitions from one to the next are often abrupt), the book as a whole is carefully constructed, and the various parts, often different in style, theme and tone, harmonize to give a fairly coherent impression of a certain man's life. (In the French *Nouvelles* we find the same technique of a series of *aperçus* combining to form a picture of one existence.) Furthermore, the style throughout *More Pricks and Dream* is characterized by a calculated and elaborate allusiveness, together with an extensively developed verbal irony; at its best this can give rise to suggestive and witty prose, at its worst it is pedantry pure and simple, which, arrogantly disdaining simpler formulations, prefers to employ an esoteric manner more effectually to cloak the vapidness or banality of the thought. It is only fair to add, however, that it is not often at its worst in *More Pricks than Kicks*, where the allusions usually have some justification, frequent as they no doubt are, with echoes and unmarked quotations, often in an altered or parodied form, constantly presenting themselves to the attentive reader. (The only other work with which *More Pricks than Kicks* can be even remotely compared for this systematic use of allusion to the literature of the past and to historical and geographical data is *The Waste Land*, where, of course, the intention is wholly different.) Here is a typical passage, with some of the echoes indicated:

Bovril into Salome, thought Belacqua, and Tommy Moore there with his head on his shoulders. Doubt, Despair [Bunyan] and Scrounging, shall I hitch my bath-chair [Emerson] to the greatest of these? . . . The Wanderjahre were a sleep and a forgetting [Wordsworth], the proud dead point. . . . Whither next? To what licensed premises? To where the porter was well up, first; and the solitary shawly like a cloud of latter rain in a waste [Shakespeare] of poets and politicians [Swift], second. . . .

Dream of Fair to Middling Women is written in much the same vein, and its main events may be summarized thus:

Belacqua has just waved goodbye from the Carlyle Pier to the Smeraldina, whom he has met only recently but with whom he has fallen head over heels in love. She has gone to Vienna to study music, and soon afterwards Belacqua abandons his own lady-friend, 'who had a great deal of the predatory masochism of the passionate Quaker', to follow the Smeraldina. One morning during his stay in Vienna, however, there occurs a disaster:

The implacable, the insatiate, warmed up this time by her morning jerks to a sexy sudorem, she violated him after tea. When it was his express intention, made clear in a hundred and one subtle and delicate ways, to keep the whole thing pewer and above-bawd.

All Bellacqua can do in the face of this catastrophe is to 'quote *le soleil est mort* in petto'. From this moment onwards their relationship enters a steady decline:

> It was always on that issue that they tended to break and did break .... One day he forgot his manners and exhorted her: 'For the love of God will you not take a loiny cavalier servente and make me horn-mad ante rem and get some ease of the old pruritus and leave me in peace to my own penny death and my own penny rapture.'

They manage, however, to avoid an open breach, and Belacqua moves on to Paris, for it is only in separation that he can love her completely:

> It was not when he ... er ... held her in his arms, nor yet when he remained remote, and shared, so to speak, her air and sensed her essence, but only when he sat down to himself in an approximate silence and had a vision on the strength of her or let fly a poem at her, anyhow felt some reality that somehow was she fidgeting in the catacombs of his spirit, that he had her truly and totally, according to his God.

> In Paris it is the Syra-Cusa who becomes 'as impotently besotted on Belacqua babylan, fiasco incarnate, Limbese, as the moon on Endymion'. Belacqua however is moved only to give her his Dante,

a beautiful book, one that he loved, that he had stolen from shelves at great personal risk, with pertinent dedication drawn by the short hairs from the text.

The time then comes round, after the receipt of the Smeraldina's *Billet Doux* which is placed here in the *Dream*, for his next visit to Vienna. Despite severe liver-trouble he goes, but the Smeraldina is displeased that he has arrived ill, and their relations gradually worsen until New Year's Eve, when Belacqua abandons her to a rival and pays a visit with the girl's easy-going father to a prostitute ('I have the address,' he says, 'of Abraham's bosom') and by the next day it is clear that it is all over between him and his *amata*. 'Extraordinary how everything ends like a fairy-tale, or can be made to, even the most unsanitary episodes,' comments Beckett sardonically.

In the second chapter of the novel Belacqua returns to Dublin, where he meets the Alba and enjoys many an intimate and sophisticated *tête-à-tête* with her (but never, the author insists, anything that could be construed as a carnal relation). The Alba, a tired valetudinarian, but also a woman of great character, meets with Belacqua's approval, and he, as far as can be, with hers. As in *More Pricks than Kicks*, they leave the Frica's party together, then have a drink *chez elle*, after which Belacqua comes out ('you didn't suppose, it is to be hoped, that we were going to allow him to spend the night there') and clashes with the policeman on his way home. At this point the manuscript comes to an end.

Both of these works are set largely in Dublin, and are permeated with the atmosphere of the city: street-names, names of bridges, the river, the canal, the College, the monuments, all continually recur. In snatches of dialogue we hear the city's brogue and feel the *ambiance* of its 'low publics' with their 'rough but kindly habitués, . . . recruited for the most part from dockers, railwaymen and vague joxers on the dole'. The working people of Dublin, whose company Belacqua seeks in preference to that of the 'incontinent bosthoons of his own class', the 'aesthetes and the impotent', are affectionately observed, albeit from a distance, for Belacqua is an outsider as far as they are concerned: he is idle, he is educated, and he is a Protestant, a 'dirty low-down Low Church Protestant high-brow'. Inevitably, therefore, one does not find here the same feeling of day-to-day Dublin as that in *Ulysses*, the sense of belonging to a society that has deservedly a reputation for being unique, with its own customs, humour and myths. The city and its citizens are contemplated in these books from a certain distance, which is hardly surprising in the work of a Protestant Irishman, but, for all that, the feeling of alienation cannot only be explained in terms of religion and class. Belacqua is not only a bourgeois communicant of the Church of Ireland, he is also the first in a line of Beckettian heroes whose condition of exile becomes gradually more painful; he is in fact the natural precursor of the *expulsé* of the *Nouvelles*.

* * *

Physically, indeed, Belacqua appears something of a clown; it is possible, for instance, for Dr. Sholto in *Fingal* to give a 'brief satirical description' of his person, which would no doubt run on these lines: a 'pale fat man', nearly bald, wearing spectacles which he delights in polishing ('ecstasy of attrition'), not particularly tall (the Smeraldina is taller than he is), shabbily dressed, and clothed on one occasion in 'filthy old trousers', with a reefer and boots, on another in a black leather coat. He always looks 'ill and dejected', with a 'baby anthrax' permanently on his nape. His appearance is in fact 'grotesque' enough 'to provoke . . . comment and laughter' in all places except those where he is best known. This grotesqueness would seem to come not only from his clothes, but also from his 'spavined gait', in which he resembles all the other Beckettian heroes: one thinks of Murphy's curious progress in his impossible suit, of Watt's outlandish way of walking, of Molloy's attempts to use crutches and bicycle at the same time. As for his personal character, Belacqua is 'naïve and a dull vain dog'; the Alba found that 'he was too irremissibly naïve for her altogether, too permanently selfish, faithful to himself . . . he lay coiled up in the shadow, always the shadow, of the dread of leze-personality . . .'; the Smeraldina sees him as 'indifferent to everything', and others as a 'live-and-let-live anchorite on leave', 'a compound of ephebe and old woman'.

Belacqua has, it is true, a decidedly eccentric attitude to most things: to his lunch, for example, which is, as we saw, an affair of pepper, mustard, Gorgonzola and burnt toast. He delights also in oxymoron and 'derives considerable satisfaction' from his inability to make himself clear to 'Mr. Beckett' on the subject of his manœuvres in *Ding-Dong*; he has a horror of clocks and chronometers, since for him the 'local publication of the hours was six of the best on the brain every hour, and even the sun's shadow a torment'. During the sacrament of matrimony he feels acutely the sensation 'of being cauterized with an outward and visible sign', and the absurdity of the metaphors of Psalm 128 'provoked him to a copious scoff that would have put the kibosh on the sacrament altogether had it not been for the coolness and skill of the priest who covered as with a hand this coarseness with a collect'. This oddity in Belacqua's reactions (or rather his incapacity for registering the normal reactions expected of him) is coupled with 'a faculty for acting with insufficient motivation' that his creator maintains to be serious enough to make a mental home the place for him. But what Belacqua (unlike Murphy) wants is not the comfort of a padded cell but a return to the bliss of the womb:

'And then', he said, 'I want very much to be back in the caul, on my back in the dark for ever. . . . No shaving or haggling or cold or hugger-mugger, no' – he cast about for a term of ample connotation – 'no night sweats'.

In default of this return, Belacqua enjoys to the full a melancholy indulged in for its own sake: 'he was in his element in dingy tears', and he 'could not resist a lachrymose philosopher', such as Heraclitus. In the *Dream of Fair to Middling Women* we are told at one point that he 'was crowned in gloom and had a wonderful night', and in *More Pricks than Kicks* that 'landscapes were of interest to Belacqua only in so far as they furnished him with a pretext for a long face'. This fondness for gloom is accompanied by a complete defeatism: 'I am what I am. That was the end of all his meditations and endeavours. . . . He had read the phrase some-where and liked it and made it his own.' Like his Dantesque namesake, he is in fact an 'indolent bourgeois poltroon', preparing for the 'new lease of apathy' that is to *follow* his death.

Belacqua often has occasion to feel pity for the sufferings of others, but even this pity is idiosyncratic. In the first place, it tends to be

devoted entirely to the living, by which is not meant this or that par-ticular unfortunate, but the nameless multitude of the current quick, life, we dare almost say, in the abstract. This impersonal pity was damned in many quarters as an intolerable supererogation and in some few as a positive sin against God and Society. But Belacqua could not help it, for he was alive to no other kind than this: final, uniform and continuous, unaffected by circumstance, assigned without discrimina-tion to all the undead, without works. The public, taking cognisance of it only as callousness in respect of this or that wretched individual, had no use for it. . . .

Belacqua, therefore, finds himself widely criticized, because he does not seem to mourn Lucy earnestly enough, wearing 'none of the proper appearances of grief' and by no means enjoying the 'delicious mucus of sympathy' that Lucy's kin insist on secreting upon him, '*viva sputa* and by letter post'. His inability to shed tears comes from his having 'as a young man exhausted that source of solace through over-indulgence' and so, when, in *Ding-Dong*, a little girl carrying milk and bread is run over by a bus in Pearse Street, his eye rests not on the accident but upon its sadly grotesque by-product:

The good milk was all over the road and the loaf, which had sustained no injury, was sitting up against the kerb, for all the world as though a pair of hands had taken it up and set it down there. . . .

In *Walking Out*, Lucy's accident is passed over in the same neutral manner:

. . . the wheels of the car jolted over what was left of the jennet, who expired there and then in the twilight, *sans jeter un cri*. Lucy however was not so fortunate, being crippled for life and her beauty dreadfully marred.

Belacqua's pity is, rather, for 'all the living [who] dare . . . continue full of misery'. It is for this reason that we find in *Dante and the Lobster* that the outcasts and the damned fill him with compassion. Here the fate of McCabe, a murderer from Malahide whose petition for mercy has been refused and who is to hang at dawn, is interwoven with that of the lobster which has to be boiled alive. Their destiny is then viewed in a wider perspective, that of damnation and the curse of God, imposed upon 'Cain with his truss of thorns, dispossessed, cursed from the Earth, fugitive and vagabond,' and upon those in the *Inferno*:

qui vive la pietà quand' è ben morta. . . .

exclaims Belacqua after Virgil, but he is concerned more with the 'superb pun' entailed by the line; 'Why not,' he wonders,

piety and pity both, even down below? Why not mercy and Godliness together? A little mercy in the stress of sacrifice, a little mercy to rejoice against judgement. He thought of Jonah and the gourd and the pity of a jealous God on Nineveh. And poor McCabe, he would get it in the neck at dawn. . . .

Belacqua, for all his eccentricity, is therefore not lacking in compassion either for the living dead in Hell or for the living dying on earth. The workings of God's justice are unfathomable to all the Beckettian heroes, and Belacqua is not alone in his bewilderment at the fate of such creatures as the lobster, McCabe, Cain and Dante's damned.

He is already an oddity, not quite at one with his fellow-men, often more an onlooker than active protagonist in the books that he appears in. One notices that Beckett frequently uses him as a means towards a primarily satirical end. The element of satire is prominent throughout Beckett's writing: satire on society and on individuals in the earlier works, changing to a sarcastic undermining of man in a more general sense in the later books. For this reason critics insist that Beckett is a comic writer, in the sardonic tradition of Swift, certainly, but genuinely comic nonetheless. His books, if they destroy, destroy with laughter, however cruel its resonance, or however close this humour comes to *humour noir*.

In his earliest works, Beckett's attitude to Belacqua is throughout what might be termed semi-associative; he speaks up for his hero but never hesitates to stand apart from him and view his weaknesses with an unbiased eye. He tells, for instance, of Belacqua's 'key-cold embrace', and of a part of the Smeraldina's life having been spent in 'ultra-violet intimacy' with him. We learn too that Winnie and the Alba feel something like contempt for their 'shabby hero', for the irresolute, moody, ineffectual person that he is: 'you and your sad and serious', says Winnie, 'will you never come off it?' and in the *Dream* the Alba feels that

all this pallor and umbilicism *à deux* might be the very thing for a certain class of *gémisseur*, it might be the very thing for him, permanent and pertinent and all the rest of it for him. But it was fundamentally all my eye for her. . . . She used to say affectionately that he would get over this and that, she bestowed *niño's* and *mamon's* on him when she felt like it, but her real opinion the whole time was that there was little hope for him.

Just like these two women, the author himself feels that Belacqua's behaviour needs justification and a 'minimum of charity' if it is to be excused at all: 'we can't straddle the fence nicer than that', he adds when he has said as much as can be said to attenuate the venality of Belacqua's fancy for Thelma bboggs. Beckett indeed goes so far as to appear as a person in his own novels, as 'Mr. Beckett' in the *Dream* and in *More Pricks than Kicks*, and as 'Sam' in *Watt*, in order to emphasize the fact that he observes his heroes from a neutral position:

'Behold, Mr. Beckett', said [Belacqua] whitely, 'a dud mystic'. He meant *mystique raté*, but shrank always from the *mot juste*.

Guardedly, reservedly, we beheld him. He was hatless, he whistled a scrap of an Irish air, his port and mien were jaunty resignation. . . . In the twilight, in the evening, in the black and dark night, after music, with the wine of music, Rhine wine, it was given to us to cotton on, to behold him as he was, face to face, even as he sometimes contrived to behold himself.

'We were Pylades and Orestes for a period,' says Beckett of his relationship with Belacqua,

flattened down to something very genteel; but the relation abode and was highly confidential while it lasted. . . . In his anxiety to explain himself he was liable to come to grief. Nay, this anxiety in itself, or so at least it seemed to me, constituted a break-down in the self-sufficiency which he never wearied of arrogating to himself, a sorry collapse of my little internus homo, and alone sufficient to give him away as inept ape of his own shadow. But he wriggled out of everything by pleading that he had been drunk at the time, or that he was an incoherent person and content to remain so, and so on. He was an impossible person in the end. I gave him up in the end because he was not *serious*.

In spite of the detachment the author preserves *vis-à-vis* his hero, he tends nevertheless to support him with something of the same indulgence that he shows towards Murphy ('all the puppets in this book whinge sooner or later, except Murphy, who is not a puppet'), and he does this by satirizing those with whom his hero comes into contact. *More Pricks than Kicks* is indeed rich in satirical portraits: Beckett has the gift of inspired caricature, of fixing the less amiable aspects of a person in few words. In doing so he is clearly more for Belacqua than against him. One thinks of the intellectuals assembled at the Casa Frica, and their empty chat for which Beckett has such a finely-tuned ear:

'Ravenna!' exclaimed the Countess, memory tugging at her carefully cultivated heart-strings, 'did I hear someone say Ravenna?'

'Allow me', said the rising strumpet: 'a sandwich: egg, tomato, cucumber.'

'Did you know', blundered the Man of Law, 'that the Swedes have no fewer than seventy varieties of Smœrrbrœd?'

The voice of the arithmomaniac was heard: 'The arc', he said, stooping to all in the great plainness of his words, 'is longer than its chord.'

'Madam knows Ravenna?' said the paleographer.

'Do I know Ravenna!' exclaimed the Parabimbi. 'Sure I know Ravenna. A sweet and noble city.'

'You know of course,' said the Man of Law, 'that Dante died there.'

'Right,' said the Parabimbi, 'so he did.'

'You know of course,' said the Professor, 'that his tomb is in the Piazza Byron. I did his epitaph in the eye into blank heroics.'

'You knew of course,' said the paleographer, 'that under Belisarius . . .'

'My dear,' said the Parabimbi to the Beldam, 'how well it goes. What a happy party and how at home they all seem. I declare,' she declared, 'I envy you your flair for making people feel at their ease.'

Others who appear in *More Pricks than Kicks* in a similar light are Otto Olaf bboggs, complacent cuckold ('any man who saved him trouble, as Walter had for so many years, could rely on his esteem'); the 'presumptive cuckoo', the effeminate Walter Draffin himself ('he expelled his words with gentle discrimination, as a pastry cook squirts icing upon a cake'); Una, Thelma's unmarried sister ('think of holy Juliana of Norwich, to her aspect add a dash of souring . . . [and] abstract the charity and prayers . . .') and finally Hairy, Belacqua's friend ('he felt his face improving as grief modelled the features'). They are, together with others, the object of a refined and pithy sarcasm which Beckett deploys in defence of his hero, while treating the latter with relative indulgence. He even shows him to be no mean wit, as for instance in his speech of thanks on the occasion of his wedding:

'I have to thank: Miss bboggs, who henceforward may be so addressed without the least ambiguity, for her as always timely reminder; Mr. Draffin, for his kind torrents of meiosis; Mr. and Mrs. small double bee, for their Bounty; the Maids, with special reference to Belle-Belle their leader, for their finely calculated offices this day, something more than merely buttress and less than *vis a tergo*; . . . my faithful friend and best of men, Tiny Hairy Capper Quin, tipping the scale, day in day out, for me and for many, whose spiritual body is by now I feel confident a *fait accompli*; the entire Church staff; the Abbé Gabriel; as many, in fine, as have found the time to witness and acclaim, in how small a way soever, this instant of the whirligig. Eleleu. Jou Jou.'

*   *   *

Turning now from the character and satirical function of Belacqua, let us examine the motifs that can be discerned not only here, but ultimately in nearly all Beckett's writings: themes of alienation from society, sexual discontent, and desire for spiritual release.

With regard to society, it should by now be apparent why Belacqua (unlike later heroes) can be called a citizen of the world, for he is still acceptable to most people in spite of his peculiarities. He is, as we have seen, eccentric in behaviour and appearance, keeping to the same grocer's and to the same public houses to avoid provoking the curiosity and laughter of those who do not know him. Nonetheless, he is invited to the Frica's party and even seems reasonably attractive to women; we have little hint here of Molloy's exile to come. But what Belacqua does show in common with his successors is a desire to shun people as much as possible; one hears for instance of his need to keep out any 'brisk tattler bouncing in big with a big idea or a petition' while he is preparing his lunch; and on his way to the public house

the great thing was to avoid being accosted. To be stopped at this stage and have conversational nuisance committed all over him would be a disaster . . . he would not have hesitated to strike any man rash enough to buttonhole and baulk him, he would have shouldered him out of his path without ceremony. Woe betide the meddler who crossed him when his mind was really set on this meal.

This aspect of Belacqua's character is frequently emphasized. In *A Wet Night* we are told that 'when intimidated he was rude beyond measure, not timidly insolent'; and 'intimidation' for Belacqua means finding himself accosted by 'poets and politicians' when he prefers to be 'where he neither knew nor was known'.

In the same way, after Lucy's death he withdraws into his garden and plays with the snapdragons:

To kneel before them in the dust and clay of the ground and throttle them gently until their tongues protruded . . . was the recreation he found best suited to his melancholy at this season and most satisfying to that fairy tale need of his nature whose crises seemed to correspond with those of his precious ipsissimosity, if such a beautiful word may be said to exist.

Before his wedding (in *What a Misfortune*) Belacqua goes into a complete retreat and sees no one except his best man Hairy and (with regret) his fiancée, from whom 'a short daily visit' has to be 'swallowed as being all in the game'.

In *Dream of Fair to Middling Women* he feels the need 'to pass, not to halt in the street, even when the man was nice', but although he thus eagerly shuns the members of his own class, it nevertheless pains him to realize that

never at any time did he mean anything at all to his inferiors. . . . He could enter at the same hour the same store to make some trifling indispensable purchase, he could receive his coffee at the same hour in the same café from the hands of the same waiter . . . and never know his assiduity to be recognised by as much as a smile or a kind word or the smallest additional attention. . . . Almost it seemed as though he were doomed to leave no trace, but none of any kind, on the popular sensibility. . . . He never grew accustomed to this boycott. . . . The fact of the matter is, we suppose, that he desired rather vehemently to find himself alone in a room, where he could look at himself in the glass and pick his nose thoroughly, and scratch his person thoroughly what is more wherever and for as long as it chose to itch, without shame.

Here Belacqua's fear of his fellows and his preference for solitude is shown in conflict with a longing for recognition of some kind from ordinary people, a recognition which in the *Dream* at least he never obtains. It is doubtful whether he even achieves it in *More Pricks than Kicks*, for all his assiduous frequenting of back-street grocers' shops and public bars, and despite his fascinated interest in pedlars, beggars and tramps, such as the woman who sells him seats in heaven, or the blind paralytic who is seen in *A Wet Night* begging from his wheel chair and, like Hamm in *Endgame*, tyrannizing over his chairman, or the tramp in *Walking Out*, a man of such 'instinctive nobility' as to inspire in Belacqua 'a paroxysm of shame for his capon belly'.

In this alienation the exile of Watt and the others is foreshadowed; the reasons for it will soon be clear. Meanwhile let us note that Belacqua, because of his oddity, is unable either to feel at ease with people of his own sort (as his sufferings at the Frica's party showed) or to persuade his inferiors to accept him as one of themselves.

*   *   *

A second characteristically Beckettian motif is sexual maladjustment. It is more than suggested in *Dream of Fair to Middling Women* that Belacqua tends to narcissism, not to mention autoeroticism. We constantly hear of the delight he takes in picking his nose – 'ah solitude, when a man at last and with love can occupy himself in his nose!' – we hear too of his 'chiroplatonism', and there are other hints at an onanism such as that so freely indulged in by later Beckettian heroes. It is stated explicitly, however, that Belacqua's perversion is that of being 'a peeping Tom in bicycle-clips', spying on lovers in the woods; on one occasion (*Walking Out*) he is soundly thrashed by an irate '*Tanzherr*' who has caught him *in flagrante delicto*. This pastime Belacqua honours with the name *sursum corda*, and mentions it both to Winnie and to his fiancée Lucy. The latter bears the shock bravely when she realizes, quite suddenly, that 'all his baby talk of her living with him like a music' and 'all his fugues into *sursum corda* and *private experience*' are merely the evasions of 'a trite spy of the vilest description, a patent cad'. Only when she is crippled for life is she able to marry him to the satisfaction of both of them.

Belacqua has in fact a manifest horror of physical love. Early on in the *Dream of Fair to Middling Women* we are told that he is in love with the Smeraldina, but only 'from the girdle up'; and it has already been seen that she is the one who insists on turning their relationship into a series of 'fiascos and semi-fiascos, he doing his poor best to oblige her and she hers to be obliged, in an absenc of all douceness'. If only she could be like the 'rapt spirit' of Dante's Sordello, huddled in a niche of rock, but

of course it was only a question of seconds before she would surge up at him, blithe and buxom and young and lusty, a lascivious petulant virgin, a generous mare neighing after a great horse, caterwauling after a great stallion, and amorously lay open the double-jug dugs.

Later, Belacqua asserts 'there is no such thing as love in a thalamus', and in *More Pricks than Kicks* the same idea of the incompatibility of love and sex is insisted upon. Lucy must take a cicisbeo, Ruby has a difficult task in inducing Belacqua to take her in his arms, and Thelma finds his indifference bewildering. Throughout the *Dream*, too, his so-called 'bloodless nonchalance' is emphasized. His most real self, we are told, is that of Belacqua the Florentine, the next most real Narcissus fleeing Echo, the least real Apollo seeking Daphne.

His indifference to nubile women is counter-balanced by his reverence for older, less intemperate ones. His Italian teacher, Signorina Ottolenghi, appears in a very favourable light:

He did not believe it possible for a woman to be more intelligent or better informed than the little Ottolenghi. So he had set her on a pedestal in his mind, apart from other women. . . . There subsisted as much of the Ottolenghi as might be expected to of the person of a lady of a certain age who had found being young and beautiful and pure more of a bore than anything else.

It is however the Alba, the woman 'full of lassitude and pain', who receives Belacqua's most enthusiastic homage; in spite of her youth she shows little interest in the pleasures of the appetite, and since Belacqua is happiest in adoration felt at a distance, her preference for sophisticated *amour courtois* suits him perfectly. In *Dream of Fair to Middling Women* they indulge in long conversations, 'all in overtones and of a fairly good standard of obscenity. They enjoyed themselves very much . . . the bandying of gross and subtle futilities, that was what she liked best, since it was a question here below of talking most of the time'. In *More Pricks than Kicks* the Alba ('you are white music' Belacqua tells her in the *Dream*, hence her name) does not figure so prominently, but at the Frica's party she shows, characteristically, no interest in the

sinister kiss-me-Charley hugger-mugger that had spread like wildfire throughout the building . . . she proceeded in her own quiet and inimitable style to captivate all those who had curbed their instinct to join in the vile necking expressly in order to see what they could make of this pale little person so self-possessed and urbane.

When Belacqua arrives, although she thinks she has 'never seen anybody, man or woman, look quite such a sovereign booby', she takes him into her care and leaves the party with him. She reappears briefly as a bridesmaid in *What a Misfortune*, where she asks Walter Draffin (of all people) to see her home. She has also, it is interesting to note, an enigmatic poem written to her in Beckett's collection *Echo's Bones and other Precipitates*, first published in 1935.

Few other women in Beckett's writings (Murphy's Celia, and Mrs. Rooney of *All that Fall*, are important exceptions) achieve the status of the Alba. Most of them are mercilessly satirized, like Miss Caleken Frica:

she visits talent in the Service Flats. In she lands, singing Havelock Ellis in a deep voice, frankly itching to work that which is not seemly. Open upon her concave breast as on a lectern lies Portigliotti's *Penombre Claustrali*, bound in tawed caul. In her talons earnestly she grasps Sade's *Hundred Days* and the *Anterotica* of Aliosha G. Brignole-Sale, unopened, bound in shagreened caul. . . . Solitary meditation has furnished her with nostrils of generous bore. . . .

Such is the Frica. There are many others like her. Belacqua generally dislikes women, and the more lascivious they are the more he dislikes them. He wishes his open, day-to-day relations with the opposite sex to be 'like a music', that is, sexless; to the secret heart of his sensuality he will only admit either autoerotic or vicarious delights that are purely solitary. Once again, therefore, there is this theme of solitude, for it is evident that Belacqua's erotic eccentricity, on which so much stress is laid in these books, is a further illustration of the fact that the first of the Beckettian heroes is a lonely man, a radical and voluntary outsider.

*　　*　　*

The spiritual problem (the last significant motif) arises from Belacqua's need to shut himself off from the outside world, to achieve self-sufficiency (that 'self-sufficiency which', we are told, 'he never wearied of arrogating to himself'), to dam himself up against the inroads the surrounding world makes into him:

The fragile dykes were caving in on him, he would be drowned, stones and thickets would flood over him and over the land, a nightmare strom [sic] of timber and leaves and tendrils and bergs of stone. He stood amidst the weeds and the shell of the Hof, braced against the dense masses, strained out away from him. Over the rim of the funnel, when he looked up, the night sky was stretched like a skin. He would scale the inner wall, his head would tear a great rip in the taut sky, he would climb out above the deluge into a quiet zone above the nightmare. (*Dream of Fair to Middling Women*)

During the Paris episode of the *Dream*, Belacqua 'throws up a ring of earthworks, to break not so much the flow of people and things to him as the ebb of him to people and things. It was his instinct to make himself captive. . . .' In this 'cup so scooped out of the world' he lies lapped in indolence, dwelling with 'the shades of the dead and the dead-born and the unborn and the never-to-be-born, in a Limbo purged of desire'. In this realm he can relish the deep peace of

. . . the mind at last its own asylum, disinterested, indifferent, its miserable erethisms and discriminations and futile sallies suppressed; the mind suddenly reprieved, ceasing to be an annex of the restless body, the glare of understanding switched off. The lids of the hard aching mind close, there is suddenly gloom in the mind; not sleep, not yet, nor dream, with its sweats and terrors, but a waking ultra-cerebral obscurity, thronged with grey angels. . . . In the umbra, the tunnel, when the mind went wombtomb, then it was real thought and real living, living thought. Thought not skivvying for living nor living chivvying thought up to the six-and-eightpenny conviction, but live cerebration that drew no wages and emptied no slops.

Belacqua's enjoyment of beatitude is of brief duration, because a letter arrives from the Smeraldina summoning him to her side. 'This was the moment if ever, to slay his old man, to give, there and then, this love the slip' but he does not seize it. 'Out from the tunnel therefore he came, it clanged behind him'; the same opportunity never again arises. Faced with the choice between a retreat into his mind and a return to the world, he opts for the latter. Murphy does not make this mistake: he makes an attempt, at least, to choose not Celia, nor a career, nor the world, but the mindless dark, and if he fails, it is because in this earthly life it is not possible to secure final release. But Belacqua, unlike Murphy, is only an apprentice in the ways of mysticism (*'mystique raté'*) and although he 'remembers the pleasant gracious tunnel, he cannot get back, not for the life of him', because he tries 'to mechanise what is a dispensation . . . instead of simply waiting until the thing happens'.

This urge to retreat into the wider freedom of the mind springs from an underlying dualistic conviction, entailing the consequence that the mental part of one's being desires continually to escape from the contingencies of the physical part. In all his writing, in fact, Beckett advances a version of Cartesianism, the belief that the mind and the body are quite distinct, the one thought, the other extension, their interaction a mystery which it is not worth trying to fathom. What matters is the *fact* of the split: 'Belacqua scoffed at the idea of a sequitur from his body to his mind', when Winnie suggested that his sudden fits of enthusiasm were an ailment resulting from his being run down. His lunch, moreover, is ritualistic because his hunger is 'more of mind, I need scarcely say, than of body'; in *Murphy* also the same idea occurs: 'Murphy's fourpenny lunch was a ritual vitiated by no base thoughts of nutrition.' The body is of no significance: 'what matter about bodies?' asks Beckett *à propos* of the Smeraldina. Belacqua's body, furthermore, shows that tendency to decrepitude which is now recognized as typically Beckettian: he suffers, among other things, from weak eyes, from 'ruined feet' which pain him continually, even in bed; and from stomach cramps and a paunch, as well as from a generally uncertain health. In addition, he takes delight in mortifying his alien flesh, as when, for instance, he puts pressure on his boil to intensify 'the pangs, they were a guarantee of identity'; and on one occasion (in *A Wet Night*), he uncovers his chest and belly to the icy rain: 'it was even more agreeable than he had anticipated, but very cold'.

There is, therefore, already discernable a theme (not quite

drowned by the wit and bombast of these early books, by their particular quality which Edwin Muir compared in 1934 to 'extremely good and calculated and quite impossible talk'), that becomes increasingly important in Beckett's fiction: the theme of the radical split between mind and body, a split which causes the former to retreat into itself, into an isolated life of its own. The nature and characteristics of this separate existence of the mind now become more and more the author's concern, and most of all in *Murphy*, the next book. For Murphy tries, however unsuccessfully, to achieve final liberation from his body; but the later heroes prefer to give up the struggle, to accept the fact of a *mésalliance* which cannot be dissolved and which leaves the body to break down like a worn-out machine, whilst the mind, terrified of ceasing, chatters on, turning over continually its never-changing futilities.

Chapter 2

MURPHY

There is no return game between a man and his stars.

MURPHY

AFTER the publication of *More Pricks than Kicks*, Beckett produced a certain amount of occasional writing, as well as the collection of verse *Echo's Bones*. About this time (between 1933 and 1935) he spent two bad years in London ('bad in every way', he told me, 'financially, psychologically'), before finally settling in Paris in 1937. He was at this period without a profession, although he had thought of literary journalism and had even met Desmond MacCarthy with a view to this, without anything coming of it. In 1933 his father had died, and his elder brother took over the family firm of quantity surveyors, leaving Beckett a small annuity, enough to live on, as his share of his father's property. To a limited extent, therefore, his second hero's situation resembled his own.

During this time in London he lived in Gertrude Street in Chelsea, and at one point visited the Bethlem Royal Hospital, a mental institution in Beckenham on the borders of Kent and Surrey, at the invitation of a doctor friend who worked there. Here he conceived *Murphy*, his second work of fiction and his finest comic achievement, which Routledge published in 1938. It was no commercial success (its predecessor had not been one either) but it was read by some and even had a certain influence (notably on Iris Murdoch and her novel *Under the Net*).

Its hero Murphy is, like Belacqua, a Dubliner. He holds in bond, albeit *malgré lui*, the affections of a 'depraved Cork County' young lady, Miss Counihan, and when the story opens he has come to London ostensibly to 'set up a habitation meet for her' where she will lack none of the luxuries to which she is accustomed. But Murphy is an even less active person than Belacqua, for his only pursuits in London are 'apperceiving himself into a glorious grave', supine on the grass in the Cockpit of Hyde Park, and various speculations of an astrological nature. He is quite without profession, occupation or trade, and survives by virtue of an arrangement with his landlady, who fraudulently adds a supplement to the bill she sends to his rich uncle in Holland, and then hands Murphy the proceeds, less a reasonable commission. The situation might continue like this indefinitely, provided that Miss Counihan's patience lasts, but for two factors: Neary and Celia.

Neary runs a Gymnasium in Cork, and Murphy, a former pupil, has failed to acquire the faculty for which Neary is famous, that of stopping his heart 'in situations irksome beyond endurance'. Murphy's heart is too irrational ('like Petrouchka in his box') to achieve what Neary calls Apmonia (or alternatively Isonomy, or Attunement). In February 1935 (dates in this book are never left vague, being most often accompanied by the relevant planetary information to ensure even greater accuracy) Murphy leaves the Gymnasium, and a month later Neary meets Miss Counihan, for whom he feels at once a frenzied adoration, which is rejected. She leaves Cork for Dublin and forbids him to trespass further near her precincts unless and until he has in hand evidence of either Murphy's death, repudiation of her person, infidelity, or economic failure. Neary dispatches Cooper, his man-of-all-work, to London to look for Murphy and see if the required evidence is available.

Not long after Neary has thus become an important factor in Murphy's destiny, Celia, an Irish girl and a prostitute with a Chelsea beat, picks Murphy up in the mouth of Stadium Street while he is inspecting the heavens on midsummer night, and goes off to live with him. He soon proposes to her, but they cannot possibly marry on his slender income, and as Murphy declares himself incapable of any remunerative occupation, Celia leaves him to go back to her own. He, unable to live without her for long, finally agrees to look for work if she will 'kindly procure a corpus of incentives based on the only system outside his own in which he felt the least confidence', that is to say, get his horoscope from a swami in Berwick Market. This, once acquired, is found to decree that not before the first Sunday in 1936 to fall on the fourth of the month will Murphy be able to seek work with the maximum chance of success. Celia throws a scene, so does Murphy, but he ends in bowing to her wishes and in setting out to find a job at once.

Meanwhile in Dublin Neary, failed by Cooper who has succumbed to the alcoholic temptations of the metropolis, is succoured by the aptly-named Wylie, another pupil, who advises him to go to London and direct operations on the spot. Once Neary has left in accordance with this counsel, Wylie becomes Miss Counihan's lover and Cooper, dismissed by Neary, returns to Dublin to work for them instead. Finally all three leave Dublin together for London, thus making (with Neary) the number of people seeking Murphy four.

Their quarry has meanwhile met one Ticklepenny: 'this encounter, on which so much unhinges, took place on Friday, October the 11th', 1935. Ticklepenny is desperate, because he fears his employment as a male nurse in 'an institution on the outskirts of London known as the Magdalen Mental Mercyseat' will drive him as insane as those in his care. Murphy, struck by a sudden congruence between two of the swami's motifs, firstly that 'the lunatic would easy succumb' to his eye, and secondly that he 'should inspire and lead, as go-between, promoter, detective, custodian', offers to replace Ticklepenny in his post. A garret is found for him at the Magdalen Mental Mercyseat and a gas-fire to heat it (the gas proceeding from a tap in a W.C.). No sooner has he started work in the wards than he feels overjoyed at finding at last a race of men who seem to have achieved that complete withdrawal from the 'contingencies of the contingent world' which he has for so long striven to achieve in the teeth of his 'deplorable susceptibility' to Celia and a few other things. *Il est difficile* (quotes Beckett from Malraux) *à celui qui vit hors du monde de ne pas rechercher les siens*.[1] Now that he thinks he has found them, Murphy leaves Celia for good.

Neary, quite cured by now of his longing for Miss Counihan, yearns for Murphy instead, no longer as a rival but as a long-lost friend. Cooper, having tracked Celia to her home, and assuming that 'where a man's woman is, there it is only a question of time before that man will be also', separately informs Wylie and Miss Counihan, who converge on Neary's room to tell him the news that Murphy is found. In a vivid scene, the two who have double-

---

[1] 'It is difficult for him who lives outside the world not to seek his own kind', from *La Condition humaine*, in *Romans d'André Malraux*, Gallimard, Paris, 1947, p. 353. (The remark is made in connection with the Chinese terrorist Tchen.)

crossed each other and together double-crossed Neary, join in
witty exchanges at Murphy's expense while Neary expresses his
tolerant contempt of them both. The next day they all take a
taxi to Celia's lodging, only to find that Murphy no longer lives
with her, and that Celia has moved into a smaller room, formerly
occupied by an old butler who has cut his throat. Two days later
word arrives from the Mercyseat that Murphy is dead. The gas-
fire he had had installed (neither he nor Ticklepenny having considered the safer possibilities of an oil-stove, or realized that chains
in lavatories are easily confused) had exploded after he had returned to his garret, abandoning his first disastrous spell of night
duty, and with it, all his obligations to the hospital. The Dubliners
go to identify the charred body (Miss Counihan is mortified that
her rival alone is capable of doing so) and to dispose of his remains,
which Murphy had willed in a note to Celia to

be burnt and placed in a paper bag and brought to the Abbey Theatre,
Lr. Abbey Street, Dublin, and without pause into what the great
and good Lord Chesterfield calls the necessary house, where their
happiest hours have been spent . . . and I desire that the chain be
pulled upon them, if possible during the performance of a piece, the
whole to be executed without ceremony or show of grief.

Neary, relieved of his search, pays off Wylie and Miss Counihan,
who will, we are given to understand, eventually get married,
faute de mieux. Cooper takes Murphy's remains, to scatter them,
not where the testator had intended, but on a public-house floor,
and Celia is left to go back to her occupation in sadness.

The plot of *Murphy*, as will be seen from this synopsis, is
occasionally quite improbable (Hugh Kenner has spoken of the
characters' 'solemn pursuit of some goal for the achievement of
which Murphy is preposterously indispensable') and can be read
as a parody of the traditional novel (the finicky precision with
which the simultaneities of the action are pointed out, as well as
the virtuosity with which the different elements of the intrigue
are harmonized and the characters made to converge, would seem
to constitute a deliberate *défi de maître*). Certain questions moreover might occur to a carping reader, for example how Murphy
came to write a will concerning the disposal of his remains and
address it to Celia when he could have had no inkling that he was

to be killed by a risky gas-connection. But such questions are futile. *Murphy* is not meant to be a good story, but the examination of an Irishman's tragi-comic quest for nirvana, of his failure and ridiculous death and of the farcical sowing of his earthly remains among the cigarette-butts and vomit of a gin-palace floor. It is in fact, despite its humour, a pessimistic book. Celia's destiny is for instance one of sadness, because she who alone truly loves Murphy loses him so soon after finding him.

The style of this novel is an advance on that of *More Pricks than Kicks*. Allusion and quotation are still prominent features, but they rarely render the meaning obscure. There is moreover a new economy in the writing: unnecessary transitions, for instance, are left out. Here is an example taken at random (the scene is a Dublin café where Neary has been telling Wylie his troubles):

> Neary again buried his head in his hands.
> 'Cathleen,' said Wylie, 'tell the Professor the worst.'
> 'Eight sixes forty-eight,' said Cathleen, 'and twos sixteen one pound.'
> In the street Neary said, 'Wylie, why are you so kind?'

A less economical writer might have filled this short passage out with such transitions as 'Wylie called the waitress', 'The waitress totted up the bill and said', and so on. The scene, lightened of these superfluities, gains in vividness by the inclusion of the waitress's actual mutterings as she makes out the bill, and at the same time an important point is subtly made: that Wylie, who has invited Neary to the café, nevertheless leaves the paying of the bill to his guest.

Another feature of *Murphy's* style is its occasional poetic quality. This springs both from Beckett's ability to fix in striking images the beauty of natural things and from his awareness of the poignancy of crises in the human heart. Here is an example of the former:

> The leaves began to lift and scatter, the higher branches to complain, the sky broke and curdled over flecks of skim blue, the pine of smoke toppled into the east and vanished, the pond was suddenly a little panic of grey and white, of water and gulls and sails.

And of the latter (Celia has just heard from the landlady that Murphy has called while she has been out):

'He took his bag and the chair', said Miss Carridge, 'but couldn't wait.'

There was the usual silence, Miss Carridge missing nothing of Celia's expression, Celia appearing to scrutinise her hand on the banister.

'Any message,' said Celia, at last.

'I can't hear you,' said Miss Carridge.

'Did Mr. Murphy leave any message?' said Celia, turning away and taking another step upward. . . .

'Yes,' said Miss Carridge, 'now that you ask me, he did say to tell you he was all right and would be writing.' A lie. Miss Carridge's pity knew no bounds but alms.

When it was quite clear that this was the whole extent of the message Celia went on slowly up the stairs. Miss Carridge stood with a finger on the switch, watching. The turn of the stair took the body out of sight, but Miss Carridge could still see the hand on the banister, gripping, then sliding a little, gripping again, then sliding a little more.

Beckett's prose thus draws its strength both from its economy and its use of poetically-charged understatement. He never over-writes tragic occurrences, choosing even to state them quite baldly, with a lack of passion that could easily appear callous. That this is not the case can be seen in the discreet sympathy of the passage that closes the novel (Mr. Kelly, a frail old man, has lost his kite in Kensington Gardens just before closing time):

Mr. Kelly tottered to his feet, tossed up his arms high and wide and quavered away down the path that led to the water, a ghastly, lamentable figure. . . . Celia caught him on the margin of the pond. The end of the line skimmed the water, jerked upward in a wild whirl, vanished joyfully in the dusk. Mr. Kelly went limp in her arms. Someone fetched the chair and helped to get him aboard. Celia toiled along the narrow path into the teeth of the wind, then faced north up the wide hill. There was no shorter way home. The yellow hair fell across her face. . . . She closed her eyes.

All out.

The humanity of the writing is nevertheless constantly informed by wit (here is one example among many):

The bed was tiny. Miss Carridge could not imagine how the two of them were ever going to manage. When not fired by cupidity, Miss Carridge's imagination was of the feeblest.

as well as by irony:

Wylie and Miss Counihan met face to face, a trying experience for them both.
'You cur,' said Miss Counihan, getting her blow in first.
'You bitch,' said Wylie.
They belonged to the same great group.

Irony of this sort runs throughout the book. The prose is moreover of such denseness that much of the humour can easily be missed: *Murphy* indeed amply repays close reading. Attention to the detail of the text will reveal stroke after stroke of wit as well as unlock the intricate allusiveness of the writing, which adds considerably to its richness; for Beckett's prose is charged with echoes, especially those of a Christian nature:

He kept on thinking it was Friday, day of execution, love and fast. Thus Bom released Ticklepenny and delivered Murphy to his folly. Remember also one thief was saved (cf. *Waiting for Godot*).

Echoes not only of the Bible, but of Dante and Shakespeare and many other writers, are so numerous that the curious reader easily discovers them for himself. Allusiveness even in *Murphy* can sometimes degenerate into wilful esotericism, but on the whole Beckett puts it to apt use:

'Oh, if you have,' cried Miss Counihan, 'if you have news of my love, speak, speak, I adjure you.' She was an omnivorous reader.

The contortions of the resistive in particular seemed to Murphy not so much an entreaty to nature's soft nurse as a recoil from her solicitations. The economy of care was better served, in the experience of the resistive, when they knit up the sleave by day.

*   *   *

Places in *Murphy* are as carefully particularized as in the preceding books. Murphy's residence at the beginning of the novel is a West Brompton Mew; the place of his meeting with Celia in Chelsea is precisely stated, and the room they occupy together is in Brewery Road in Islington, equidistant between York Way and the Caledonian Road, near to both Pentonville Prison and the Metropolitan Cattle Market (between which we are expected to see a connection, for dumb beasts, especially cattle in or on their way to slaughter-houses, are objects of compassion in Beckett's work: both Molloy and the Unnamable are affected by their lowing and sufferings). In Dublin, Wylie discovers Neary beating his head against the buttocks of the statue of Cuchulain set up as a memorial in the General Post Office to the heroes of the 1916 rising, and stays the wrath of the Civic Guard on duty with the assurance that the culprit is an inmate of the House of St. John of God, a mental hospital at Stillorgan, to which he shall promptly be returned. In the same specific way the Magdalen Mental Mercyseat is described and one obtains a good impression of what a mental hospital must look like from the inside (though it should be emphasized, 'lest', to borrow a phrase of Beckett's, 'an action for libel should lie', that the Bethlem Royal Hospital served only as a point of departure for Beckett's story, and that his description of the Mercyseat and of its buildings is purely fictitious).

Together with this detailed accuracy with regard to place and time, there is the creation of vivid characters. One finds here further evidence of Beckett's skill at portraiture, especially of a satirical nature. Wylie, for example, is a small-time sensualist on the lines of Walter Draffin but without his intelligence; Miss Counihan, whose deadly sins are lust, ambition and avarice, is turpitude incarnate, a ruthless egoist who is only vulnerable through 'her erogenous zones and her need for Murphy'. He represents for her the potentialities at least of a substantial income and the place in high society that she, in many ways a Madame Verdurin *manquée*, covets so highly (though it is one of the little mysteries of the book how she came to imagine the 'seedy solipsist' a likely stepping-stone to the presidency of a *coterie*). Indeed she would have all the cocktail-party hostess's sophisticated artificiality but for the fact that her education has been of the slightest. She is the Smeraldina of the social gehenna, and where she falls short of the robustness of the former's sensuality, she amply compensates for it by her ambition and greed, vices of which the

Smeraldina was innocent. But if we do not wish to be too severe to her, we may say that she is the Mr. Facing-both-ways of the novel, and as such is constantly condemned out of her own mouth:

> She went on to say that she could not very well renounce a young man, such a nice young man, who for all she knew to the contrary was steadily amassing a large fortune so that she might not be without any of the little luxuries to which she was accustomed, and whom of course she loved very dearly, unless she had superlative reasons for doing, such for example as would flow from . . . overwhelming evidence of infidelity and economic failure. She welcomed the happy chance that allowed her to communicate this – er – modified view of the situation to Mr. Neary, looking so much more – er – youthful without his whiskers.

Of Neary we learn little, except that he instructs in Apmonia, which faculty he exercised frugally,

> as when he wanted a drink and could not get one, or fell among Gaels and could not escape, or felt the pangs of hopeless sexual inclination.

He is in fact greatly given to 'pangs of hopeless sexual inclination' since it is usual with him to sigh for a lady and then to tire of her as soon as, or even before, she has bowed to his wishes.

Several minor characters in the novel come over vividly, such as Mr. Kelly, grandfather to Celia and almost bedridden, whose attention

> could not be mobilised . . . at a moment's notice. His attention was dispersed. Part was with its caecum, which was wagging its tail again; part with his extremities, which were dragging anchor; part with his boyhood; and so on. All this would have to be called in.

Mr. Kelly is in fact extraordinarily like the Malone of *Malone Dies*:

> He did not look a day over ninety, cascades of light from the bed-lamp fell on the hairless domes and bosses of his skull, scored his ravaged face with shadow. He found it hard to think, his body seemed spread over a vast area, parts would wander away and get lost if he did not keep a sharp look-out, he felt them fidgeting to be off. He was vigilant and agitated, his vigilance was agitated, he made snatches and darts in his mind at this part and that.

In a similar way Cooper is somewhat like Molloy or Macmann:

Cooper's only visible humane characteristic was a morbid craving for alcoholic depressant. . . . He was a low-sized, clean-shaven, grey-faced, one-eyed man, triorchous and a non-smoker. He had a curious hunted walk, like that of a destitute diabetic in a strange city. He never sat down and never took off his hat.

After Murphy's death he finds he can both sit down and take off his hat, an ancient bowler. He takes advantage of both at the end of the book, by sitting heavily on his hat and destroying it.

Among many other characters, such as the landlady Miss Carridge whose affliction is acute body-odour, and the spiritualist medium Miss Dew who suffers from duck's disease, one of the best rapid sketches is that of the absent-minded Coroner:

'These remains', said the coroner in his nancy soprano, 'were deposited just within my county, my county, I am most heartily sorry to say. Another long putt and I would be sinking them now.' He closed his eyes and struck a long putt. The ball left the club with the sweet sound of a flute, flowed across the green, struck the back of the tin, spouted a foot into the air, fell plumb into the hole, bubbled and was still. He sighed.

Celia, however, is the most subtly-drawn secondary character in the whole novel. She is an attractive green-eyed, yellow-haired Irish girl, lacking all guile. She goes off to live with Murphy because she loves him, and she continues to love him to the last: on the way to the post-mortem she feels nothing any longer, her 'affective mechanisms seemed to be arrested'. But earlier she insists that he find a job to support them both (thus relieving her of the need to continue in a profession she finds dull and disagreeable) and fails to see why work is anathema to him. Little by little, however, she begins to recognize the force of his arguments: 'it struck her that a merely indolent man would not be so affected by the prospect of employment'; and before long she ceases to enjoy walking in the nearby Market,

where the frenzied justification of life as an end to means threw light on Murphy's prediction, that livelihood would destroy . . . his life's goods. This view, which she had always felt absurd and wished to go on feeling so, lost something of its absurdity when she collated Murphy and the Caledonian Market. Thus in spite of herself she began to understand as soon as he gave up trying to explain.

And soon she begins to feel 'the impulse stirring tremulously, as for an exquisite depravity, to be naked and bound', and to adopt Murphy's old pursuits, whereby he spent the long hours of the day in a 'less precarious abeyance than that of sleep':

> She got out of her clothes and into the rocking chair. Now the silence above was a different silence, no longer strangled. The silence not of vacuum but of plenum, not of breath taken but of quiet air,

a silence in which she 'teases the oakum of her history' in order to be able, that accomplished, to 'lie down in the paradisal innocence of days and places and things and people'.

But in so far as her lover is concerned, she has failed in what she has attempted to do: 'all her loving nagging had gone astray . . . her efforts to make a man of him had made him more than ever Murphy', and death comes to him before he decides to return to her.

Celia enjoys instant respect: Wylie 'staggers reverently to his feet' when he first sees her and Neary and he 'feel more and more swine before a pearl' as they observe her. She was, she tells them, only a recalcitrant part of Murphy that he had to lose to be able to go on: 'he had to leave me to be what he was before he met me . . . I was the last exile'. The novel ends with her broken grief, which prevents her from seeing, as she formerly would have done, the beauty of the wind tearing up a cloudy sky, or of the kites flying before it: she 'looked at the sky . . . simply to have that unction of soft sunless light on her eyes that was all she remembered of Ireland'. Like the woman in the short story *Assumption*, she has loosed her man into the unknown; and although not an intellectual like Murphy, she has common sense and an innate intelligence which enables her to gain an insight into what he is striving for in life. She has, moreover, a fundamental goodness and purity that distinguishes her from the Wylies and the Counihans of the story, and she is not only Beckett's most completely developed female character, but one of his most human figures altogether.

Although important and impressive, she is a less significant

character than the protagonist. All Beckett's fictional works re-
volve completely round their hero, and *Murphy* is to such an
extent the story of Murphy, that it is by him that it stands or falls.

He is a youngish man, with gull's eyes and yellow complexion;
he suffers from violent heart attacks (his heart being so irrational
that Neary could do nothing for him) and from pains in neck and
feet, like Belacqua. He never wears a hat ('the memories it awoke
of the caul were too poignant, especially when he had to take it
off') and his suit, originally black, is now the colour of verdigris,
and is tubular in form, 'exhibiting a proud and inflexible autonomy of hang'. Apart from his mystical activities, he is interested
only in astrology and chess. He is plunged in the study of the
former when Celia meets him, and he plays the latter with Mr.
Endon in the Magdalen Mental Mercyseat.

Murphy believes the future holds great things in store for him,
but at present he is a 'chronic emeritus', as indolent as Belacqua.
He is tolerant ('his respect for the imponderables of personality
was profound') and resilient ('to die fighting was the perfect
antithesis of his whole practice, faith and intention'). He is also
as much out of sympathy with his times as Belacqua: even his
vagitus was off the note, and now as a grown man he meets
'derision tinged with loathing' from his fellow men, and the
oddity of his appearance causes the boys playing football to mimic
and ridicule him as he trudges along Brewery Road.

In the past he has been a theological student, 'an adherent (on
and off) of the extreme theophanism of William of Champeaux',
'lying awake night after night with Bishop Bouvier's *Supplemen-
tum ad Tractatum de Matrimonio* under his pillow . . . or ponder-
ing Christ's parthian shaft: *It is finished*'. This may explain his
present mystical pursuits.

For Murphy, like Belacqua but with more determination and
therefore more success, is for ever striving to cut himself off from
the importunities of the world of sense and to retire into the calm
of his mind. An essential mechanical aid is his rocking chair, into
which he ties himself, naked, with scarves, and then sets himself
rocking at speed. The chair, like a centrifuge, sends his mind
spinning away from his unquiet body, and by the time it stops
rocking, his body is still and he himself is far away in his Elysium,
'in the freedom of that light and dark that did not clash, nor alter-

nate, nor fade nor lighten except to their communion'. His mind 'functions not as an instrument but as a place' and it is only there that he can perceive truly (like Belacqua who, we saw above, could only have his Smeraldina 'truly and totally, according to his God' when she was 'fidgeting in the catacombs of his spirit'):

Before he could see, it had to be not merely dark, but his own dark. Murphy believed there was no dark quite like his own dark.

Half-way through the novel a mock-serious chapter is devoted to a *deffence et illustration* of the term 'Murphy's mind'.[1] This pictures itself as a hollow sphere, a universe unto itself, excluding nothing it does not itself contain. There is both a physical mode and a mental mode, and the latter has three zones: the light, containing forms with parallel in the physical mode; the half light, containing forms without such parallel; and the dark, 'a flux of forms . . . forms becoming and crumbling into the fragments of a new becoming'. Murphy's metaphysic is therefore not so much Idealism as solipsism. It is unashamedly eclectic, owing something both to Leibnizian monadism and Geulincxian dualism; from the former it takes the theory of the autonomy and self-sufficiency of the individual monad, which concords with others not by means of any interaction but by virtue of the pre-established harmony; from the latter the theory that the physical and mental modes are completely distinct (there being neither logical entailment nor casual connection between them), although equally real (Murphy is no Berkeleian). He rejects however all of the post-Cartesian explanations of interaction and is 'content to accept the partial congruence of the world of his mind with the world of his body as due to some . . . process of supernatural determination. The problem was of little interest. . . . Of infinitely more interest than how this came to be so was the manner in which it might be exploited'. He exploits it in the following way:

In the *first zone*, the light, he enjoys full sovereignty and reconstructs the real world in accordance with his own wishes. 'Here the kick that the physical Murphy received, the mental Murphy

[1] It is headed, characteristically, by a twisted quotation from Spinoza (*Ethics*, Bk. V, Prop. 35): *amor intellectualis quo Murphy se ipsum amat*, 'the intellectual love with which Murphy loves himself'. Spinoza, of course, has: 'with which God loves himself'.

gave . . . here the whole physical fiasco became a howling success'; and here he can exact retribution for the world's blows and indulge in the pleasures of reprisal, by exposing 'Miss Carridge to rape by Ticklepenny, and so on.'

In the *second zone*, the half light, 'the pleasure was contemplation'; here he indulges in his 'Belacqua fantasy' by virtue of which he imagines himself in Antepurgatory with the late-repentant,

looking down at dawn across the reeds to the trembling of the austral sea and the sun obliquing to the north as it rose, immune from expiation until he should have dreamed it all through again, with the downright dreaming of an infant, from the spermarium to the crematorium. He thought so highly of this post-mortem situation, its advantages were present in such detail to his mind, that he actually hoped he might live to be old. Then he would have a long time lying there dreaming, watching the dayspring run through its zodiac, before the toil up hill to Paradise.

The *last zone* is the dark, where he is no longer merely free and sovereign, but 'a mote in the dark of absolute freedom . . . a point in the ceaseless unconditioned generation and passing away of line'. This is the most beatific of all the zones:

It was pleasant to kick the Ticklepennies and Miss Carridges simultaneously together into ghastly acts of love. It was pleasant to lie dreaming on the shelf beside Belacqua, watching the dawn break crooked. But how much more pleasant was the sensation of being a missile without provenance or target, caught up in a tumult of non-Newtonian motion. So pleasant that pleasant was not the word.

Murphy's mind, as analysed in this parody of the classifications dear to hermetic philosophers, is, therefore, a blissful place of retreat, a closed system subject to no laws but its own. His apparent indolence is in fact a carefully reasoned indifference to the events of the realm in which he is completely impotent, according to the ethics of Arnold Geulincx (1624-69), the Belgian philosopher and follower of Descartes whose work Beckett discovered, and was deeply affected by, while at Dublin. He taught (*ubi nihil vales, ibi nihil velis*) that the reasonable man, knowing he is nowhere independent except in his own mind, and able to govern only his own mental states, therefore wastes no energy in futile attempts to control any part of the external world, not even his own body. Such a man, if he follows Geulincx, does not act against passion, but in indifference to it.

But the trouble with Murphy is that he still is subject to certain passions which he cannot subdue, notably his need for Celia. He goes to the Magdalen Mental Mercyseat in the hope that constant association with those who seem to have achieved 'that self-immersed indifference to the contingencies of the contingent world, which he had chosen for himself as the only felicity' will enable him to clinch the issue in favour of the serenity of the mind for once and for all: 'stimulated by all those lives immured in mind, as he insisted on supposing, he laboured more diligently than ever before at his own little dungeon in Spain'. But the key-words here are 'as he insisted on supposing'; for Murphy over-simplifies the matter, the patients are not as blissfully happy as he imagines, and the 'therapeutic vexations' they suffer at the hands of the medical staff are not the only sombre notes heard in their inner symphony; and what is supremely painful to Murphy, is that although they successfully differentiate him, a sympathizer, from the rest of their tormentors, they are nonetheless incapable of admitting him into their company and even of instructing him in the way. Moreover he finds it less and less easy to 'come alive in his mind', even after he has returned to Brewery Road for his rocking-chair, and his astrological meditations mean less and less to him. Matters are already serious enough when he begins night duty for the first time, but worse follows. To pass the tedious night hours he starts a game of chess[1] with Mr. Endon his favourite patient, 'a schizophrenic of the most amiable variety', and not only do neither of them attempt to attack each other, but Mr. Endon's game shows that he is concerned only with the aesthetic symmetry of his play, with returning to the positions he has set out from, just as if his partner did not exist and he were playing alone. The realization that he is a mere 'speck in Mr. Endon's unseen' determines Murphy to abandon the Mercyseat and per-

---

[1] Characteristically, Beckett lists the 86 moves of the game in the usual way, under two columns, White (Murphy) and Black (Mr. Endon), and adds a detailed commentary. Similarly, Celia is first introduced by the enumeration of her measurements.

haps return to Celia, after first returning to his garret to recuperate his energies by spending a few hours in his chair, but it is while he is in his chair that he is killed.

Although Murphy's vocation is more serious than that of Belacqua, he is no less of a *mystique raté*. He fails because even if it is possible to come alive in one's mind, it is not possible this side of the Styx to cut oneself off completely from the body, and this is what Murphy basically wants, but unhappily cannot achieve. It is moreover impossible for him to tell whether the insane are blessed mortals who have managed to become permanently free in their minds or automata whose bliss is only apparent, whose inhabitation of earthly paradise an illusion. The situation in which Murphy finds himself is tragi-comic, and it becomes steadily more tragic as its consequences unfold in Beckett's fiction, the hero of which is *par excellence* an agile but despairing mind tied to, and unable to escape from, a decaying and disgusting body which it holds in contempt and the appetites (sexual as well as alimentary) of which are fit only to be the butt of the crudest ridicule. The dualistic split foreshadowed in Belacqua is acute in Murphy, and the fact that the latter feels profoundly divided is ultimately the cause of the catastrophe that kills him: for 'all things hobble together for the only possible', comments Beckett, with Geulincxian fatalism.

*   *   *

Murphy is as alienated from society as he is split from his body, and the world of everyday labour is, we find, continually derided in this novel. Celia 'could not go where livings were being made without feeling that they were being made away'; and Murphy asks himself 'what was all working for a living but a procuring and a pimping for the money-bags, one's lecherous tyrants the money-bags, so that they might breed'. The scene in which he defrauds a firm of multiple caterers 'to the honourable extent of paying for one cup of tea and consuming 1·83 cups approximately' is very funny, not least because his principal if unwitting ally is the waitress Vera, a 'willing little bit of sweated labour'. But despite the cunning of this feat of misappropriation, Murphy is fundamentally indifferent to the whole system of 'pensums and prizes' the elaboration of which the world considers one of the highest achievements of human genius, but which is merely, as far as Beckett is concerned, the carrot that keeps the donkey treading on his rounds.

In this refusal to earn his living, Murphy shows that he is even more an outsider than the eccentric Belacqua, whose responses to the characteristic situations of human life were nevertheless often the reverse of normal. Murphy's solitude is in fact complete, and quite voluntary. We learn that he does 'not speak at all in the ordinary way unless spoken to, and not always even then' and that 'had Ticklepenny been Cleopatra herself, in the last years of her father's reign', Murphy would still have refused to share a room with him. Never, except in the case of the mental patients, and then only for special reasons, does he seek fellow-ship of his own accord: Celia has to approach *him*, for instance, and not the other way round. His love of solitude is most clearly demonstrated by his nostalgia for the womb, which is insisted upon (the padded cells of the Mercyseat he sees to be as cosy as a womb), and by his tendency to look upon his birth as a calamity.

Even more lonely than Belacqua, Murphy seems nonetheless to be free from the former's finicky refusal of sex. His enthusiasm for 'music' (by which he means quite the opposite from Belacqua) is considerable, and Neary admits regretfully that women find him attractive, in spite of the fact that the *plaisir de rompre* is for him 'the rationale of social contacts'. Women, especially Miss Counihan, are ridiculed in *Murphy* as much as in *More Pricks than Kicks* for their insatiable 'instinct for artificial respiration'; but Murphy's nights with Celia are nonetheless an untroubled series of 'serenade, nocturne and albada' from June to October, and he certainly appears to feel no disdain for them on that account.

*   *   *

In the *Sunday Times* during March 1938, D. Powell wrote of *Murphy*: 'beneath the traffic-roar of crudeness, there can be heard the small voice of a genuine horror and disgust. The book may be sterile, but it is not negligible'.

It is, indeed, *not* negligible, for it occupies an important place in Beckett's fiction as first clearly setting the tone of the hero defeated by a maleficent destiny which dallies with him rather than crushes him outright. Nor can it with justice be called *sterile* – stylistically, it is a rich and skilfully written book, and has as many interesting characters as one can reasonably ask of such a work. It is in fact as far as Beckett is prepared to go with the traditional novel, and within that form it is, if not a great book, an amusing and attractive one. Moreover, the note of horror and disgust which D. Powell remarked on when it was first published becomes considerably less muted as Beckett's work develops, for Murphy is the last of the heroes who can be described as a citizen of the world; in *Watt* the tone comes much nearer to the strident cry of loneliness and despair that is characteristically Beckettian. For the present, moreover, the dualistic issue slips into the background, and the main preoccupation now, at least for a while, is with the terrors of exile, which means not only exclusion from the world of men but also the painful bewilderment of inhabiting a universe where little seems to make sense any longer and where it is painfully difficult to decide what is, or is not, truly known.

Part Two

THE HERO AS OUTCAST

WATT
Between 1942 *and* 1944

A CASE IN A THOUSAND
About 1934

NOUVELLES, MERCIER ET CAMIER,
MOLLOY, MALONE MEURT
Between 1945 *and* 1949

Chapter 3

WATT

Wovon man nicht sprechen kann, darüber muss man schweigen.
WITTGENSTEIN

To know you are beyond knowing anything, that is when peace
enters in.
MOLLOY

BEFORE the publication of *Murphy* Beckett had settled in Paris,
where the outbreak of war found him. In spite of his being a
citizen of a neutral nation, he was, it seems, associated for a while
after the fall of France with a resistance group, and eventually
fled from Paris to the Rhône valley (to Roussillon in the *département* of Vaucluse) where for two years or so (1942-44) he lay in
hiding among peasants and farmers. During this period he wrote
Watt, set in the Ireland of his boyhood, in order, he has said, 'to
get away from war and occupation'. This was his third novel, and
the last to be written in English. Extracts from it appeared in
Irish and Parisian periodicals between 1950 and 1953, but the
complete work was not published until certain of the author's
American friends undertook to issue it in a limited edition in the
Collection Merlin series at the Olympia Press, Paris, in 1953. The
same press issued an unlimited edition in 1958, in the 'Traveller's
Companion' series.

* * *

Watt is a novel consisting of four parts, or long chapters, followed by an appendix comprising addenda, of which the author
ironically says: 'The following precious and illuminating material
should be carefully studied. Only fatigue and disgust prevented
its incorporation.' This section of addenda does, in fact, contain
notes towards a possibly indefinite expansion of the novel, notes
such as are provided also in Durrell's *Alexandria Quartet*.

In the first chapter, Mr. Hackett, an elderly gentleman, is taking
the air on a summer's evening somewhere in Ireland. He decides to
sit down on a public bench the better to enjoy the fading light,

but finding it occupied by two lovers, he calls a policeman to remove them and secures his seat. Soon he is saluted by a scarcely less elderly couple, Mr. and Mrs. Nixon, who join in conversation with him. Before long a tram stops opposite them, and when it moves on it discloses

on the pavement, motionless, a solitary figure, lit less and less by the receding lights, until it was scarcely to be distinguished from the dim wall behind it. Tetty was not sure whether it was a man or a woman. Mr. Hackett was not sure that it was not a parcel, a carpet for example, or a roll of tarpaulin, wrapped up in dark paper and tied about the middle with a cord.

This object turns out to be Watt, with whom Mr. Nixon, alone of the party, is acquainted. The latter crosses the street to remonstrate with Watt. He returns to his wife and Mr. Hackett with the news that Watt is still unable to repay a six-and-ninepenny debt of seven years' standing, although he offers to pay four shillings and fourpence of it, a compromise which Mr. Nixon has humanely refused since it would leave the man penniless just as he is setting out on a journey. Mr. Hackett is greatly bewildered by Watt but can obtain very little information about him from Mr. Nixon, who indeed knows very little himself.

The scene changes to the railway station, where Watt bumps into a porter, is rudely shouted at, and finally enters a compartment which he shares with a Mr. Spiro, editor of a popular Catholic monthly called *Crux*. This gentleman harangues him on farcical pseudo-theological subjects until Watt reaches his destination, whence he sets out on foot to Mr. Knott's house. It is by now already late at night. As he advances along the road a Lady McCann, faithful to 'her traditions, Catholic and military', hurls a stone at him, hitting him but fortunately not drawing blood. 'This was indeed a providential escape . . . for Watt had a poor healing skin'; but he pays no attention to the insult. He then takes a rest in a ditch, listens to the 'voices, indifferent in quality, of a mixed choir' singing a threne, and finally reaches Mr. Knott's, enters he knows not how, and soon finds himself being addressed, in the kitchen as he rests after his journey, by a man who has mysteriously appeared, called Arsene. The latter is the outgoing servant whom Watt is to replace in the service of the strange Mr.

Knott. In a long speech Arsene introduces him to life at the house, and tells Watt that he will not do the same for *his* successor. The first part of the novel ends with Watt, Arsene having as mysteriously vanished, watching the dawn light creep into the silent kitchen.

The next chapter tells of Watt's service on the ground floor of Mr. Knott's house (the first floor being looked after by a servant called Erskine). He is, very early on, greatly troubled by a visit from the Galls, father and son, piano tuners, since this apparently simple and straightforward incident soon loses all definite meaning for him and begins troubling him with haunting uncertainties. During this period he does however learn of the extremely elaborate arrangements for the preparation of Mr. Knott's food and for the disposal of the leftovers (to which disposal the teeming Lynch family is an indispensable accessory); but at the same time he is perplexed by other problems, such as who presses the bell that occasionally rings in Erskine's room at night, and what is the meaning of the strange picture he finds hanging there when eventually he secures entry.

When the third part opens, we learn that Watt has been telling the whole of this story to Sam, a fellow-inmate of an institution that is evidently a mental hospital. Sam, speaking in the first person, now describes the difficulties he has met with in learning the history of Watt's service on the first floor, after the departure of Erskine and the arrival of a man called Arthur to work on the ground floor in Watt's place. The chief difficulty is that Watt, in speaking to Sam in the grounds of the hospital, inverts 'the order of the letters in the word together with that of the words in the sentence together with that of the sentences in the period'. This peculiarity makes communication almost impossible between the two men. Moreover, the only thing that Watt can clearly remember to tell Sam of the last period of his service is the story that Arthur only began to recount to Mr. Graves the gardener of the fortunes of one Ernest Louit, sometime student of the 'College' (Trinity?) and later managing director of the house of Bando, which is, as its French connotation implies, a product to cure impotence, an affliction from which Mr. Graves suffers. Watt learns little else on the first floor, for of Mr. Knott, whom he serves all day long and most of the night, he cannot speak. Then, in the last chapter, Sam describes Watt's departure from the house on the arrival of Mr. Micks, who will replace Arthur on the ground floor while Arthur is promoted to replace Watt on the first floor: for Mr. Knott's servants are not allowed to make his house their last refuge, but must move on when a successor arrives, either to the first floor if they are on the ground floor, or return to the outside world if they are already on the first floor, 'for the coming is in the shadow of the going and the going is in the shadow of the coming'. Watt arrives, and departs, in summer, but he cannot say how many years have elapsed between the summer he came and the summer he went:

Watt was never to know how long he spent in Mr. Knott's house, how long on the ground floor, how long on the first floor, how long altogether. All he could say was that it seemed a long time.

And as Arsene had predicted, Watt makes no attempt to initiate Mr. Micks, nor even to utter 'the few simple words at parting, that mean so much, to him who stays, to him who goes'.

Once clear of Mr. Knott's house, Watt arrives at the station, spends the night in the waiting-room with the signalman's permission, but is stunned the next morning when the door is swung violently open by the porter. To revive him a bucket of slops is thrown over him by the railwaymen, but it slips out of their hands and falls, injuring him. Nevertheless he gets up, ignoring the incident, and buys a ticket to the further end of the line. The train arrives, taking him away, and the railwaymen are left to exult in their joy at being alive:

All the same, said Mr. Gorman, life isn't such a bad old bugger. He raised high his hands and spread them out, in a gesture of worship. He then replaced them in the pockets, of his trousers. When all is said and done, he said. . . .

And they say there is no God, said Mr. Case.

All three laughed heartily at this extravagance.

*   *   *

The setting of this strange and enigmatic story is far less precise than that of *Murphy*: we know merely that Mr. Knott's house is in the Irish countryside, by a racecourse, not far from the sea, and also near a railway-station, which is connected by a

direct line to a city, probably Dublin. But there is so little commerce between the house and the outside world, that it is as if it
stood nowhere on the known globe: even its dependence on such
outsiders as the Lynch family is preposterously unreal.

The minor characters of this novel are, perhaps deliberately,
more clearly delineated than the chief actors, Watt, Sam and Mr.
Knott. Arsene, the first servant, reveals a gloomy disposition in
his parting speech, for he regards life as 'an ordure, from beginning to end' and mentions the 'bitter and I blush to say even blas-
phemous words' that have escaped him now and then during his
service. Arthur, on the other hand, is much more easy-going,
ready to gossip light-heartedly in the garden with Mr. Graves,
and Erskine, again, is completely silent, rarely deigning to address
a single word to Watt while the latter serves under him on the
ground floor. And Mr. Spiro, the talkative latitudinarian Catholic
layman, Lady McCann the belligerent *châtelaine* and Mrs. Gorman the fishwoman, all have their own characteristics, as do
the three railwaymen, Mr. Gorman *fils* the station-master, Mr.
Case the signalman and Mr. Nolan the porter. The Irish voices
of the latter, incidentally, ring as authentically true in *Watt* as
do those in the radio play *All that Fall*.

Watt himself, on the other hand, is a much hazier character,
a deliberate enigma. Although it is stated explicitly that he is a
reincarnation of Murphy ('he had once known [the stars] famil-
iarly by name, when dying in London') – Watt, like all the
Beckettian heroes to come after him, is in this way clearly linked
to his predecessor in the series – he has nevertheless little of the
distinct personality that Murphy has. He never appears to be a
credible or living human being, but rather a shadowy figure whose
experiences are presented to us as if Watt himself takes little or
no part in them, as for instance on the occasion when Mr. Spiro
speaks to him without any reaction being recorded on his own
part. In fact, apart from his confused tale to Sam, he speaks only
three or four times in the book; and he has moreover artificially
to construct a smile on his face whenever his dealings with men
demand it, on the basis of what he has observed others to do, but
this is so far from seeming a spontaneous and natural expression
that it seems to many 'a simple sucking of the teeth'. When he
does speak, it is with an 'extraordinary accent' and with attention

closely paid to the rules of grammar (Watt says for example 'the nearer end' of the line while Mr. Nolan the porter is content with 'the nearest end'), and this is perhaps to be accounted for by the fact that, as Mrs. Nixon suggests, 'he is a university man'. He is not however very good at arithmetic (he has 'no head for figures'), for he counts out three-and-one for a ticket that costs only one-and-three.

Watt's habitual expression is 'that of Judge Jeffreys presiding the Ecclesiastical Commission', and Micks, for one, is frankly terrified by it. His way of walking is eccentric:

Watt's way of advancing due east, for example, was to turn his bust as far as possible towards the north and at the same time to fling out his right leg as far as possible towards the south, and then to turn his bust as far as possible towards the south and at the same time to fling out his left leg as far as possible towards the north. . . . So, standing first on one leg and then on the other, he moved forward, a headlong tardigrade, in a straight line. The knees, on these occasions, did not bend.

In the mental institution he even takes to walking backwards, as if in his gait to imitate his inverted speech:

His progress was slow and devious, on account no doubt of his having no eyes in the back of his head, and painful too, I fancy, for often he struck against the trunks of trees, or in the tangles of underwood caught his foot, and fell to the ground, flat on his back.

About Watt's physical appearance we are given few details; merely that he is a big bony man and middle-aged, his hair being red and streaked with grey. He has a 'huge big red nose' and his ears are 'stuck out wide on either side of his head'. And as Belacqua had his anthrax, so Watt has 'on his right ischium a running sore of traumatic origin'. As for his dress, he wears a hat (he is in fact the first of the Beckettian heroes regularly to do so; Belacqua wore one only after Lucy's death and Murphy never), a 'block hat of a pepper colour'. He also wears an enormously long, enveloping greatcoat, once green in colour; baggy trousers; and on one foot a boot, and on the other a shoe, both 'happily of a brownish colour':

This boot Watt had bought, for eight pence, from a onelegged man who, having lost his leg, and *a fortiori* his foot, in an accident, was happy to realize, on his discharge from hospital, for such a sum, his unique remaining marketable asset. He little suspected that he owed this good fortune to Watt's having found, some days before, on the sea-shore, the shoe, stiff with brine, but otherwise shipshape.

(Let us note in passing that the play on boots that is an important feature of *Waiting for Godot* is thus foreshadowed in *Watt*.)

Unlike some of the later heroes, Watt is 'a man of some bodily cleanliness' and carries about, in two grousebags, 'his toilet necessities and change of body linen'. Moreover he is a teetotaler, drinking nothing but milk.

So much for his physical characteristics. His personality is an eccentric one: he much prefers rats to dogs, for instance, and he is an experienced traveller, happiest living without fixed address, sleeping in a grassy ditch, becoming almost vegetational himself in the pleasure he takes at the cool dampness of it. He can reason, sometimes very rapidly, but sometimes only very slowly, so much so that he is 'greatly worried by this disparity. And indeed it contained cause for worry'. He moreover prefers, like Murphy, to 'see in his own dark', and is a 'sullen silent sot . . . always musing', either talking to himself, or listening to voices which whisper and sing to him continually:

Now these voices, sometimes they sang only, and sometimes they cried only, and sometimes they stated only, and sometimes they murmured only . . . and sometimes they sang and cried and stated and murmured, all together, at the same time . . . . And sometimes Watt understood all, and sometimes he understood much, and sometimes he understood little, and sometimes he understood nothing.

The voices play as important a part in Watt's existence as mental retreat plays in Murphy's. A 'little voice' tells him, for instance, that Mr. Knott does not keep his own housedog because he once knew a man bitten by a dog; and in the railway station, just before he leaves Mr. Knott's district, Watt hears the voice of a woman named Price telling him about the seating capacity of the station waiting-room. But most of the time the voices simply 'whisper their canon . . . like a patter of mice, a flurry of little grey paws in the dust', or exist as 'the soundless tumult of an inner lamentation'.

Watt is thus clearly an introvert, and these voices people his world as completely as Murphy's visions inhabit his: it is, in fact, interesting to note that Murphy's retreat is spoken of in semi-visual terms (contemplation of Belacqua in the lee of his rock, and so on) and Watt's in terms of hearing, of listening to an inner discourse. The purpose of this motif is of course to emphasize the hero's separateness from the surrounding physical world, Watt's general passiveness also giving the same impression of detachment:

Watt suffered neither from the presence of Mr. Knott, nor from his absence. When he was with him, he was content to be with him, and when he was away from him, he was content to be away from him. Never with relief, never with regret, did he leave him at night, or in the morning come to him again.

In a similar way, acts of hostility never cause him to bear a grudge:

There was no more room in his mind for resentment at a spit in the eye, to take a simple example, than if his braces had burst, or a bomb fallen on his bum.

Again, when he first comes to Mr. Knott's house, Watt's attitude towards perplexing incidents like the visit of the Galls, father and son, is described as 'anxious'; but at the end of his period of service on the ground floor, the question is asked, 'Of his anxiety to improve, of his anxiety to get well, what remained? – Nothing.' And at the end of his last period in Mr. Knott's house the same idea recurs:

Of the strange doings above stairs, that had so preoccupied Watt during his time below stairs, no explanation was to be had. But they did not preoccupy Watt any longer.

Watt is, therefore, a quite passive creature. Sam on the other hand is more active, for his has been the formidable task of assembling the information on which the whole chronicle of *Watt* is based; he describes himself as Watt's 'mouthpiece' but adds that he has had only 'scant aptitude to give' as well as to receive the information which Watt imparted. Add to this that Sam's hearing began to fail at this time, that Watt spoke to him in a voice both rapid and low, and that the whole tale took 'some years' to tell, then

some idea will perhaps be obtained of the difficulties experienced in formulating, not only such matters as those here in question, but the entire body of Watt's experience, from the moment of his entering Mr. Knott's establishment to the moment of his leaving it.

Sam used a notebook to record Watt's story, and this in itself could well have resulted in inaccuracies:

I may . . . have left out some of the things that Watt told me, though I was most careful to note down all at the time, in my little notebook. It is so difficult, with a long story like the story that Watt told, even when one is most careful to note down all at the time, in one's little notebook, not to leave out some of the things that were told, and not to foist in other things that were never told, never never told at all.

We learn little else about Sam except that he has a 'glossy skull' and wears a 'pretty uniform' as a mental patient, although neither he nor Watt have any 'truck with the other scum' of the institution,

cluttering up the passageways, the hallways, grossly loud, blatantly morose, and playing at ball, always playing at ball.

He and Watt only meet when the weather is right for them both, since

the kind of weather we liked was a high wind and a bright sun mixed. But whereas for Watt the important thing was the wind, the sun was the important thing for Sam. With the result that though the sun though bright were not so bright as it might have been, if the wind were high Watt did not audibly complain, and that I, when illuminated by rays of appropriate splendour, could forgive a wind which, while strong, might with advantage have been stronger. It is thus evident that the occasions were few and far between on which, walking and perhaps talking in the little garden, we walked there and perhaps talked with equal enjoyment.

Once they do manage to meet, their pursuits are sadistic: the rats, to whom they feed birds' eggs, frogs and fledgelings,

would come flocking round us at our approach, with every sign of confidence and affection, and glide up our trouser-legs, and hang upon our breasts. And then we would sit down in the midst of them, and give them to eat, out of our hands, a nice fat frog, or a baby thrush. Or seizing suddenly a plump young rat, resting in our bosom after its repast, we would feed it to its mother, or its father, or its brother, or its sister, or to some less fortunate relative. It was on these occasions we agreed, after an exchange of views, that we came nearest to God.

Sam, whose ironic savagery is revealed by this last remark, seems to be the author of the meditation which in the third part is to be found somewhat incongruously inserted into the *compte rendu* of Watt's service on the first floor:

To think, when one is no longer young, when one is not yet old, that one is no longer young, that one is not yet old, that is per- haps something. To pause, towards the close of one's three hour day, and consider: the darkening ease, the brightening trouble; the pleasure pleasure because it was, the pain pain because it shall be; the glad acts grown proud, the proud acts growing stubborn; the panting the tremb- ling towards a being gone, a being to come; and the true true no longer, and the false true not yet. And to decide not to smile after all, sit- ting in the shade, hearing the cicadas, wishing it were night, wishing it were morning, saying, No, it is not the heart, no, it is not the liver, no, it is not the prostate, no, it is not the ovaries, no, it is muscular, it is nervous. Then the gnashing ends, or it goes on, and one is in the pit, in the hollow, the longing for longing gone, the horror of horror, and one is in the hollow, at the foot of all the hills at last, the ways down, the ways up, and free, free at last, for an instant free at last, nothing at last.

From this it would seem that Sam, although at first sight a mere onlooker and recorder of events, has the resigned pessimism of Arsene, who had been driven to say:

And yet it is useless not to seek, not to want, for when you cease to seek you start to find, and when you cease to want, then life begins to ram her fish and chips down your gullet until you puke, and then the puke down your gullet until you puke the puke, and then the puked puke until you begin to like it. The glutton castaway, the drunkard in the desert, the lecher in prison, they are the happy ones. To hunger, thirst, lust, every day afresh and every day in vain, after the old prog, the old booze, the old whores, that's the nearest we'll ever get to felicity, the new porch and the very latest garden. I pass on the tip for what it is worth.

The bane, as well as the fascination, of all these different people is Mr. Knott, the owner of the house in which Watt works. It is impossible, however, to give any idea of his appearance, for this changes continually:

For one day Mr. Knott would be tall, fat, pale and dark, and the next thin, small, flushed and fair, and the next sturdy, middlesized, yellow and ginger, and the next small, fat, pale and fair, and the next middle-sized, flushed, thin and ginger, and the next tall, yellow, dark and sturdy . . . .

In the same way

the clothes that Mr. Knott wore, in his room, about the house, amid his garden, were very various, very very various. Now heavy, now light; now smart, now dowdy; now sober, now gaudy; now decent, now daring (his skirtless bathing-costume, for example). Often too he wore, by his fireside, or as he mooched about the rooms, the stairs, the passage-ways of his home, a hat, or cap, or imprisoning his rare his wanton hair, a net. And as often his head was bare.

Small wonder, then, that

the figure of which Watt sometimes caught a glimpse, in the vestibule, in the garden, was seldom the same figure, from one glance to the next, but so various, as far as Watt could make out, in its corpulence, complexion, height and even hair, and of course in its way of moving and of not moving, that Watt could never have supposed it was the same, if he had not known it was Mr. Knott.

Mr. Knott's routine is a rigid one, but inside that framework he allows himself a certain freedom. His food is served to him 'cold, in a bowl, at twelve o'clock noon sharp and at seven p.m. exactly, all the year round', but the bowl is removed again an hour after being left in the dining-room. Mr. Knott can then either eat his meal, or leave it, or eat only part of it, but whatever he does, the same time-table of the serving and removal of his food is always adhered to. If part, or whole, of his meal is left, it is given to a

famished dog brought to the back door every evening for that purpose by Art and Con Lynch, two members of a local indigent
family. Watt tells Sam in great detail how Mr. Knott's food is
prepared (it is cooked mixed all up together, once a week), how
the dog is kept by the Lynches and how they themselves live;
the whole structure has a ludicrous and rigid inevitability in its
functioning that also characterizes the movements of the servants,
from ground floor to first floor, from first floor to the outside world
again, so much so that

in this long chain of consistence, a chain stretching from the long dead
to the far unborn, the notion of the arbitrary could only survive as the
notion of a pre-established arbitrary.

In what seems an infinite series of servants, dogs and dog-keepers,
one taking over the functions of his predecessor and then surren-
dering them to his successor, Mr. Knott appears to be the only
permanent and unchanging element. In the addenda section,
however, there is a passage which tells of Arthur's meeting in the
garden with an old man who implies that there was once a time
when even Mr. Knott was not. For the old man can remember
Mr. Knott's father, and he mistakes Arthur for the present Mr.
Knott. Arthur runs to Watt with the news, that he has met an old
man formerly employed 'by the Knott family':

This was the first time Watt had heard the words Knott family.
There had been a time when they would have pleased him, and the
thought they tendered, that Mr. Knott too was serial, in a vermicular
series. But not now.

Watt's own observation of Mr. Knott on the first floor yields very
little information. He learns that his master subjects the 'solid
and tasteful' furniture of the room in which he lives to frequent
changes of position, but for all that the 'empty hush, the airless
gloom' that surrounds him is constantly maintained. Mr. Knott is
however given to vanishing suddenly from his room, and to
returning just as mysteriously. When he is perceived, he is usually
muttering or singing to himself in a language that Watt, 'a very
fair linguist', cannot understand; but the latter is nevertheless as
much gladdened by the sound, 'as by the rain on the bamboos, or
even rushes, [or] the land against the waves'. Mr. Knott is also

70

given to 'solitary dactylic ejaculations of extraordinary vigour, accompanied by spasms of the members. The chief of these were: Exelmans! Cavendish! Habbakuk! Ecchymose!' However, he never seems to engage in actual conversation with anyone. Watt never heard him speak to Erskine, and between himself and his master no conversation is ever exchanged. Knott is even such an extraordinarily negative figure that Sam in the course of his narrative occasionally confuses his name with Watt's, and by the end of the novel we are successfully convinced that for all of us, just as for Watt, Mr. Knott is unknowable and his essence unattainable. The purpose of this *mystification* is considered below. Before it can usefully be discussed, however, something must first be said about the formal aspects of the work in which Mr. Knott figures.

*   *   *

The style of *Watt* is quite different from that of the preceding novels. There can still be discerned, however, traces of the economy of *Murphy* and of the leaving out of transitions:

Taking a pace forward, to satisfy himself that the gentleman's other hand was not going to waste, Mr. Hackett was shocked to find it limply dangling over the back of the seat, with between its fingers the spent three quarters of a cigarette.

I see no indecency, said the policeman.

There is here no mention of Mr. Hackett's calling the policeman, or of the policeman's inspection of the lovers on the bench. In the same way, changes of scene are often abrupt; we move suddenly, for instance, from Mr. Hackett talking with the Nixons to Watt at the railway station, and in the second part from Watt's puzzles about the theory of the changes in the servants to the details of his affair with the fishwoman. In a similar way, the imagery of the novel often has an almost violent quality, certainly an unfamiliar ring about it, that one associates also with Beckett's verse (my italics):

in the height of summer the doorstep was not dark . . . but burning with all the *raging dying summer light*, for it looked west, the backdoorstep.

looking . . . with *listening* lacklustre eyes out of the window, at the sky *supported* here and there by a cupola, a dome, a roof, a spire.

On the other hand, and this is the important point, most events in the book are narrated at fussy, unnecessary length:

Finally suddenly he focussed the wicket.

Watt climbed the wicket and found himself on the platform, with his bags. For he had the foresight, before climbing the wicket, to hoist his bags over the wicket and let them fall, to the ground, on the other side.

Watt's first care, now that he was safe and sound, with his bags, within the station, was to turn, and to gaze, through the wicket, the way he had come, so recently.

Fastidious completeness and extreme precision of this sort are in fact what strikes one at once on reading *Watt*, and examples of it are so frequent throughout the novel that it is hardly necessary to explore all the forms it can take. Fullness can sometimes, for instance, reside in a slightly archaic, formal or even baroque choice of language:

The lady held the gentleman by the ears, and the gentleman's hand was on the lady's thigh, and the lady's tongue was in the gentleman's mouth;

Similarly, dogs do not die, but 'pay nature's debt', and a small wooden bridge 'bestrides the dark waters' of a brook.

Another form, a very common one, of exactitude is the exhaustive setting out of *all* the facts of a given situation, suggesting anxiety lest by chance any be overlooked:

The dog [brought to eat Mr. Knott's leftovers] was seldom off the chain, and so got no exercise worth mentioning. This was inevitable. For if the dog had been set free, to run about, as it pleased, then it would have eaten the horsedung, on the road, and all the other nasty things that abound, on the ground, and so ruined its appetite, perhaps for ever, or worse still would have run away, and never come back.

This exhaustiveness frequently has a nightmarish quality about it:

He wondered what the artist had intended to represent (Watt knew nothing about painting), a circle and its centre in search of each other, or a circle and its centre in search of a centre and a circle respectively, or a circle and its centre in search of its centre and a circle respectively, or a circle and its centre in search of a centre and its circle respectively, or a circle and a centre not its centre of its centre and its circle respectively, [and so on].

As we are thus told all the possible things this picture (the one in Erskine's room) can represent, so too we are told all the many ways in which the five members of a committee may look at each other, all the different movements and variations of movements that Mr. Knott can make from window, to door, to bed, to fire, and all the changes of position he can subject his furniture to, the tall-boy, the washstand, the nightstool and the dressing-table. These descriptions frequently stretch over many pages.

But detail of this kind is not the only means towards precision: repetition, very like that of a schoolmaster, is frequently employed, as, for instance, the word 'clasp' in:

he contrived, for the dog's dish, a little lid that could be fastened down, by means of clasps, of clasps that clasped tight the sides, of the dish;

and the word 'not' in:

the little that is known about it has not yet all been said. Much has been said, but not all. Not that many things remain to be said, on the subject of the Galls father and son, for they do not;

and the word 'never' in:

Art and Con were great chewers of tobacco twist, and never had enough, never never had enough tobacco twist, for their liking.

This repetition of simple words, punctuating the discourse, leads us to notice a stylistic habit which is typically Beckettian and first becomes noticeable in *Watt*: that is the insertion, between commas, of 'oh', or 'no', or 'was it not', into the body of the narrative:

This was indeed a merciful coincidence, was it not, that at the moment of Watt's losing sight of the ground floor, he lost interest in it also.

He was not so foolish as to found in this a principle of conduct, or a precedent of rebelliousness, hò no, for Watt was only too willing to do as he was told.

Moreover, the careful use of subjunctives, and also of commas placed wherever possible (almost as an illiterate person would

place them), gives *Watt* the fastidious, finicky aspect that characterizes and indeed makes possible the painstaking exposition of
such enormous fantasies as that of the disposal of the leftovers,
entailing such detail about the dog and its antecedents. The purpose of this fullness is throughout comic; indeed most of the odd
humour of *Watt* results from the peculiarities of its style. Farcical
elements, for instance, are made more so when told with a
straight face and in exaggeratedly formal terms:

He could recall . . . the time when his dead father appeared to him in a
wood, with his trousers rolled up over his knees and his shoes and socks
in his hand; . . . or the time when an old lady of delicate upbringing,
and advantageous person, for she was amputated well above the knee,
whom he had pursued with his assiduities on no fewer than three
distinct occasions, unstrapped her wooden leg, and laid aside her
crutch.

The ridiculous event also gains by being recounted in an odd
blend of a literary and colloquial style, frequently to be found in
Watt:

Had his whistle been less piercing, and his entry less resounding, he
might have heard, behind the door, a disquieting sound, that of soliloquy, under dictation, and proceeded with care. But no, he turned the
key and dealt, with his boot, the door a dunt that sent it flying inwards,
at a great speed.

Stylistic humour of this kind is accompanied by more explicit
humour in the form of asides on the part of the author:

Officer, he cried, as God is my witness, he had his hand upon it.
God is a witness that cannot be sworn.

Or else in the form of witticisms tossed off in the course of the
narrative:

to the spoon, the knife, and even the fork, considered as aids to inges-
tion, she had never been able to accustom herself, in spite of excellent
references.

Naturally enough, some of the humour is in what is usually considered bad taste:

Watt's smile was further peculiar in this, that it seldom came singly, but was followed after a short time by another, less pronounced it is true. In this it resembled the fart.

Irony, too, is no more absent from *Watt* than from anything Beckett has written, although it is often less overt than usual:

[Ernest Louit] was a close companion of the College Bursar, their association (for it was nothing less) being founded on a community of tastes, and even I fear practices, all too common in academic circles, and of which perhaps the most endearing was brandy on awakening, which they did habitually in each other's society.

Parody is often found, as in this passage with its echoes of Defoe's *Robinson Crusoe* manner:

Being now so near the fence, that I could have touched it with a stick, if I had wished, and so looking about me, like a mad creature, I perceived, beyond all possibility of error, that I was in the presence of one of those channels or straits described above, where the limit of my garden, and that of another, followed the same course.

In this book, as elsewhere, biblical parody is frequent, as in the scene of the rats quoted above: 'and then we would sit down in the midst of them, and give them to eat'. The style in fact varies with the mood. Academic language is parodied in the Ernest Louit story, and frequently, in the text, snatches of doggerel are quoted, the best of which is perhaps the song to his Nelly of the solicitor Grehan, jailed for seven years:

> To thee, sweet Nell, when shadows fall
> Jug-jug! Jug-jug!
> I here in thrall
> My wanton thoughts do turn.
> Walks she out yet with Byrne?
> Moves Hyde his hand amid her skirts
> As erst? I ask, and Echo answers: Certes.

Watt is, indeed, even more a stylistic *tour de force* than its predecessors. The literary allusions have largely gone, but the verses, the elements of parody and pastiche, the wit and the systematic exploitation of paradox, as in the following passage, all make for prose of considerable intricacy:

Watt's eyes filled with tears that he could not stem, and they flowed down his fluted cheeks unchecked, in a steady flow, refreshing him greatly.

In this connection the use of absurd understatement is noticeable, as in the following example:

Watt might have broken the door down, with an axe, or a crow, or a small charge of explosive, but this might have aroused Erskine's suspicions, and Watt did not want that.

The intention behind this diversity of style seems often to be a debunking of the whole act of literary creation. Digressions are, for example, embarked upon, albeit within the symmetrical structure of the four parts, with a zest and a frequency that strongly suggests the influence of Sterne, for this device is employed in *Watt* with the same skill and deliberateness as in *Tristram Shandy*. The story of Ernest Louit, for example, forms a vast digression, thirty pages long, and the tales of Mary the gluttonous housemaid, and of the quasi-incestuous activities of the Lynches, are scarcely less copious. Beckett affects occasionally not to know what to say, and so either leaves a question mark, or inserts, like Swift in *Tale of a Tub*, phrases like *hiatus in MS* into the body of his text. Then again, he intervenes with expressions like 'tired of underlining' and 'how hideous is the semicolon', and even goes so far as to flaunt the illogical nature of his tale: 'haemophilia is, like enlargement of the prostate, an exclusively male disorder. But not in this work'. He repeats himself endlessly; and all this in continual mockery of a craft in which he is, for all that, well skilled, for if this book cannot be described as highly readable, it can certainly be said to contain interesting and original prose. Besides, the deliberate flouting of the logical sequence which is usually required of the traditional novel, and which Beckett respected with tongue-in-the-cheek punctilio in *Murphy*, shows that he has broken with the conventional form, with the 'vulgarity of a plausible concatenation', of which he speaks impatiently in his monograph on Proust. *Watt*, as Christine Brooke-Rose has pointed out, is in fact an 'anti-novel' in the tradition of Cervantes,

Furetière and of course Sterne, a novel which disdains 'to tell a story about persons recognizable as human beings in recognizable situations', and which introduces such extraneous matter as digressive anecdotes, snatches of song, exhaustive lists of objects and of logical (and illogical) combinations of possibilities, with an addenda section to contain the rejectamenta from the rest of the book; moreover, it develops minor characters at the expense of major ones, and, finally, fails to show any real action, any progression to a *dénouement* such as for instance we find, although of a particularly violent kind, in *Murphy*. Nevertheless this tenuous action, continually and wilfully erratic and inconsequential, does contribute, as do the excessive complications of the style and the impression of great tact and care in the handling of immensely difficult subject-matter, to the plausible rendering of the issues of the novel. It is to these issues, to the philosophical content, as it were, of *Watt*, that we now turn.

*　　*　　*

The most obvious theme of *Watt*, the one that strikes the reader at once, is that of the alienation of the hero from the rest of humanity. At the very beginning, he appears as a mysterious and uncertain person to his fellow men – Mr. Hackett and Mr. and Mrs. Nixon cannot decide who he is or what he does, and Mr. Hackett himself is almost frantic in his wish to gain some information about Watt:

> He did not know when he had been more intrigued, nay, he did not know when he had been so intrigued. He did not know either what it was that so intrigued him. What is it that so intrigues me, he said . . . I burn with curiosity, and with wonder.

Watt is therefore an unknown quantity to Mr. Hackett and his friends, for although Mr. Nixon says 'I seem to have known him all my life,' he can say nothing much about him: 'he does not invite mention, there are people like that', and finally, exasperated by Mr. Hackett's insistence, he cries 'I tell you nothing is known. Nothing.' The friends finally resign themselves with the thought 'what does it matter who he is? What can it possibly matter to us?'

Apart from exciting people's curiosity, Watt also arouses their anger: the conductor of the tramcar carrying Watt at the beginning of the story raises his voice at him, as does Mr. Nixon too, and the porter, whose milk-can Watt almost upsets, curses him for his clumsiness. Lady McCann, we saw, hurls a stone at him, for no reason except that she dislikes the look of him walking along the public road, and the railwaymen at the end of the book injure him with their slop-bucket. When he comes round, they feel impelled to ask him 'who the devil are you, and what the hell do you want?', but Watt's only form of reply is to put his hat on. In fact he behaves everywhere as if oblivious of the people around him: only when he sees a face on the other side of the ticket-window does he ask for a ticket, ignoring completely the commotion around him of people asking each other who he is. In a similar way, at the beginning of the book, as Watt watches the porter moving the milk-cans, he cannot discover the purpose of the manœuvre: 'he is sorting the cans, said Watt. Or perhaps it is a punishment for disobedience, or some neglect of duty'. The railwaymen at the end refer to him coarsely as 'the long wet dream with the hat and bags'; and in Mr. Micks, his successor, he inspires nothing but terror.

Watt is indifferent to this situation of exile. Why should he care about it, since his own body is deserting him?

It was now fully two hours since Watt had passed water . . . he who hourly passed an urgent water, a delicious water, in the ordinary way. This last regular link with the screen, for he did not count as such his weekly stool, nor biannual equinoctial emission in vacuo, he now envisaged its relaxation, and eventual rupture, with sadness, with gladness.

Little wonder then that Watt should end up in a mental institution, in the 'windowlessness', the 'bloodheat', the 'hush' of a padded cell, the 'separate soundless unlit warmth' of what Murphy considered 'indoor bowers of bliss'.

Watt's exile is exactly that which Murphy had longed to share with the mental patients. But the former only arrives at this exile after great suffering, and there is little indication that a 'slap-up psychosis' is for Watt the joy that Murphy had believed it would be. Watt indeed reaches the plenitude of his exile from the world of men only *after* his stay with Mr. Knott, which destroys for him the world of objects, of logic, and of names, and which takes him a step further in the dolorous calvary that is the way of the Beckettian hero from Belacqua's Dublin to the muddy netherworld of Pim.

*　　*　　*

Sexual unease is quite as prominent a feature in *Watt* as in *More Pricks than Kicks*. Great play is made, for instance, of the fact of Mr. Graves' inability 'to get on well with his wife', and Arthur, in a clever piece of parody, gives out in copy-writer's patter a recommendation for Bando to cure it. We find, too, the committee, set up to examine Mr. Louit, observing intently Mr. Nackybal's rapt air as he scratches himself, and exclaiming: 'What vitality! At his age! The open-air life! Ego autem!' But the biggest sexual joke of all is that of Watt's halting affair with the fishwoman Mrs. Gorman:

Further than this, it will be learnt with regret, they never went, though more than half inclined to do so on more than one occasion. Why was this? Was it the echo murmuring in their hearts, in Watt's heart, in Mrs. Gorman's, of past passion, ancient error, warning them not to sully not to trail, in the cloaca of clonic gratification, a flower so fair, so rare, so sweet, so frail? It is not necessary to suppose so. For Watt had not the strength, and Mrs. Gorman had not the time, indespensable to even the most perfunctory coalescence. The irony of life! Of life in love! That he who has the time should lack the force, that she who has the force should lack the time!

If we put with this the ironies about Mr. Louit's homosexuality, a general picture emerges of a detached disdain on sexual matters; all manifestations of the erotic impulse, from inversion and onanism on the one hand, to conjugal love (sardonically termed at one point in the story 'cloistered fornication') on the other, are exposed in this novel to ironical contemplation. In the books which follow *Watt* they are exposed to something much harsher than amused irony of this kind.

*　　*　　*

But the questions of exile and sexuality are in *Watt* subordinated to the really burning question, which concerns the difficulty, the impossibility in fact, of all knowledge, even of the simplest kind, such as the knowledge of physical things. We are, in this connection, not told why Watt undertakes his baleful journey to Mr. Knott's house, whether he has been sent for, as K. was in *The Castle*, or whether he is answering a newspaper advertisement for a servant; we only know that he leaves the city, with very little money in his pocket, one summer evening, and before dawn the next day he has arrived at the house. Very soon mystery begins for him, for 'Watt never knew how he got into Mr. Knott's house. He knew that he got in by the back door, but he was never to know, never, never to know, how the backdoor came to be opened.' In the same way he is never to know at exactly what moment Arsene comes into the kitchen, and finds it 'strange to think of all these little things that cluster round the comings, and the stayings, and the goings, that he would know nothing of them . . . as long as he lived.' (Frequently in this book, in fact, we are told of an event, or practice, 'the reasons for this are not known', or else that some pseudo-explanation given is 'merely the reason offered to the understanding'.) Arsene himself gazes long at Watt, and Watt notices Arsene's dress in minute detail; the latter then disappears, returns in a short time dressed for the road, and makes an important speech in which he surveys his experience in the service of Mr. Knott.

Watt, it seems, in his 'weary watchful vacancy', reminds Arsene of his own arrival, and the latter describes to the newcomer his feelings of that period, when wounded (like Christ) 'in his head, in his side, in his hands and feet', he felt stretching before him 'the long blue days, for his head, for his side, and the little paths for his feet, and all the brightness to touch and gather', and 'at night rest in the quiet house . . . by a window opening on refuge, the little sounds coming that demand nothing . . . explain nothing, propound nothing'. For, Arsene says, one comes to Mr. Knott's as to 'sites of a stirring beyond coming and going, of a being so light and free that it is as the being of nothing'; one comes as to a conversion, 'a face offered, all trust and innocence and candour, all the old soil and fear and weakness offered, to be sponged away and forgiven'. At last one knows that here one is the 'right man', for 'the sensations, the premonitions of harmony are irrefragable', when one seems to be 'in one's midst at last, after so many tedious years spent clinging to the perimeter', in complete unity with 'all outside', the flowers, the earth, the sky, which in fact seem to have become oneself. One's euphoria is not dissipated by the fact that one has to work at Mr. Knott's, for any servant of the latter soon realizes that

he is working not merely for Mr. Knott in person, and for Mr. Knott's establishment, but also, and indeed chiefly, for himself, that he may abide, as he is, where he is, and that where he is may abide about him, as it is. Unable to resist these intenerating considerations, his regrets, lively at first, melt at last, melt quite away and pass over, softly, into the celebrated conviction that all is well, or at least for the best.

But this conviction is eventually shaken, for no explicable reason, and Arsene describes how this occurred in his own case. It came, he says, at a time of perfect health and in fine weather and seemed to be a slip and rearrangement of things, both internal and external, since the distinction between the two was then difficult to draw.

And thereafter, everything was changed, the sun looked different on the wall, and his pipe ceased so completely to be the solace to which he was accustomed that he feared it might have become 'a thermometer, or an epileptic's dental wedge'. He cannot, however, say in what the change really consisted. He hazards a guess: 'what was changed was existence of the ladder. Do not come down the ladder, Ifor, I haf taken it away'; it was, as it were, 'the reversed metamorphosis, the Laurel into Daphne, the old thing where it always was, back again'; it was a realization that attainment is far less agreeable than longing (the 'drunkard in the desert' is the happy one), and an intuition of the 'presence of what did not exist'. Arsene ends his speech (after much digression) with the implication that Watt's experience will be like his own: 'For in truth the same things happen to us all, especially to men in our situation, whatever that is, if only we chose to know it'.

It seems clear that Watt has come to Mr. Knott's house fundamentally for religious reasons; he explains his quest to Sam later in these terms (I transcribe his inverted jargon):

Abandoned my little to find him. My little to learn him forgot. My little rejected to have him. To love him my little reviled. This body homeless. This mind ignoring. These emptied hands. This emptied heart. To him I brought. To the temple. To the teacher. To the source. Of nought.

The resemblance to the suffering Jesus, which Arsene remarked upon, is further underlined ('his face was bloody, his hands also, and thorns were in his scalp'), and it is in this state that Watt came to the 'nought' that is Knott on a day which seems to him to be 'without precedent at last'. And when he arrives, the world still accepts his names and his categories:

He had experienced literally nothing since the age of fourteen, or fifteen, of which in retrospect he was not content to say, That is what happened then;

for things do not yet show any 'tendency to vanish in the farce of their properties'. But Watt has not long served at Mr. Knott's before there occurs the incident to which he is unable to attach any meaning, and which announces the disastrous crumbling of his faculties of cognition.

An old man and a middle-aged man call at the house, and introduce themselves as the Galls, father and son, piano-tuners. The younger man carries out the work, both men then exchange gloomy comments on the fate of the piano, its tuner, and its pianist, and finally take their leave. But simple as the incident sounds, it is not at all simple for Watt: it 'gradually lost, in the nice processes of its light, its sound, its impacts, and its rhythm, all meaning, even the most literal', and

became a mere example of light commenting bodies, and stillness motion, and silence sound, and comment comment. This fragility of the outer meaning had a bad effect on Watt, for it caused him to seek for another, for some meaning of what had passed, in the image of how it had passed. The most meagre, the least plausible, would have satisfied Watt, . . . who had lived, miserably it is true, among face values all his adult life, face values at least for him.

He feels 'the need to be able to say . . . Yes, I remember, that is what happened then'. But this need is not satisfied, and the Galls incident is followed by others, 'of a similar kind, that is to say of great formal brilliance and indeterminable purport' which Watt cannot accept 'for what they perhaps were, the simple games that time plays with space'; instead he feels obliged 'to enquire into what they meant, oh not into what they really meant, . . . but into what they might be induced to mean'. For what really distresses him is that 'a thing that was nothing had happened, with the utmost formal distinctness . . . with all the clarity and solidity of something', and his distress is constant, as it was also for his predecessors, Erskine, Arsene, Walter and Vincent, in the same predicament. When he manages to evolve a hypothesis to dispel his doubts about the incident he usually finds that 'the hypothesis evolved lost its virtue, after one or two applications'. How, then, can one be sure, 'with reference to two or even three incidents related by Watt as separate and distinct, if they are not in reality the same incident, variously interpreted', that is, how can one be sure that one is not merely being presented with two, or even three different hypotheses erected by Watt to explain only one occurrence? Especially as Watt is obliged, we are told, to devise so many hypotheses which so soon cease to apply? That is, Sam feels, the chief problem, and this is why he asks us to realize 'the difficulties experienced in formulating . . . the entire body of Watt's experience' at Mr. Knott's establishment.

Such incidents as these are only the beginning of Watt's troubles. He needs someone to apply words to his situation, because now he 'found himself in the midst of things which, if they consented to be named, did so as it were with reluctance'. A pot, for some reason, ceases, for Watt, to be a pot any more, and soon he discovers 'that of himself too he could no longer affirm anything that did not seem false'. His 'need of semantic succour was at times so great that he would set to trying names on things, and on himself', but he can no longer apply the term 'man' to himself 'as he had used to do, with the intuition that he was perhaps not talking nonsense'. The unwillingness of things to accept the 'time-honoured names' does not always grieve him, even though (as for Murphy) things have always been his best friends; on the whole, however, he does long for a voice, if only Erskine's, 'to speak of the little world of Mr. Knott's establishment, with the old words, the old credentials', at least before his world has 'become unspeakable' and he 'grown used to his loss of species'. When Watt does learn to bear the fact that 'a nothing had happened . . . and even, in a shy way, to like it', it is by then 'too late', for his world is in ruins.

Watt is, in fact, alert to all sense-data, he is even described as 'lacerated with curiosity', but 'the results, on the whole, were meagre', both on the ground floor, and on the first:

Of the many excellent reasons for this, two seemed to Watt to merit mention: on the one hand the exiguity of the material propounded to his senses, on the other the decay of these. What little there was to see, to hear, to smell, to taste, to touch, like a man in a stupor he saw it, heard it, smelt it, tasted it, touched it.

Besides, phenomena are never fixed, even 'the stairs were never the same', but 'the number of steps seemed to vary, from day to day', and even 'the clouds seen from Mr. Knott's premises were not quite the clouds that Watt was used to'.

He does, however, manage to learn something about the immense trivialities of Mr. Knott's nourishment, but although he successfully turns this particular 'disturbance into words', his knowledge of Mr. Knott himself is still absolutely nil, he is quite without conception of the latter. One day they do meet on the lawn, but even then Watt fails to see Mr. Knott's face, so that 'little by little Watt abandoned all hope, all fear, of ever seeing Mr. Knott face to face'; and, at about the same time, when a friend of Mr. Knott's telephones to enquire after his health, Watt troubles himself no further with finding a formulation that will fit the facts of the incident. Only too frequently has he 'opened tins with his blowlamp' to find them empty. When he eventually leaves his service on the ground floor on Arthur's arrival, he is exhausted, 'sicker, aloner', and, as we saw, 'of his anxiety to get well', nothing remains. All that he has discovered is the unwillingness of words to fit things, the reversibility of logic ('it is rare that the feeling of absurdity is not followed by the feeling of necessity . . . [and] it is rare that the feeling of necessity is not followed by the feeling of absurdity'), the agonizing infinitude of all series, and the uncertainty of number ('the figures given here are incorrect. The consequent calculations are therefore doubly erroneous').

On the first floor, where his duties bring him into daily contact with Mr. Knott, he remains 'in particular ignorance of Mr. Knott himself' who lives in hush and gloom 'dimming all, dulling all, stilling all, numbing all, where he passed'. Watt summarizes his relationship with Mr. Knott in these terms (I again transcribe his jargon):

Side by side, two men. All day, part of night. Dumb, numb, blind.
Knott look at Watt? No. Watt look at Knott? No. Watt talk to Knott?
No. Knott talk to Watt? No. What then did us do? Niks, niks, niks.
Part of night, all day. Two men, side by side.

'For except, one, not to need, and two, a witness of his not needing, Knott needed nothing, as far as Watt could see.' Of himself
Knott 'knew nothing, and so he needed to be witnessed . . . that he
might not cease'. He therefore depends upon his servants' perception of him in order to be able to continue in existence. His
being is certainly a fragile one, for he seems to be unfamiliar
with his own house, and his physical appearance is, as we saw,
constantly altering. He is both very ordinary in his habits and
very strange. What interests Watt most during his stay on the
first floor is Arthur's tale, which has nothing to do with it, for now
that he is near Mr. Knott, he feels only 'ataraxy' and is quite
immune to the oddness of the things that once so perplexed him,
as for instance the painting in Erskine's, now his own, room.

Numbed by his unnerving contact with the nothing that is
Knott, he does not know whether he should feel grief or not when
he leaves the house: he sheds tears, but calculates that these must
soon evaporate, and as Arsene had clearly foretold, the knowledge
Watt acquires at Mr. Knott's 'partakes . . . of the nature of . . . the
unutterable or ineffable'. Once at the station he sees a figure
advancing along the road whose gait closely resembles his own,
and he at first 'falls into his old error' of wanting to know 'what
the figure appeared to be, in reality', but apart from this lapse,
he behaves with more 'reserve' vis-à-vis the tactile and olfactory
stimuli of the station waiting-room than he would have done
before his stay at Mr. Knott's: for this stay has destroyed his innocence, and he now seems fully to realize that the world is fraught
with uncertainty and mystery, and only great patience will resolve some of its enigmas. He therefore waits, in the waiting-
room, for a chair and a picture to materialize from the chaos of
phenomena, and he no longer feels impelled to rush things. But
otherwise his situation is little changed: 'from naught come, to
naught gone', his trip to Knott's was that 'of a dim mind way-
faring / through barren lands'. Who knows, the whole tale
may have been enacted only in Watt's 'soul-landscape', which in

the addenda section is described as dark and vast, just as all Bom's adventures, in *Comment C'est*, turn out to be mere fictions of his own invention; and, of course, Watt-Knott, what-not, means 'anything', and Watt is the eternal question what? driving up against the eternal answer Knott, nothing, *néant*.

Perhaps the only other Beckettian hero Mr. Knott closely resembles, apart from Mr. Endon and Hamm with whom there are also some similarities, is Godot, who never actually appears but who plays games with the hopes and fears of Vladimir and Estragon. Knott, too, plays with his servants. For them, his house is haven, approached with awe, but their stay is of finite duration. Arsene sees a purpose behind these changes in personnel ('for what is this shadow of the going in which we come . . . if not the shadow of purpose?') but his dreams of peace are nonetheless destroyed and he leaves embittered and hopeless. As for Arthur, he is both drawn and repelled by Mr. Knott, who is at once the object and the derision of his servants' quest, and who can never be known, although at one point Sam suggests that something might be discovered if it were ever possible to collate all the experiences of all the servants who had ever worked for him: 'that would have been a very interesting exercise', he says, 'but they all vanished, long before my time'. In any case, Mr. Knott is inexpressible ('ineffable'): Watt's syntax breaks down under the strain when he tries to tell Sam of his master, who appears as a negative god, the great Nothing of which nothing can be predicated. That he is a god-figure is left in no doubt: to speculate about him is to be guilty of an 'anthropomorphic insolence'. He is, furthermore, directly compared to a sun, able to be glimpsed in 'an eastern window at morning, a western window at evening'; he does the circuit of his bed in twelve months, and round him his servants eternally turn 'in tireless love'. And yet, when Watt himself has vanished from the scene, nature continues on its triumphant way, and the railwaymen exalt its creator. Nothing much has changed. That is perhaps the point: Knott is nothing, the experience has no effect, just as, when Berkeley calls the physical universe into question in his *Principles*, we yet carry on afterwards as if no doubt could ever be cast on the substantiality of what we see and touch. Experience of Mr. Knott is like a dream left over in the bright sun that shines on the railway-station and on its busy life;

the contented realism of the railwaymen contrasts sharply with the sombre uncertainties of the house and with the strangeness of the asylum to which Watt eventually goes. (In a similar way, the world of Jacques Moran is contrasted with the dark forest inhabited by Molloy.) The negative vision of Mr. Knott results merely in a rearrangement of things, 'the old thing where it always was'; but, as in concussion, the reshuffling leaves everything out of focus, and Watt never recovers from the disturbing effects of the Galls incident. Shaken and troubled by the perplexing difficulties of his recent experiences, he withdraws, more in indifference than in deep pain, to an asylum, and wanders aimlessly in the grounds, a bizarre and even terrifying figure.

This novel, clearly a somewhat uncertain and transitional composition, a sort of extended doodle in words, leads us nevertheless into unfamiliar country, the land of windy heaths and lonely roads, where Mercier and Camier undertake their journey and Molloy crawls in search of his mother, and introduces us to a new kind of literary hero: an antisocial vagabond, a decayed intellectual, a decrepit savage muttering on the hopeless incongruity of the world.

TWO NOTES ON CHAPTER THREE

1. Jacqueline Hoefer, in an article in *Perspective* (Washington University, St. Louis, Missouri, number for Autumn 1959), made a clever guess that Arsene's words, 'what was changed was existence of the ladder', etc. (*Watt*, 1958 ed., pp. 47-48), were a reference to the closing sentences of Wittgenstein's *Tractatus Logico-Philosophicus*, as follows:

'My propositions are elucidatory in this way: he who understands me finally recognises them as senseless, when he has climbed out through them, on them, over them. (He must so to speak throw away the ladder, after he has climbed up on it.) He must surmount these propositions, then he sees the world rightly. Whereof one cannot speak, thereof one must be silent.'

Jacqueline Hoefer supports her interpretation, which indeed would explain much in *Watt*, by the German pronunciation in 'I haf' and 'Ifor'. Unfortunately this interpretation is quite erroneous. Mr. Beckett told me in 1961 that the 'ladder' is a reference to 'a Welsh joke' (an *Itma* classic, I'm informed), making the pronunciation not German but Welsh, and that he had read the works of Wittgenstein only 'within the last two years'.

Other references to the 'ladder' joke are to be found on p. 16 of *Watt* and p. 188 of *Murphy* ; see also p. 81, above.

*   *   *

2.   A question that also springs to mind when one reads *Watt* is how far Beckett was influenced by Kafka in writing the novel. Ruby Cohn in an excellent and thorough article in *Comparative Literature*, Eugene, Oregon, Spring 1961, sees in both *The Castle* (the only large work of Kafka's that Beckett says he has read in the original German) and in *Watt* further manifestations of the theme of the quest, which is such a common one in European literature. 'In both novels', Ruby Cohn says, 'mystic forces prove impregnable to weak human siege' and these forces continue to remain indifferent to that siege, for 'the tools of this world do not render [Mr. Knott] sapient', nor do they make the Castle accessible to K. It is evident that there are definite similarities between *The Castle* and *Watt*, but whether this means direct influence of the former on the latter is another matter. At one point, however, the expression of the two books is too close for there to be much question of coincidence. I refer to the following passages, the first from *Watt*, the second from *The Castle*, the one almost a paraphrase of the other:

> The incident of the Galls, on the contrary, [heard] long before, an instant in the life of another, ill told, ill heard, and more than half forgotten.
> (*Watt*, 1958, p. 81)
> *Es war mir, als sei es vor vielen Jahren geschehen, oder als sei es gar nicht mir geschehen, oder als hätte ich es nur erzählen hören, oder als hätte ich selbst es schon vergessen.* (*Das Schloss*, 1951 ed., p. 76)

There are however important differences between the two books. The theme of guilt for instance does occur in *Watt* (cf. p. 127) but never is it of such importance as in *The Castle*. Guilt in Kafka, of course, extends to the whole situation in which the hero finds himself; his liability is as extensive as that of Oedipus. Beckett's situations are quite different from this, for Watt is never held to be undergoing *punishment* in Mr. Knott's house. Moreover, Mr. Knott, despite interesting similarities which Ruby Cohn points out, is not like Klamm, who is an object of terror, alarmingly masked by a harmless exterior and by physical inaccessibility: K. misses his only chance (in the interview with Bürgel) through his insuperable fatigue, a situation which occurs in nightmares everyone is familiar with. Watt, however, does not seem to fail because of any such moral weakness: he fails because his attempt is quite vain from the outset. We, like Watt, suffer not so much because of a *malignant* God, who truly exists, but because we clutch at phantoms – Knott, Godot – in our frenzy to know, to hope, to believe, and we suffer ludicrously as a result. *Watt* is therefore a much more comic book than *The Castle*, and this is true of most of Beckett's work, where humour constantly tempers an otherwise oppressive sense of disaster.

Stylistically, moreover, there seems to be little parallel between the two novels. Beckett himself (quoted by Ruby Cohn) has said that 'Kafka's form is classic, it goes on like a steam-roller – almost serene'; and Ruby Cohn adds that Kafka follows conventional chronology, causally links chapters, etc. This firmness of structure is, as we have seen, far less evident in *Watt*, for within the admittedly symmetrical framework of four chapters, and two phases, ground floor and first floor (cf. the two acts of *Godot* and *Happy Days*), incongruous matter abounds.

Both novels are however similar in that they are myths, the interpretation of which must be a subtle and complex affair, for they have the power of haunting the mind on many levels without being explicit: they fulfil the functions of a symbol of *unassigned* value: it is we who lend the symbol meaning, from our own hopes and fears.

The last word on this subject should go, perhaps, to Maurice Nadeau:

'La créature de Kafka supporte le poids d'une faute, ignorée sans doute, mais qu'elle a commise, et dont elle cherche obscurément et comme à tâtons le pardon; celle de Beckett est innocente, entraînée dans un monde qui se suffit à lui-même et dont l'absence de signification ne postule aucun ordre transcendant . . . chez Beckett [l'homme] se désagrège dans le même mouvement qui mène le monde au désastre.'

(*Temps Modernes*, janvier 1952)

Chapter 4

THE FIRST FRENCH HEROES

'That sentence has a wonderful shape. It is the shape that matters.'

SAMUEL BECKETT TO HAROLD HOBSON, 1956

I THE HERO OF THE *NOUVELLES*

THE liberation of France made it possible for Beckett to visit his mother in Ireland for the first time since the outbreak of war; but returning to France afterwards seemed to present difficulties, and therefore on the advice of a doctor friend he applied for a post as interpreter at the hospital set up at St.-Lô by the Irish Red Cross. This appeared at the time to be the simplest way he could return to the country of his adoption, although he subsequently discovered that he had to act as storekeeper in the hospital as well. A poem in English called *St.-Lô* dates from this period. Before long, of course, the appointment ended and Beckett was able to resume the simplicity and seclusion of his pre-war existence in Paris, which despite his accession to fame has altered very little since. Although he prefers to remain somewhat inaccessible, he has a reputation with those who know him for kindness, affability and good humour. The only outstanding public events in his life since the war have been the great and unexpected success of *En attendant Godot*, and the subsequent performance of three of his plays by state-sponsored companies in Paris; an honorary Doctorate in Letters conferred by his old university; the first *Prix international des Editeurs*, awarded *ex æquo* with Jorge Luis Borges in 1961; and the supreme honour, the Nobel Prize, in 1969.

This recognition was not, however, easily come by: the printing history of Beckett's post-war work written in French is a record of struggle and slow acceptance. Soon after the war, in the tenth number of Jean-Paul Sartre's review *Les Temps Modernes* (July 1946), there appeared Beckett's first piece of fiction written

90

directly into French, a short story entitled *Suite*. Sartre had been a student at the Ecole Normale Supérieure just before Beckett's period as *lecteur* there, and this fact could perhaps explain why it was to his review that Beckett submitted the story. A few months later, in the fourteenth number of the same review, appeared twelve of Beckett's short French poems (since collected) written between 1937 and 1939, and then at the turn of the year Max-Pol Fouchet's periodical *Fontaine* contained another short story, *L'Expulsé*. In the course of that year (1947) Beckett's French version of *Murphy* appeared, but thereafter there was virtual silence until Jérôme Lindon issued *Molloy* in 1951 at the Editions de Minuit. The same publisher in 1955 collected the two stories *Suite* and *L'Expulsé*, and added a third, till then unpublished (*Le Calmant*), together with the *Textes pour rien* (written later), to form the *recueil* entitled *Nouvelles et Textes pour rien*. The first half of this volume contains the definitive texts of the early French stories which are the subject of the present chapter.

They were written, according to Beckett himself, in the following order: firstly, *La Fin* (as *Suite* is now entitled), secondly, *L'Expulsé*, and thirdly, *Premier amour*, which the author has not wished to be published; these were then followed by a fourth *nouvelle*, *Le Calmant*.

Before proceeding to examine these stories, we should first consider the problems raised by Beckett's definitive adoption of French as his medium soon after the liberation. Such a changeover is indeed a striking occurrence, but not by any means unique in the history of literature: for Edward Gibbon wrote a journal in French with a view to composing the *Decline and Fall* in the same language, and William Beckford wrote his *Vathek* in French, a fact which excited the surprise and interest of Mallarmé, who in his preface to *Vathek* called it *un des écrits les plus intéressants qui aient été jadis composés en français*. Beckett's adoption of French did not however take place as abruptly or as suddenly as may seem, nor did it occur as unexpectedly as did, for instance, Beckford's. In fact, Beckett carried out the translation of *Murphy* into French (with some assistance from his friend Alfred Péron, *normalien* and sometime *lecteur* at Trinity) before the war, when he was also writing poetry in French; and by the time he wrote

Watt, gallicisms were already creeping into his English prose style. Here are a few of the more obvious ones:

I do not rise, not having the *force* (French *la force*).

I was not found *under a cabbage* (humorous combination of English *under a gooseberry bush* and French *dans un chou*).

But does the penny fare end here, . . . at a merely facultative stop? (French *arrêt facultatif*).

Certain fish, in order to *support* the middle depths . . . (French *supporter*).

He quoted *as well* from his ancestors' experience *as* from his own (French *aussi bien . . . que*).

. . . we should ever have *embraced* . . . and never on the mouth (French *embrasser*).

. . . dives from dreadful heights . . . before a *numerous public* (French *public nombreux*).

Mrs. Penny-a-hoist Pim, . . . that old *put* (French abbreviation for *putain*).

Several of these gallicisms, especially the last quoted, have evidently a humorous function and can be explained by the fact that for a man used to hearing French spoken all the time such transpositions as 'facultative stop' would seem amusing. (British students in France frequently indulge in a similar kind of humour.) But other gallicisms, especially 'as well . . . as', seem to have resulted from a genuine mental habit which the author did not manage to rid himself of, cut off as he was from spoken English by the fact of the Occupation, and thinking and living as he did the whole time in French; so that even when he sat down to compose in English certain French turns of phrase kept intruding. (In such circumstances this is a common experience.) It is furthermore interesting to note that *Watt* translates easily into French, which is a further indication that Beckett, in his last English novel, was already moving towards a more distinctly French idiom.

Again, we find definite anglicisms lingering on in the *Suite* of 1946, whereas in the definitive 1955 version, *La Fin*, these have been completely eliminated. Here are the principal anglicisms that can be noted, together with the corrected version:

1946: je vous suis très *obligé pour* ces vêtements;

1955: je vous suis *reconnaissant*;

1946: un petit garçon . . . demanda à sa mère *la cause de cela;*

1955: un petit garçon . . . demanda à sa mère *comment cela était possible;*

1946: il *offrit* d'envoyer chercher un taxi;

1955: il *proposa* d'envoyer chercher un taxi;

1946: les longs mois de calme, *oblitérés* en un instant!

1955: les longs mois de calme, *anéantis* en un instant! (oblitérer, by which Beckett meant 'wiped out', has usually only the technical meaning of 'cancel (a stamp)'.)

1946: il répéta l'histoire . . . que j'avais oubliée. *Même alors* c'était comme si je l'entendais pour la première fois;

1955: il répéta l'histoire . . . je l'avais oubliée, c'était comme si je l'entendais pour la première fois; (*même alors*=English 'even then', left out.)

1946: il était très *amical et hospitalier;*

1955: il était *bon.* (*amical*, 'friendly', can usually only be applied to an attitude, etc.; *accueillant* would be better French than *hospitalier* in this context.)

These examples suggest that Beckett's early French prose contains anglicisms that ten years later, when he was much surer of his new medium, he took good care to eradicate. In the translation of *Murphy*, too, we find (as we might well expect), a French style that still has an English flavour, and that is still not yet fully naturalized. In *Murphy*, however, this seems to spring mainly from the attempt, doomed in advance, to transpose unaltered the dense, allusive fabric of the original into French, the genius of which is alien to such virtuosity. One sentence in particular, with its religious echoes that the English reader responds to, falls rather flat translated literally into French:

She stormed away from the callbox, accompanied delightedly by her hips, etc. The fiery darts encompassing her about of the amorously disposed were quenched as tow.

Elle quitta le kiosque en coup de vent, voluptueusement suivie de ses hanches, etc. Comme un lumignon furent éteints les traits enflammés des affamés d'amour.

This sort of verbal wit is amusing in English, but a Frenchman would not find it so. Nevertheless Beckett usually tried very hard in his translation to render faithfully as many of his jokes as possible, but his book was received in France with even less enthusiasm than it had been in England, and even now, when the Editions de Minuit have taken it over from Bordas, it seems to be little read in France. Where he could not translate, however, Beckett was content to delete and compensate elsewhere, as Ruby Cohn has pointed out in a valuable article that goes deeply into the whole question. Murphy's 'clonic' joke, for instance ('why did the barmaid champagne? – because the stout porter bitter'), is omitted and replaced merely by the sentence *il fit une plaisanterie de fort mauvais goût*, and the long commentary on the joke is also omitted. In the same way, a paragraph describing Murphy's joys on a number eleven bus is deleted, since the difficulties of transposing the details to a Parisian context proved evidently too formidable. On the other hand, ironic asides are added by way of compensation: we are told, for instance, that Neary cursed the night in which he was conceived, *car il avait toujours été un fils respectueux*.

In *La Fin* and the other stories, however, Beckett no longer attempts to write in his *Murphy* manner, but adopts from the outset a more French personality: as he has expressed it in a frequently quoted remark, *en français c'est plus facile d'écrire sans style*, and it was without style no doubt that he originally intended to write: but the clever *prosateur* that he is could not long remain simple even in a foreign language, so in his French writing we usually find that *ars est celare artem*, although he eschews the verbal play, the intricately-contrived allusiveness and surface wit of the English novels.

A study of the successive versions of *La Fin* (there are at least four: the 1946 *Temps Modernes* version, the one Richard Seaver translated with the author for *Merlin* (1954), the 1955 Editions de Minuit text, and Seaver's revised translation for the *Evergreen Review*, 1960) provides useful insight not only into the way Beckett carefully works over his prose, but also into the evolution of his French style from somewhat hesitant beginnings into the smooth instrument that it becomes in the trilogy. In *Suite*, apart from the obvious anglicisms that have been noted, there are other differences between his early and his mature style; for in that story, as in the translation of *Murphy* too, the language has a colloquial freedom that Beckett restricts and controls more tightly in later writing.[1] Examples of this in *Murphy* are, as Ruby Cohn has pointed out, the stronger oaths and vulgar expressions in the French, as opposed to the English text, as in this tirade:

My God, how I hate the charVenus and her sausage and mash sex. . . . How can I care what you DO?

Putain de putain, ce que ça m'emmerde, la Vénus de chambre et son Eros comme chez grand'mère. . . . Qu'est-ce que ça peut me foutre, ce que tu FAIS?

Much the same thing can be observed in *Suite*: the man whose clothes the hero inherits is called *le type* in *Suite* but, more accurately as well as more elegantly, *le mort* in *La Fin*. In the former we find: *elle avait un accent bizarre. Moi-même je parlais d'une drôle de façon*, and in the latter: *elle avait un accent bizarre. Mais moi aussi*; in the former, again: *ça commençait à me fâcher*, and in the latter: *cela m'indignait*. Moreover, the vocabulary in *La Fin* is wider and richer, for we do not find the obvious word in the obvious place; instead of: *j'envoyai rouler la chaise* (1946) we have: *j'envoyai valser la chaise* (1955); *ce n'était pourtant pas un site classé* (1955), instead of the banal *un lieu d'excursion* (1946); the more precise *peu après cette transaction* (with the Greek woman) instead of the neutral *peu . . . après cet événement*; and, this time more pedantically, *j'enfourchai l'âne* (1955) instead of

[1] The essay 'La peinture des van Velde, ou le monde et le pantalon' (1945), Beckett's very first French publication, is written in a style closely akin to that of *Suite* and of the French version of *Murphy*. The article shows immense sympathy for the two painters Bram and Geer van Velde: Beckett was among the first to champion their work (the elder of the two brothers, Bram, born in Holland in 1895, has been Beckett's close friend for many years, and they have much in common: for B. van Velde, whose total *œuvre* does not far exceed one hundred paintings and gouaches, creation is just as difficult, just as total a form of self-involvement and self-betrayal, as it is for Beckett – at least, so the latter's numerous commentaries on the artist's work imply). Despite the penetration and understanding revealed in this study, it is marred by an indiscriminate use of slang, which tends to alienate the reader's sympathies from the cause Beckett seeks, somewhat belligerently it is true, to promote. Words like *emmerder*, *déconner* and *foutre la paix* have a hollow ring about them in this context, and would not be used by a native, as Beckett soon came to realize. The study has never been reprinted.

je montai sur l'âne (1946) and *je m'agrippais à l'arête de l'encolure* (1955) instead of *je tenais l'âne à la crête du cou* (1946).

Suite is, moreover, generally more wordy than *La Fin*, being much longer as far as it goes (for only a truncated piece was printed[1]), and occasionally even more pompous: we read for example *je présenterai ma requête* instead of simply *je demanderai*.

Not always, of course, is it easy to explain the changes in expression, but on the whole two main reasons seem to dictate improvements: the first is the desire to be less explicit or less definite about the circumstances in which the story takes place. Examples of this are numerous: *fournisseurs* (of the town) becomes the more general *commerçants*; *pendant des années* is replaced by the vaguer *pendant longtemps*; and *un jour j'étais tellement faible que je ne pouvais plus me lever, et j'aurais certainement perdu connaissance sans la vache* is pruned drastically to: *un jour je ne pus me lever. La vache me sauva.* We find also that a phrase like *non, faux, enfin, je ne sais pas* is inserted to introduce a further element of uncertainty, and whole sentences (in one case a whole paragraph), which the author evidently thought gave too much particularity and definiteness to his 1946 story, are omitted: one interesting omission informs us that the hero, had he been in the London area, would (like any other Irishman, one feels) have sought a lodging in the Euston-King's Cross-Islington area.

The second general reason for modifications arises from a more developed sense of euphony, of elegance, or simply of correctness of style: *Que signifie ceci? dis-je. Est-ce un sauf-conduit?* becomes in 1955 the more euphonious *qu'est-ce que c'est, dis-je, un sauf-conduit?*; and *je me mis les autres vêtements* becomes the more elegant *je finis de m'habiller*; and *c'est alors que je reçus* the more grammatically correct or literary *ce fut alors que je reçus*.

This polishing of the style, which can be discerned wherever it is possible to study variants[2] in Beckett's texts (I indicate all the

---

[1] Mr. Beckett wrote to me that this occurred due to 'a misunderstanding with the *rédaction*, who thought the first half, sent separately, I forget why, was the whole story, and declined to publish the second half in the next issue – for reasons I could not understand; something to do, according to S. de Beauvoir, with the "tenue de la revue". . . '.

[2] The two versions of *L'Expulsé* also differ considerably from each other; in fact all the observations here made concerning changes between *Suite* and *La Fin* apply equally well to this *nouvelle*.

possibilities I am aware of in the bibliography below) reveals clearly that he has worked painstakingly to fashion himself a prose instrument that is accurate and sensitive, that functions as he wishes, that has no throw-away shows of brilliance which tend to distract the reader from his purpose, as in *Murphy* or *Watt*. Moreover, by purifying his French, by resisting the temptation to which he succumbed in the French *Murphy* to indulge wildly in slang and obscenities for their own sake, irrespective of any purpose they are intended to serve, he can give full explosive force to such oaths and curses and vulgar expressions as are couched in otherwise correct and elegant language, as we find for instance in the skilfully achieved contrast between the style of the following meditation and the woman's unexpected, cruel obscenity that shatters it:

Il faisait cette étrange lumière qui clôt une journée de pluie persistante, lorsque le soleil paraît et que le ciel s'éclaircit trop tard pour pouvoir servir. La terre fait un bruit comme de soupirs et les dernières gouttes tombent du ciel vidé et sans nuage. Un petit garçon, tendant les mains et levant la tête vers le ciel bleu, demanda à sa mère comment cela était possible. Fous-nous la paix, dit-elle.

Moreover, we soon notice that the French heroes usually speak correctly (as Watt did also), whereas other people, especially policemen with whom they come into contact, do not: this serves to differentiate the exiled heroes all the more from the crude, cursing tribe of the rest of mankind. At one point, for example, the hero with polite *préciosité* asks someone for *l'heure juste, de grâce!*, whereas at another point a policeman rudely tells him not to take up the whole pavement as he walks, adding coarsely *si vous n'êtes pas foutu de circuler comme tout le monde . . . vous feriez mieux de rester chez vous*. This device gives rise to a certain amount of humour. When, however, the hero does express himself vulgarly or with violence, the effect is doubly striking:

On devrait aménager, dans les rues passantes, des pistes reservées à ces sales petits êtres [children in general], leur landaus, cerceaux, sucettes, patinettes, trotinettes, pépés, mémés, nounous, ballons, tout leur sale petit bonheur quoi.

Nevertheless the French heroes are somewhat restricted as far as verbal humour is concerned: they can occasionally exploit possibilities of paradox (*une espérance accablante*) and incongruously distort common expressions (*si j'ose dire, et j'ose*). But if such jesting is from now onwards largely excluded by the very nature of French prose, the possibilities of irony, of irony directed against the world and life in general, are greatly increased. It is in his French fiction, in fact, that Beckett employs ironic effects reminiscent of those of Jonathan Swift.

There have been many attempts to explain why Beckett adopted French, ranging from the improbable (that he was reacting against Ireland, and/or English civilization) to Mrs. Jolas' more astute surmise, namely that Beckett, knowing of Joyce's envy of French writers and their sophisticated public, determined to woo this audience for himself. Neither of these explanations is convincing, nor is it enough to say that he chose to write in French as a discipline, a deliberately self-imposed difficulty, since for such a man, of more than ordinary linguistic gifts who has lived for many years in France, it is no harder to write well in French than in English. He was not, in fact, seeking an antidote to virtuosity, but a different kind of virtuosity: his French is just as subtly expert as his English, but it is a different sort of expertise, and one that better serves his present purposes. Perhaps this is what he meant when he said to Israel Shenker that he turned to French because he 'just felt like it. It was a different experience from writing in English. It was more exciting for me – writing in French'.

A more likely explanation, therefore, for his adoption of French is the following. Being already drawn in that direction by the gallicisms which he could not or would not keep out of *Watt*, since he now had things he wanted to say (for he was no longer the aloof and rather disdainful intellectual who had conceived Belacqua and Murphy), things about exile and the self, about death, about the body and the mind, and since, perhaps as a result of suffering under the Occupation, he felt this need strongly, he realized that he no longer wished, or no longer could, indulge in the ironic brilliance of *Murphy* or the Sternian intricacies of *Watt*, but wanted to turn away from the language in which he naturally expressed himself elaborately and tortuously, and adopt what amounted to another literary personality in a language in which he could make a fresh start and refashion, after an austerer mould, sharper tools for his trade. The naked, first-person, clipped sentences in French thus replaced the veiled, third-person, elaborate periods in English: and yet, despite the change from *he* to *je*, the prose remained just as impersonal, and even gained a new universal application: *le son de sa voix dans nos oreilles,* Maurice Nadeau once said, *c'est notre propre voix, enfin trouvée.*

Watt is therefore especially significant in Beckett's fiction as the turning-point, a work written in farewell to the native language, and announcing already the works of considerable importance that Beckett was to contribute, in another language, to another literature. And having forged his tool, he must in fact be fairly satisfied with it, because his only attempt since *Watt* at writing fiction once again in English has been the fragment, aptly named, which is all that remains of an English novel begun and then left: *From an Abandoned Work* (1955).

*   *   *

La Fin (The End) tells – in the first person, for as has been said, all Beckett's French fiction (except *Mercier et Camier*) is written from the point of view of 'I' – of the nameless hero's expulsion from a 'charitable institution'. He is given money to start him on his way, and a dead man's set of clothes still reeking of fumigation: shoes, socks, trousers, shirt, coat and bowler hat. When his bed is broken up he throws a scene to avert expulsion, but he is soon cowed and warned never to attempt to return. Allowed to wait awhile in the cloister for the rain to stop, he is then ordered on and finds the town unrecognizable. Despite his elaborate manners, he cannot secure a lodging, until he finds a basement where he lives contentedly enough, having his food brought to him and his chamber pot emptied once a day by his Greek (or Turkish) landlady. Some time later she offers him a reduction in return for six months rent in advance, and promptly disappears. The new landlord expels him at once, even though the hero offers to share the room with the man's pig.

He wanders from town to country until a man with an ass whom he once knew invites him to share his sea-cave, but the hero cannot abide the sea, and soon leaves to occupy the man's abandoned cabin in the mountains. Winter succeeds summer, and he nearly dies of starvation, until a cow, which he manages to milk, saves him. Eventually he ends up begging in the streets of the town, sleeping at night in a shed on a deserted estate near the river, protected from the ravenous water-rats by the boat in which he makes his bed. He can feel the end drawing near: he goes out less and less, feeling too weak and indolent to stir. He begins to have visions, and sees himself gliding out to sea in his boat, opening a hole to let the water in, and then swallowing the sedative which he has been carrying in a phial. The sea, sky, mountains and islands seem as in a huge systole to close and compress him, and then to scatter to outer space. He thinks *faiblement et sans regret* of the story he might have told, the true one (or rather just a slightly truer one, since this is a world of the mind and there are no absolutes) in which his life, instead of ending dramatically as he has told, merely dwindles away, *sans le courage de finir ni la force de continuer*, a slow transformation through cold and inanition, into the shadowy state in which he finds himself when *Le Calmant* (*The Sedative*) begins.

This story opens with his remark that he does not know quite when he died, but perhaps it was at the age of ninety, when he was greatly decayed in any case. Being too frightened to lie listening to the rotting of his body, he decides to tell himself a story, a sedative story, but in it he will be older than ever he was in life: it may even tell of a return to earth after his death, except that he does not think it likely he would return to earth after his death. The story he decides to tell will therefore take place in fact at the moment of its telling, but he will nonetheless tell it in the past, *comme s'il s'agissait d'un mythe ou d'une fable ancienne*, because this evening he requires the age, at which he became what he was, to become another age: he gleefully contemplates the muddle in which this must leave the reader in a sardonically provocative sentence, *ah je vous en foutrai des temps, salauds de votre temps*. So he finds himself before long even using the future tense (hence his comment *me voilà acculé à des futurs*), but soon he begins his story proper, which he tells throughout in the past historic.

He enters his town by the *porte des Bergers*, and finds it both brightly lit and totally deserted. He is wearing a green greatcoat, his father's, the hem of which rubs along the ground, it is so stiff and he so short. He goes to the port, in the hope of exchanging a few words with a seaman so that he can carry them back to his hut like a trophy. A boy leading a goat offers him a sweet, which he accepts, but he is so unaccustomed to speaking that his mouth only emits a rattle instead of words, and he has hardly found the use of his tongue before the boy disappears. Re-entering the town, he goes into a brightly-lit but empty cathedral, climbs to the top where he sees a man, a little girl, and another man, before returning to the street again. This dream-like sequence continues (*car nous sommes bien entendu dans une tête*, he says) until eventually a man speaks to him, to his delighted surprise. This man tells him his life story, asks for a kiss, and gives him a phial in exchange. Left alone once more, 'hidden in his ancient flesh', *tendu vers une voie. de sortie* but missing them all, he finds a vast crowd assembling around him as darkness falls. Flat on his stomach, *j'étais bien*, he says, *abreuvé de noir et de calme, au pied des mortels*, happy now that the deserted incandescence has at last been replaced by a thronged darkness; but soon 'reality' (*trop fatigué*, he says, *pour chercher le mot juste*) re-establishes itself, the bright light returns, the crowd vanishes, and he goes on his way. He does not seem to have achieved much in this rambling story, except that he has at least succeeded in speaking to one or two people, and in giving himself a factitious existence for a while.

The other story, *L'Expulsé* (*The Expelled*) is much simpler and he tells it as if it happened a long time before. 'In the prime of life' (he gives his age as being between forty and fifty in the *Fontaine* version) he is ejected from a house which he has known since childhood and 'they' throw his hat after him, the same hat that his father bought him when he was a boy; he then hires a cab for the day to look for a lodging, and, not being able to find one, accepts the cabman's offer of shelter, and spends the night in the latter's stable, leaving at dawn without paying either for his cab-hire or his night. The expelled man nevertheless still possesses some money, left him by a woman whose name he has forgotten. He thinks that she must have taken him on her lap as a baby and that some childish love-making went on between them. This apparently incongruous idea is not new to the French *nouvelle*, for it first occurred in *A Case in a Thousand*, a short story which appeared in 1934 and which has not been mentioned until now because it is only of marginal interest in Beckett's fiction. It nevertheless repays careful reading, telling of an eminent young physician, Dr. Nye, who is described as a 'sad man', perhaps because phrases like 'myself I cannot save' keep recurring to his mind. He cannot 'save himself' because of a childish trauma that continues to trouble him. In the course of his practice, a boy under his care dies after an operation which he has recommended and after it has transpired that the boy's mother, Mrs. Bray, is Nye's old nurse. The doctor sees her frequently in the course of his attendance on her son and both are embarrassed by an unexorcized memory, behind which Dr. Nye's trauma seems to lie. The memory is connected with the fact that as a child he was impatient to grow up so that he could marry Mrs. Bray, and eventually she relates

a matter connected with his earliest years, so trivial and intimate that it need not be enlarged on here, but from the elucidation of which Dr. Nye, that sad man, expected great things.

The trauma at the root of Dr. Nye's childhood attachment for Mrs. Bray no doubt sprang from the nostalgia for the womb that afflicts so many of the Beckettian heroes in one form or another, and that, in this case perhaps, caused erotic feelings in the child which the nurse indulged but the memory of which troubles them still in later life, until chance brings them together again, allowing them to exorcize it. The *mamours* of which the French hero speaks seem therefore to be a clear echo of the something that occurred in another story written over ten years previously.

* * *

In the synopses of the stories given above, it has been assumed that the hero who figures in all of them is the same man, more or less. It seems reasonable to do so, firstly because Mr. Beckett has said that they can be taken as three phases of one existence (or four, with the story ironically entitled *First Love* or *Premier Amour*): prime, death and limbo; and secondly because there is internal evidence for there being a single protagonist throughout. In both *The Sedative* and *The End*,[1] for instance, the hero's hat, of which in all the stories he is very fond, is tied with string to his buttonhole, and in both, too, he possesses a phial containing a

[1] And also in the *Fontaine* version of *L'Expulsé*, a detail omitted from the definitive version of that story.

tranquillizing drug (for the title *Le Calmant* refers both to the fact that his story is to calm him and to the phial he receives in return for a kiss), a drug he swallows in *The End*. The expelled man, as we saw, sleeps in a stable, and in *The End* he finds a kind of clothes-brush, also in a stable, and comments 'stables have always been my salvation'. Finally in both *The End* and *The Expelled*, the hero has running sores on the top of his skull, except that in the latter story there is still only one pustule, which has developed into several by *The End*. Furthermore, the setting of the stories is practically identical, consisting of a town which he has known from his youth, and which he describes as a walled *cité* in a plain, with mountains in the distance and the sea close by, with its estuaries, port, islands and promontories.

Although we are not told in so many words that the hero is a reincarnation of Watt, this seems often to be hinted at: like Watt, he has a wide, stiff walk, he is a milk-drinker, does not share the common phobia of rats, wears a heavy greatcoat, and (in *Suite* at least, a detail suppressed in *La Fin*) a block hat. The 'charitable institution' he is ejected from in *The End* does not however resemble Watt's asylum at all, but we nevertheless still seem to be in Ireland, for the coinage is shillings and pence and the proper names (Nidder, Weir, Ward, Maxwell, Joe Breem or Breen) are certainly not French: moreover (curious detail) when the hero, in *La Fin*, cries *Exelmans!* in anger, this name, dear to Mr. Knott also, of a marshal of France, is not understood by Mr. Weir. Of course, the stories take place in no definite country, and this imprecision is indispensable to the oneiric nature of the narrative, but if it is anywhere, the setting is in Ireland. With imprecision of place goes imprecision of time: no names of days or months are ever mentioned, and only very occasionally is a change of seasons referred to; little or no idea is given of the lapse of time between any two events in *The End*, and in *The Sedative* temporal indications are wilfully juggled with.

As deliberately imprecise as the spatio-temporal framework is the personality of the hero. The first thing we notice is that he is nameless, and with this namelessness goes a character that changes imperceptibly from that of the relatively self-assured man in the prime of life to the lonely pathetic beggar of *The End*. The former reveals a sadistic but cowardly temperament that would love to see children lynched, but he does not wish to take a direct hand in it himself; and later he thinks of setting fire to the cabman's stable, but refrains, no doubt because this would naturally entail self-destruction. These are aggressive feelings which the beggar, who merely wants to be left in peace, would not harbour. But apart from such slender indications of the hero's character, we learn little about him, for although he says a great deal he talks very little about the sort of man he is: we merely glean fragments of information, such as that he finished his schooling in the third form, and that his tutor (another curious detail) had given him a copy of the *Ethics* of Geulincx.

The style in these stories is a bland kind of literalness, betraying no subjective emotion on the part of the hero-narrator in the telling of events, however terrible or repulsive these may be. In *The End*, for instance, the narrator speaks of his harrowing existence dragging from one shelter to another in the same neutral, almost urbane tone in which he discusses the relative merits of masturbation as against systematic scratching. Such an absence of emotional colouring attains, by the agency of that very absence, considerable force, and this is just the effect the author wishes to achieve. For in blandness of manner there are rich possibilities for irony, as Swift was well aware in the *Modest Proposal*, and it is this irony of literalness that Beckett perfects in the *Nouvelles*. The hero of these is a meticulous observer who does not reason about what he sees, and his eye falling on the activities, however sadistic, callous or obscene, of himself or of others, is uncommitted and the reports of what he sees are literal reports, which are also quite unorientated ethically. Moreover, the strong physical reaction of disgust that is often provoked in the reader (Swift, again, knew how to arouse visceral reactions to further his satirical ends) is transformed by the very neutrality and unselfconscious progression – free as it is from all simpering and conniving – of the narrator's descriptions, which even when they are obscene are the reverse of prurient, into something approaching a sad realization of the weary absurdity of the human situation. An example of this is to be found in *The End*, soon after the hero has described his autoerotic activities in detail; he goes on without transition to say that he began to excrete, and to eat, less and less at this time and adds, in an ironic but touching parenthesis of the kind

Beckett handles discreetly and well, that God was in this way making life easier for him: *Dieu me mesurait le vent.* Our disgust thus turns to a sort of pity, and the pity is for ourselves perhaps as much as for the hero.

The latter's narrative is, furthermore, subtly employed to indict the over-confident world that is ranged against him: when for instance a communist orator points out the hero to his audience as a human derelict, fit only for the rubbish-heap, a victim of capitalist society, the hero moves away, saying only:

But generally speaking it was a quiet corner, busy but not over-crowded. . . . He must have been a religious fanatic, I could find no other explanation. Perhaps he was an escaped lunatic. He had a nice face, a little on the red side;

and at that moment, although we recognize some justice in the orator's remarks, we feel more sympathy for the inoffensive man whose peace has been disturbed by the interfering hostility of those representing ideologies of universal improvement. Yet, at the same time, any simple identification between the reader and the hero is avoided by the latter's unattractive character. Beckett's purpose is in fact to employ these methods of ambiguity and irony to make us continually reconsider our attitude to his hero (whom we can neither wholly reject nor readily associate ourselves with) and, by extension, to make us question our assumptions on the usually too easily accepted constants of illness, poverty, loneliness, old age and death which the hero represents and to make us face up to our repressed guilt or fears *vis-à-vis* these constants. In much the same way, as John Cruickshank has pointed out, it is by the deliberate ambiguity of his attitude to Meursault in *L'Etranger* that Camus makes us aware of the universal tragedy of death. Through Beckett's French fiction, indeed, we attain to a sharper realization of what it really means to be an outcast and a reject from society, and, what is perhaps more important, how hypocritical and cruel our society appears to those who see it only from the gutter and dungheap. But such is the nature of the author's deliberately ambiguous treatment that neither hero nor society emerge wholly evil or wholly good. Largely lacking here is the ferocity which, in the best of Swift's writing, lies dangerously and precariously concealed under the surface blandness of tone – and which we find so often ready to break out in *Molloy* and *Malone Dies*. In the latter, the Swiftean combination of savagery and neutrality is consummately imitated, whereas in the *Nouvelles* Beckett is content to leave the harsh conclusions largely implicit, and few ripples appear on the calm surface of the hero's tale.

The *Nouvelles* hero is nevertheless allowed to make several pithy remarks at the expense of his persecutors, just as in Swift indignation can take more straightforward forms than the subtle exploitation of the possibilities of ironic mask (as Ewald has termed it). For Gulliver is not always made to play the naïf unconsciously indicting his creator's butts; occasionally he can himself point out abuses and absurdities. In a similar way the expelled hero comments, when he realizes that his ejectors have thrown his hat after him instead of keeping it, 'they were very correct, according to their god' and later he looks up at the heavens *d'où nous vient*, he says, *le fameux secours*; and in *The Sedative* he says that the advantage of death by drowning as against death on land is that the crabs, unlike the ravens, never arrive too soon.

Apart from these varied uses of irony, there is another feature of style in the *Nouvelles* which remains to be noted: the unexpected insertion into the text of incongruous details, apparently for no reason except to accentuate the inconsequential, oneiric nature of the narrative. I have mentioned '*Exelmans!*' and Geulincx, and there are many other instances of this irruption of incongruity, as for instance in *The End*, where without warning we hear of a red-bearded town planner whose gall-bladder was removed, causing his death three days later, in the prime of life. Furthermore, even the most elementary narrational transitions are now considered unnecessary, for in *The End* we are not told how the hero left the cabin in the mountains and got back to the main road to the town, and in *The Sedative*, events follow each other with as little connection as in a dream (*est-ce que j'ai rêvé, est-ce que je rêve?* he pertinently asks).

* * *

The principal theme in all these stories is the theme of exile. 'They' are against the hero continually, ejecting him from one place, slamming the door of another in his face, cheating him, robbing him (the street-urchins steal his begging-gains), abusing him from the soap-box, and pursuing him with the arm of the law – for policemen are the greatest menace of all; they accuse the hero of disturbing the peace, of obstructing the sidewalks, and of being a suspicious character who needs to be watched. The hero responds to hatred with hatred, contemplates with a sombre satisfaction *l'aversion qu'inspirait ma personne, même dans ses attitudes les plus veules et plates*, loathes children, especially his own son whom he one day catches sight of (*l'insupportable fils de putain* as he calls him), and remarks that it is small wonder he has become *aigre, méfiant . . . fervent de la cachette et de la station horizontale.* He is quite used to being singled out for abuse and mockery (*je prêtais toujours à rire, de ce rire robuste et sans malice qui est si bon pour la santé*) and his only longing is for a room lit with artificial light where he can be snug and warm and have his meals brought to him, and from which he will not have to stir abroad: 'I did not need affection fortunately.' When obliged to communicate with others he finds it difficult, for his speech is strange, all vowels and no consonants, and he frequently fails to understand the ways of the world: a solicitor's secretary seems to him to be a woman for hire. Nevertheless he shows even in his alienation an incompatible desire for human contact such as we remarked in Belacqua also; even a seaman's words addressed to him would be a precious gain, and he goes so far as to feign a fictitious citizenship, saying to a stranger to the town *vous pensez demeurer longtemps parmi nous? dis-je. Cette phrase me sembla particulièrement bien tournée.* Generally speaking, towns are hostile and unfamiliar, the open sky and the countryside being more bearable (although they too form part of the *merde universelle*), but even so he never has more than the *quasi-certitude* of being still of this world: *même les mots vous lâchent, c'est tout dire.* Such life as he does lead is reduced, economically speaking, to the barest necessities, to a daily bottle of milk or less, and he implies that even total penury holds few terrors for him.

His body, like Watt's but more obviously, also abandons him, it rots away through sores, eczema, cysts and crablice, it simply runs down like an unwound clock (for we remember that the Cartesians often compared the body to a clock, and moreover it is Cartesian physiology that here inspires such remarks as *à peine l'impulsion parvenue aux jambes je me portai en avant*), and at one point, so alien and unknown is the body, we are told it has five or six legs.

Furthermore, the identity of the self is unfixed, and memory, the only link between the selves of the past and of the present, is too decayed to serve (*je ne sais plus quand je suis mort*): names, numbers and places are rarely remembered, and it is hard for instance for him to say if the town is the same one: *c'était peut-être une tout autre ville.* As blurred is the distinction between life and death: Malone's words, *c'est vague, la vie et la mort,* hold as true here as they did even in *More Pricks than Kicks,* where we were told that Belacqua

had often looked forward to meeting the girls, Lucy especially, hallowed and transfigured beyond the veil. What a hope! Death has already cured him of that naïvety . . .

and we remember the striking idea that the incompetent anæsthetist has accorded him in death 'a new lease of apathy'. The Beckettian heroes are in fact not allowed any abrupt termination to their sufferings, for death merely consummates the body's lifelong putrefaction which began in the womb, it does not wipe out the mind. This explains the frequent references in *Murphy* to spiritualism, and in *Watt* the mention of the soul of Mrs. Price; it also accounts for *The Sedative, The Unnamable* and the rest, those incantations that the mind transmits from limbo, for Beckett's *Inferno* is rather an eternal and solitary state of suspension than a Dantesque torture-chamber thronged with popes and lechers. All three of the *Nouvelles* are in fact told from *l'outretombe* (those who listen to them are addressed as *âmes vives*) and this helps to explain the odd pointlessness of the stories: for once *tout est dit, tout sera à recommencer,* as the hero says in *The Sedative,* clearly foreshadowing the whole theme of *The Unnamable.* So that he may have *something* to say, the hero says anything that comes into his mind, tells first a little tale about a day spent riding about in a cab, then another tale, about his last days, and finally a third, this time a piece of pure imagination, in which he has to keep finding people to meet, to address, to be spoken to by, in a brightly-lit but silent town, in order to be able to continue, in order not to have to listen to his body rotting. In this life in death, or *vie de survie* as it is called in *Mercier et Camier,* little wonder he says (in *The Expelled*) 'I don't know why I told this story, I could just as well have told another,' because all is grist to the mill, as the Unnamable, who pounds every available stone to powder, well knows.

It is quite natural that, beneath this compulsion to tell stories, should lie a profound contempt for the whole activity, a contempt which accounts for the continual annulling of what has been said: *tout ce que je dis s'annule, je n'aurai rien dit.* Expressions of fatigue are frequent – 'enough', 'some other time', 'worn out' – but there can be no giving up, for *il faut toujours ressasser la même chose, histoire de ne pas l'oublier.* One sees what Beckett meant when he once said 'in my work there is consternation behind the form', constantly threatening it, continually liable to bring it to grief. His art is in fact self-destructive, liable to be consumed on its own pyre – as Nadeau has said of it, *la négation triomphante s'installe à l'intérieur de l'œuvre même et la dissout dans un brouillard d'insignifiance à mesure qu'elle se crée* – but only from the conflagration can something of value emerge, that which paradoxically remains said when all the saying has destroyed what has been said.

Only one further matter needs to be remarked upon in connection with the *Nouvelles*: that they are haunted by the figure of the Galilean, not the Christ of the Resurrection but an eternally crucified Jesus. One remembers Estragon's words: *toute ma vie je me suis comparé à lui*, and the *Nouvelles* hero does the same, referring unconsciously to the triumphal entry into Jerusalem:

> To my amazement I got up on the ass and off we went, in the shade of the red chestnuts springing from the sidewalk. I held the ass by the mane, one hand in front of the other. The little boys jeered and threw stones. . . .

'The stones' here is perhaps an inverted echo of Luke xix. 40, 'if these [my disciples] should hold their peace, the stones would immediately cry out', and further on, the hero, after Jesus, says 'my hour had not yet come', and in *The Sedative* the eyes of the crucified one are called *puits de tant d'espérance*. The Beckettian hero thus feels a decided kinship with one whose situation resembles his own: for it is not without significance that Richard Seaver translated at the author's instigation, or at least with his approval, the insult *espèce d'immolé*, which the orator hurls at the beggar, as: 'you crucified bastard'.

* * *

The above discussion of the *Nouvelles* has perhaps shown that they cannot be neglected in any examination of Beckett's work. For they are interesting from many points of view: as journeyman-pieces in which he practised a new style and wielded for the first time in his fiction a new language; as some of the most forceful and poignant statements of his theme of the hero as outcast; as pointers to some aspects of *The Unnamable* and of the most recent developments in Beckettian fiction; and as applications, conscious or otherwise, of some of the ironic methods of Jonathan Swift. Unfortunately these stories are not widely known in France, and the two in English translation have not as yet been collected, and *Le Calmant*, in many ways the most important if the most difficult, is only at the present time of writing being translated by the author and Mr. Seaver. Let us hope that it will not be long before the *Nouvelles* appear in their rightful place, in a volume accompanying the trilogy, to which they are in many ways an indispensable introduction.

II MERCIER AND CAMIER

J'ai naturellement pensé au pseudocouple Mercier-Camier
L'INNOMMABLE

Mercier et Camier is, like *Dream of Fair to Middling Women*, a jettisoned manuscript, not a novel carefully revised and exposed by the act of printing to the hazards of unrestricted reading and criticism. The author's intentions concerning it should therefore be respected, and if I discuss it here, in the place it occupies in the chronological order of the writing of Beckett's fiction, it is because certain elements in it are of considerable interest towards an understanding of the published work. In what follows I try therefore to confine my remarks to those aspects which are of immediate concern, avoiding as far as possible an inappropriately detailed consideration of what the author wishes to remain an unpublished novel.

* * *

The entire plot of *Mercier et Camier* consists of an account of a journey, *un voyage matériellement assez facile, sans mers ni frontières à franchir*, undertaken by the two men whose names figure in the title. Camier is a kind of private detective, but when the story opens he has already taken the decision to abandon his profession, and soon afterwards tears all the leaves from his *calepin* and throws them away (*calepin* is not the ordinary French word for notebook; it is, rather, the sort that detectives use, and usually one that buttons up. Gaber also carries one, in his work as messenger). Camier is a short, fat man, with small eyes, flushed complexion and sparse hair. Mercier on the other hand is tall and thin, with a grey unkempt beard, large nose, sunken eyes and a mass of dirty hair. The first is a *petit pléthorique*, the second a *grand exsangue*, and their only similarity lies in their age, for they are both old men.

The first mishap that occurs in their journey is that they waste nearly an hour round their rendezvous looking for each other, Mercier standing at the spot while Camier is looking in vain for him elsewhere, and vice-versa: and in a *Watt*-like piece of precise detail we are given a table showing the comparative times of their arrivals and departures. Then, as it is raining, the whole day is also wasted, and they put up for the night in the flat of a rather indefinite female character, Hélène, whose lodging thereafter serves as their base camp. They are both evidently on intimate sexual terms with her, especially Camier, who assures her, when later she feels sick, *c'est d'un bon augure*. Eventually they set out on their journey, but to Mercier's annoyance, Camier, perhaps because he could not bring himself to leave finally and irrevocably, has put them on a stopping train and not the express rushing southward that Mercier had expected. In this *omnibus* they have to submit to an unendearing character called Monsieur Madden who insists on telling them his life-story. They get off at a village halt and put up at the local inn, only to leave again before dawn and sit in a field where Camier jettisons his notes and they abandon their only raincoat. They decide to go back to town to look for their other possessions, haversack, bicycle and umbrella (they only have one of each between them – their persistent anxiety about their vanishing possessions announces *Malone Dies*). At this point duration of time becomes uncertain – *ils avaient perdu la notion du temps* – but, at last, they reach town and the refuge of Hélène's flat. From there they soon make to move off again, but this time separately, Camier to arrange for needed repairs to the umbrella, Mercier to look for their haversack and bicycle. Camier is next seen in a bar, where he is afterwards joined by Mercier. The umbrella is now lost, the haversack impossible to find, and of the bicycle all that remains is the frame (with its pump) firmly chained to a railing. Mercier, in the face of this appalling situation, is tempted to give up:

> Why do we persist, Camier, you and I for instance, have you ever asked yourself that question, you who ask so many. Are we going to discard the little of us that is left in the tedium of escapes and in dreams of freedom? Do you not glimpse, as I do, by what means to make your peace with this absurd chastisement and tranquilly abide the coming of the executioner, to ratify what is? – No, said Camier.

They leave the bar, batter to death a policeman who refuses to direct them to a brothel, find themselves at night on a *haute lande* made treacherous by bogs, collapse exhausted and in great pain in a ruin, and then go back to the town, where they separate at a road-fork, Mercier going to the left, Camier to the right. When they next meet it is summer, and their reunion is brought about by Watt, who appears from nowhere. He takes them to a bar, and there vociferates loudly against life (*la vie aux chiottes!*). Mercier and Camier rush out into the street, leaving him to the fury of the bar-people. It is dark, it is raining: Mercier tries to keep Camier with him, they indulge in desultory conversation:

> Ça va, à présent? dit Mercier.
> Pardon? dit Camier.
> Je te demande si ça va, à peu près, maintenant, pour toi, dit Mercier.
> Non, dit Camier . . . [he weeps].
> Et toi? dit Camier.
> Non plus, dit Mercier.

Camier remarks that they have talked of everything, during their association, except of themselves; then he leaves Mercier, who listens to 'sounds that the long day had hidden from him, human murmurs, for instance, and the rain on the water': for rain ends, as it began, this story.

The setting of this haunting tale is once again vaguely Ireland, a country ruined by rain, a land of stout and of bogs. In this island Mercier and Camier indulge continually in dialogue that is so often reminiscent of the exchanges of *En attendant Godot* that it was perhaps in favour of his play written later that Beckett suppressed this novel. However that may be, the linguistic humour of *Godot*, the play on the intricacies of French syntax represented for example by Vladimir's hesitations over *il s'en est fallu d'un cheveu qu'on-ne-s'y-soit-pendu*, is here paralleled by this sort of service and return:

Si on s'assoyait, cela m'a fatigué.
Tu veux dire s'asseyait, dit Mercier.
Je veux dire s'assoyait, dit Camier.
Assoyons-nous, dit Mercier.

Mercier says that his father always told him to show respect to a stranger, *quelqu'humble que fût sa condition*, and Camier comments: *quelqu'humble, que cela sonne drôlement*. Thus the possibilities of humour in French are exploited in this novel with a zest which confirms what was said above about Beckett's virtuosity in French being as marked as his virtuosity in English, although the different genius of the former naturally makes manifestations of this quality different in kind, for we now find syntactical games rather than recondite puzzles of echo and allusion.

Other parallels with *En attendant Godot* can be remarked in this work: Mercier, like Estragon, forgets things that have happened before, and the two men indulge here also in the now familiar cross-talk of the play:

This is worth looking into, [said Camier].
We shall confer, said Mercier, we shall make a broad survey.
Before venturing any further, said Camier.
Exactly, said Mercier.
To do that we need to be in complete possession of all our many faculties, said Camier.
That would be preferable, said Mercier.
And are we? said Camier.
Are we what? said Mercier.
In complete possession of our faculties, said Camier.

I trust not, said Mercier.
We are in need of sleep, said Camier.
Exactly, said Mercier.

and even the *je t'ai coupé* games of *En attendant Godot* are to be
found again here:

Je t'ai interrompu, dit Mercier.
C'est moi qui t'ai interrompu, dit Camier.
Mais non, dit Mercier.
Mais si, dit Camier.

The events, too, often recall those of the play: the need to embrace
on the part of the one, followed by the refusal to do so on the part
of the other; the unwillingness to listen to accounts of dreams;
the exchanges like *qu'avons-nous fait à Dieu? – nous l'avons renié*;
the question *on ne t'a pas battu?*; and finally, a reference to Christ
and the thieves.

Furthermore, as in all the novels up to and including *Watt*, the
narrator frequently intervenes, an 'I' figure who informs us
in the opening sentence that he can, if he wishes, recount the
journey of Mercier and Camier, *car j'étais avec eux, tout le temps*,
and who, rarely losing sight of them thereafter, comments frequently on their activities. In this as in a few other respects,
Mercier et Camier looks backwards rather than forwards (its
relatively sunny mood, for example, makes it more like *Murphy*
than like any of the other novels); but the remarks which the
narrator makes to undermine and annul his own narrative are
more typical of later work: *que cela pue l'artifice* he murmurs at
one point, and at another:

on sait à quoi on s'engage lorsqu'on fait de la littérature, à des décep-
tions qui feraient insérer au peintre ses pinceaux dans le cul,

a remark (implying that writing gives rise to deeper disappoint-
ments even than painting) that takes on added significance when
one recalls the Duthuit dialogues (1949) and Beckett's sympathy
for painters, especially Bram van Velde, 'the first', he has said,
'whose hands have not been tied by the certitude that expression
is an impossible act'. And finally, we come across the statement,
which occurs also in the *Nouvelles*, *ce serait le moment de finir*;

après tout, c'est fini, a gesture of impatience with a tale that takes too long to be told.

On the subject of style it should be noted that *Mercier et Camier* is both a warm and funny book, despite its sombre overtones. Some of the characters are amusing and well drawn: Monsieur Madden the sardonic farmer, for instance, and Monsieur Conaire, who is so like Pozzo that he even asks people what age they consider him to be. One entertaining passage relates how Camier overhears, and tries in vain to contribute to, an animated discussion in a café on the attitude of the Church to artificial insemination.

The chief preoccupation in this novel is, naturally, with the journey that leads the heroes nowhere, or only to the dissolution of their association. The theme of the journey is in fact a recurrent one in Beckett's fiction, from Belacqua's impulsive wanderings around Dublin, through Murphy's flight to London and through Watt's 'dark mind stumbling / through barren lands', to its full working-out in *Molloy*, where the two journeys, Molloy's and Moran's, are protracted and painful, leading nowhere except to the breakdown of each hero's body and the isolation of his mind. Such a journey is a calvary ordained by a tyrannical kind of god, *la malignité universelle* as he is called at one point here, against whom Mercier shakes his fist angrily, saying *quant à toi, je t'emmerde*, to which Camier wittily replies *lui est inemmerdable, omni-omni l'inemmerdable*. Such a journey, too, is perhaps a symbol of fruitless questing, of the turning into derision of 'seek and ye shall find'.

If in this important respect *Mercier et Camier* clearly looks forward to *Molloy*, it also looks back to *Watt* in its insistence on the erosive action of the unknowable on the known: 'there are some things we will never know' we are told at the beginning, and at the end: 'from now onwards nothing is know with certainty any more', for as the journey becomes progressively more disastrous, knowledge of it becomes harder to arrive at.

These two men do not however suffer the acute exile that is the lot of the *Nouvelles* hero, although they are irritated by park-keepers, barmen, and of course policemen; but their situation is one that results rather from their opting out of society than from any brutal expulsion. It is, for instance, they who rudely ignore the park-keeper's remonstrances about their bicycle, and who attack and kill the policeman: they themselves on the other hand seem to suffer little from the usually hostile attitude of others.

Ruby Cohn interprets this story as the dialogue between the body (Camier) and the mind (Mercier). Unfortunately it seems difficult to establish any such neat identification. Camier may seem to represent the physical side in that he is, for instance, usually the more concerned with food, but at the same time he is the bachelor whereas Mercier is married with children, and it is the latter who describes himself as the wreck and his friend as the tugboat, and not the other way about. Either can take, at any moment, the initiative for their movements, and although they certainly need each other, this need is not so much the enforced union of body and mind as the unstable association of two human beings who, like Vladimir and Estragon, must stay together if only to avoid the horrors of solitude, of the Unnamable's situation:

> Strength was certainly required to remain with Camier, just as strength was required to remain with Mercier, but less than was required for the battle of soliloquy.

They eventually fall apart, of course, but this cannot represent (although it may suggest) the final separation of body and mind, for Beckett is not likely to have descended to allegory when he treats this problem in far less obvious and more forceful terms elsewhere, especially in the next works.

More interesting than such questions are the striking instances of the reappearance of characters from other works. Quite suddenly, for instance, Mercier espies the hero of *La Fin*, *un vieillard d'aspect excentrique et misérable*, carrying under his arm the very hinged begging-board which in the *nouvelle* in question he proudly tells us he has perfected. Mercier feels he has seen the old man somewhere before; and the latter, who by an 'extraordinary chance' has caught sight of Mercier too, also feels a sensation of *déjà vu* and wonders where they could have met. Soon afterwards, Mercier catches sight of the man with the ass, *un vieillard hirsute et déguenillé*, who succoured the hero of *La Fin*, and exactly as in that story, the ass is carrying sand and seashells for sale to the townsfolk.

Watt's reappearance is, however, the most significant of all. Early on, Mercier and Camier see a man in frock-coat and top-hat walking stiffly, who is perhaps Watt. The latter in any case certainly appears at the end, a tall, aged, shabbily-dressed and evil-smelling man, telling the two that he is still little known but will be better known one day, not universally however, he adds with irony, for there is little chance that his notoriety will reach the inhabitants of either London or Cuq-Toulza (a small village in the *département* of the Tarn). He informs Camier that he knew him in the cradle; Mercier then says that he once knew a man called Murphy, who resembled Watt a little, although he was much younger and died ten years before in mysterious circumstances (Mercier has his facts right: Murphy did in fact die in 1935). Watt is wearing this time a huge bowler hat and a heavy greatcoat under which he is probably naked. In the bar to which he takes his companions he summarizes the vain search that is recounted in *Watt*: *moi aussi, j'ai cherché, tout seul, seulement moi je croyais savoir quoi* – and adds that he will be born of them, is born of them, who having nothing will wish for nothing, if only that he be left the nothing he has. Perhaps Watt is referring here to Molloy, or Malone, certainly to one of the later heroes. Then he shouts two insults against life: the first is excused, the second causes uproar. Mercier and Camier escape with Watt's last words *vive Quin!* ringing in their ears. Soon afterwards Mercier tells Camier that he met Watt near a hospital for skin diseases; and there ends Watt's last reappearance outside the novel of which he is the hero. But he is to be mentioned a few times more, notably by Molloy and by Moran.

There is no call to strive for a simple explanation of this phenomenon, for one accepts easily that in the special world of Samuel Beckett's fiction, it is not only natural, but appropriate and even inevitable that the successive heroes should know each other and sometimes converse. The books thus linked by the inter-reference of names (with Belacqua's recurring, as has been said, even in the latest novel *Comment C'est*) form a closed circle, a unity, almost one extended novel, which is sealed progressively to the world without, first to Dublin and London, then to the unspecific but still vaguely Irish milieu of the *Nouvelles* and *Mercier et Camier*, until finally we find ourselves within the limits of the mind, a mind only remotely connected by the tenuous uncertainty of memory to the human realm that is simply referred to as *là-haut, dans la lumière* – a long and remorseless novel which searches for the essential *persona* of a hero whose progressive manifestations are not established and then ignored, but all faithfully remembered and recorded.

* * *

Mercier et Camier is chiefly interesting as the first thorough working-out of the journey theme that crops up next in *Molloy*, and also as the scene of Watt's return and of the *Nouvelles* hero's brief reappearance. In itself it is touching, serious and yet frequently amusing, unlike the sombre, concentrated work that the books of the trilogy are: it is written in a lighter mode a little like *Murphy*. In fact, although it does frequently echo *En attendant Godot*, this is not likely to have been the finally determining reason why Beckett suppressed this novel. He must have been dissatisfied with it on its own account, because it did not strike the same hard pure note of solitude as the *Nouvelles*, and constituted a kind of hiatus between the latter and *Molloy*, a hiatus that this novelist, seized with what has been called an *amour fou pour la beauté formelle*, was unwilling to tolerate. It is, in fact, neither Mercier nor Camier who is the true prototype of Molloy, but rather the despised, sick beggar of *The End*.

Chapter 5

MOLLOY AND MORAN

... myself the last of my foul brood, neither man nor beast.

MOLLOY

... this is a nursery tale.

IBID

BECKETT'S most impressive novel, *Molloy*, was published by the Editions de Minuit in Paris in April 1951, the first of his works to receive this imprint and the first of any of his books to bring him fame. Unlike its predecessors, *Molloy* was from the start a modest commercial success, as well as an amazing *succès de critique:* eminent French critics like Georges Bataille, Max-Pol Fouchet, Robert Kanters, Maurice Nadeau and Jean Pouillon reviewed it favourably on publication. With this novel, in fact, Samuel Beckett was immediately recognized as a writer of considerable importance, and furthermore as a French writer making a positive contribution to French literature, by authorities who do not easily grant a foreigner this distinction; Nadeau, for instance, asserted that *avec 'Molloy' il s'établit parmi les grands écrivains et prend place dans notre littérature*. After this striking reception, the Editions de Minuit rapidly brought out *Malone meurt* (late 1951), *En attendant Godot* (October 1952) and *L'Innommable* (June 1953), the works that constitute the essential core of Beckett's *œuvre*, on which his reputation ultimately rests.

This is not, however, to say that it was an easy matter to find a publisher for these books, which had neither popular appeal nor a widely-known author's name to recommend them. Mme. Suzanne Beckett had offered her husband's manuscripts to all the major *maisons d'édition*, since he was unwilling to do so himself, but without success. Beckett in fact insisted on a contract for the whole trilogy, and refused to allow any one of the novels to be issued alone. Eventually a man was found prepared to publish on these terms. He was Monsieur Jérôme Lindon, who had taken over from Vercors in 1948 the direction of the then moribund Editions de Minuit, one of the most important of the clandestine presses during the Occupation, which in spite of numerous *saisies*, today still continues to put out books, like *La Gangrène* and *La Question*, which embarrass the authorities. Monsieur Lindon has said that he had long been unsure whether, had Proust's or Kafka's works been offered to him in manuscript, he would have been able to recognize their importance. Accordingly, after assuming direction of the firm, he read with sympathetic interest the manuscript of *Molloy* which had been rejected elsewhere. Convinced at once that he had, as he has said, *entre les mains quelque chose de génial*, he signed the contract with Beckett which not only launched the latter but was also to give Lindon both self-confidence and a reputation for being able to recognize and support valuable new work. The Editions de Minuit, which publishes all Beckett's French books, is therefore at the present time a firm of international repute which has successfully attracted other novelists like Robbe-Grillet, Butor, Pinget and Simon. Lindon is the sort of publisher who considers his authors as his friends, and who believes that his task is to educate the public to accept their work: for he insists that a writer should never trouble himself with what the public will or will not take, that this is the concern only of his *éditeur*. Thus he sees his role almost as a missionary one; he was certainly the right man to launch Beckett, and the importance of what he has done in that connection can hardly be overestimated.

* * *

Molloy, as is well known, is the first part of the trilogy which also includes *Malone Dies* and *The Unnamable*. In English they are now available in one volume as the author has always desired. The three novels were written between 1947 and 1949 when Beckett was working at an intense level of concentration: from this period date the plays *Eleuthéria* and *Godot* also, and at the end of it the *Textes pour rien* were composed. The order, according to the author, was as follows:

Molloy – Eleuthéria (abandoned) – *Malone meurt – En attendant Godot – L'Innommable – Textes pour rien.*

In the chapters that follow each novel of the trilogy is considered separately, although even more than any of the other elements in the Beckettian canon, they stand together as one work.

The most obvious feature of *Molloy* is its division into two parts or, alternatively, into two long chapters. Both chapters contain first-person narratives, the first by an individual whose name, we eventually learn, is Molloy, the second by Jacques Moran, one of the few Beckettian characters to be given a christian name.

At the beginning of Part I, Molloy tells us that he is in his mother's room, having been brought there 'perhaps in an ambulance, certainly a vehicle of some kind', since it was 'last year' that he ceased to walk. Having taken his mother's place, he does not know what has become of her. He tells us he has to write out his story for a man who comes to collect his pages once a week and then describes, in a sort of vision, how his last journey began. He was on a hill-top, crouched, he says, in the shadow of a rock, 'like Belacqua, or Sordello, I forget', and from there he watched two men walking towards each other along a country road, meeting, exchanging a few words, and then going their separate ways.

In the French text, these men are designated as A and B, and they are still largely A and B in the English *New World Writing* extract of 1954, but in the definitive translation of 1955 they have become A and C, a possible reference to Abel and Cain whose legend (which first received mention in *Dante and the Lobster*, 1934) illustrates Beckett's preoccupation with the unpredictable nature of God's favours, for Cain was 'cursed from the earth', after seeing his brother's offering preferred to his own for no apparent reason. But A and C also recall Camier and Mercier respectively: they 'know each other perhaps', one is short, the other tall, one of them at least looks old, and A, like Camier at one point in the manuscript, walks with his head bowed on his chest. (A and C also suggest, moreover, the two thieves of whom so much is said in *Godot*, for Molloy later on refers to them unambiguously as *mes deux larrons*.)

The man C has a cocked hat which Moran describes, when he sees it later in the story, as 'quite extraordinary, in shape and colour . . . like none I had ever seen', and he carries a stout stick which Molloy later calls a club, when he thinks of him again at the edge of the forest; and it is with this club in hand that C approaches Moran in the woods. The preliminary apparition is therefore of considerable significance for the rest of the story, but Molloy soon dismisses what he calls 'these rags to cover my shame' and declares that on waking he determined to go and see his mother. 'I needed, before I could resolve to go and see that woman, reasons of an urgent nature', and the reasons that now impel him are connected with the need to establish 'our relations on a less precarious footing'. He fastens his crutches (without which he cannot walk, having one stiff leg) to the crossbar of his bicycle and sets out. On reaching the ramparts of his town he is arrested, and later questioned by a sergeant at the police-station for some obscure irregularity in his manner of resting on the bicycle. Released only late in the afternoon, he goes to the country and some time afterwards finds himself back in the town (he is no longer sure it is his mother's town) where he runs over a dog, whose owner, a woman called Lousse, protects him from the indignation of the bystanders and gives him lodging in her own home. He in some way replaces the dead animal in her affections, and stays 'a good while' with her, quite unable to leave, no doubt (he thinks) because she drugs his food. There he loses track of his bicycle, and eventually leaves without it, on crutches only, his initial concern to discover its whereabouts having changed to indifference. Molloy strongly hints that Lousse kept him for sexual reasons, but she nonetheless makes no attempt to prevent his departure, 'except perhaps', he says, 'by spells', for she is, as Hugh Kenner has pointed out, the Calypso (or Circe?) of this *Odyssey*, just as the woman who later approaches Molloy on the seashore is its Nausicaa and the police-sergeant its Cyclops. After leaving her, Molloy wanders around the town and contemplates settling in a blind alley; he even attempts unsuccessfully to commit suicide. Finally, leaving the town in some haste, he spends a while at the seaside, renewing the stock of sucking-stones that keep him from feeling hungry. Soon, however, his mother's image begins again to harry him, and he moves inland through a forest, where his progress becomes slower and slower. A charcoal-burner, 'sick with solitude probably', offers his unwanted affections to Molloy (just as the donkey-man does to the hero of *La Fin*) and is soundly belaboured for his pains. No longer able to hobble, Molloy next takes to crawling, hears a distant gong, then a voice saying 'don't fret, Molloy, we're coming', and finally sinks into the bottom of a ditch at the very edge of the forest. It is from this ditch, evidently, that he is rescued in order to be made to write his story in his mother's room, not knowing what has become of her in the meantime. Thus the end of Part I refers to the beginning, and vice-versa, making the tale circular.

At first sight, the second part is quite different. The speaker gives his name at once, and is soon revealed as a fastidious individual, a practising Catholic, a fairly affluent householder very proud of his property, and as one of the employees of a mysterious agency (run by a man called Youdi) which has asked for the report we are to read. Moran's story begins one Sunday in summer. Gaber, an agency messenger, disturbs his day of rest and gives him urgent instructions to leave at once with his son, also called Jacques, and look for an individual called, according to Gaber, Molloy, but whose name, to Moran, seems more like Mollose: for the man in question 'was no stranger to me'. Throughout that Sunday, Moran's disquiet grows: the affair, at first dismissed by Gaber as 'nonsense', soon shows itself to be 'no ordinary one', and begins to make Moran 'anxious', then 'confused', until finally he admits that he is 'losing his head' and 'floundering, I so sly as a rule'. Having missed the last mass, he solicits private communion which brings him no relief, and his lunch, eaten too late, lies on his stomach. Painfully and laboriously, he prepares himself to set out. He feels for the first time a sharp pain strike his knee, while he is giving an enema to his son in the bathroom.

Moran's employment, we are told, consists in tracking down certain individuals, such as on one occasion a man called Yerk, and then in dealing with them in accordance with particular instructions; sometimes he is asked for a report. 'Oh the stories I could tell you', he says, 'If I were easy. What a rabble in my head, what a gallery of moribunds. Murphy, Watt, Yerk, Mercier and all the others'. Moran is therefore already quite familiar with most of his Beckettian predecessors; he even asks himself later whether they will 'all meet again in heaven one day . . . Molloy, his mother, Yerk, Murphy, Watt, Camier and the rest?' In the case of Molloy, however, Moran is not clear what he should do with his quarry once he finds him, as he cannot remember what Gaber said on this point. He never finds out.

For he has not long been on his journey before the pain strikes his knee again, paralysing his leg. He sends his son to the nearest town to buy a bicycle so that they may proceed unhindered; the boy is away three days. During this period two important things happen to Moran. First, the man whom Molloy designated as C, or else someone very like him, approaches Moran in the woods and asks for a piece of bread. The man carries a massive stick, or club, wears a heavy greatcoat, and there is a cold thrust in his stare 'the like of which I never saw'; furthermore

his face was pale and noble, I could have done with it. . . . He had a huge shock of dirty snow-white hair . . . . His face was dirty and hairy, yes, pale, noble, dirty and hairy. . . . His accent was that of a foreigner or of one who has lost the habit of speech.

The man, from this description, sounds so like Mercier that perhaps it is he. Moran gives him a piece of bread, and in return asks to be allowed to feel the weight of the man's stick. The latter then departs:

he walked with swift uncertain step, often changing his course, dragging the stick like a hindrance. I wished I could have stood there looking after him, and time at a standstill. I wished I could have been in the middle of a desert, under the midday sun, to look after him till he was only a dot, on the horizon. I stayed out in the air for a long time.

Next day Moran breaks himself off a heavy stick like C's club and is poking the fire with it when another very different man accosts him:

He was on the small side, but thick-set. He wore a thick navy-blue suit (double-breasted) of hideous cut and a pair of outrageously wide black shoes . . . but all this was nothing compared to the face which I regret to say vaguely resembled my own . . . same little abortive moustache, same little ferrety eyes, same paraphimosis of the nose, and a thin red mouth. . . . Have you a tongue in your head? he said. I don't know you, I said. I laughed. I had not intended to be witty. [The French has: *Je ris. Elle était bonne, en effet.*]

He asks Moran if he has seen the old man with the stick pass by. Moran, 'trembling all over', replies in the negative and orders the short man out of his way, to no effect. Then he clubs the latter to death. 'He no longer resembled me' adds Moran with evident relief, and his stiff leg, for a short while at least, bends normally again.

On his son's return with a bicycle he tells him nothing of these events, and eventually, the son riding, the father on the carrier, they reach Molloy's region. After a violent quarrel, Jacques one night abandons his father, and soon afterwards Gaber appears with an order for Moran to return home. The latter is naturally worried whether his employer Youdi is angry with him or not: but no, Youdi has, it seems, simply been chuckling to himself, telling Gaber that 'life is a thing of beauty . . . and a joy for ever'. 'Do you think he meant human life?' asks Moran, but Gaber has already disappeared.

Then Moran begins his painful return, assailed by a growing decrepitude. One evening, in the pouring rain, a farmer menacingly orders Moran off his land, and the latter only escapes violence by pretending he is accomplishing a vow in making in a straight line for the Madonna of Turdy, who preserved his wife when he lost his baby son (the reverse evidently having in fact occurred, 'not that I miss Ninette', he blandly adds). In this way Moran arrives safely home. His house is deserted, his bees are dead and his hens running wild. It is spring when he arrives; he spends May and June in his garden, and in August he determines, after writing his report, to leave again, to try and become free, to reject his manhood, and to live close to the earth. Thus this second part, in which the report is mentioned both at the beginning and at the end, is also circular.

The setting of this story is country by now familiar: a town (Molloy's birthplace) with ramparts and vaulted entrances, traversed like Dublin by two canals, and a countryside of hills (*que d'aucuns appellent montagnes*), plain, woodland and sea. The country is certainly Ireland, called once again 'the island', but Molloy speaks of it as if he knew it well only some time ago: he says of its weather and of the reticence on sexual matters of its people, 'things have perhaps changed since my time'. Once again, too, the coinage is pounds, shillings and pence. Names of places are English obscenities—Turdy, Bally and Hole—and names of persons are either Irish or French: Jacques is of course French and Moran Irish, the combined name standing for the Franco-Irish nature of the work. It may not be without interest to note in passing that on the subject of Beckettian names *Thom's Dublin Directory* yields useful information. We there find in large numbers nearly all the principal names, for besides the obvious

Murphys and Molloys, there are several Morans, Malones, Watts, Knotts, Erskines, Spiros, Camiers and Mahoods. Mercier is of course French, and *Bottin* contains many of them, but few Camiers: Mercier and Camier therefore also represent to some extent a Franco-Irish duality. Arsene and Louit in *Watt* and Joly and Ambroise in *Molloy* Part II are French names; and the Elsner sisters, Moran's neighbours, seem to be named after the lady who ran the Stillorgan kindergarten Beckett attended as a child.

The setting of the second part is substantially that of the first with certain differences: firstly, whereas the latter is distinctly Irish in atmosphere, the former seems more French; it is almost as if Beckett were symbolizing in this way his own mind, thoroughly Irish in substratum, completely French on the surface, and the dual inspiration of his art, which draws its strength and its substance from the native land (the country, as Vivian Mercier has said, of the wake and the Sheela-na-gig, mocking death and sex respectively through the comic grotesque) and which draws its expression and form from the land of adoption.

Secondly, there is the significant dissimilarity in setting entailed by the fact that the place which Molloy describes as a fairly large region of hills, forest, plain, sea and distant islands, exists for Moran merely as a small area of copse, pasture, bog, creek and muddy sands, at the hub of which stands the fortified town that Molloy speaks of but which is dismissed by Moran as little more than a village. This difference in perspective is of course essential to the theme of the novel; for Molloy is a figure of myth moving in a mythical country whereas Moran is a fairly prosaic wage-earner inhabiting a world of suburban villas and farms.

Molloy's character has, in fact, all the strangeness of Watt's while not showing any of the latter's peculiar indistinctness. The man who emerges from the soliloquy of Part I is a clearly-defined person, one of the least easily forgotten that Beckett has created. Details about his appearance, however, are few: he is toothless, has a scant beard, and wears trousers, hat, greatcoat and long boots. There is no indication as to his height, but the hat seems to be a bowler. He sleeps very little, 'and that little by day', and he is a light eater, albeit a voracious and uncouth one. Like all the Beckettian heroes he is an intellectual, or was so once: he speaks ironically of the *Times Literary Supplement*, and he used to read

travellers' tales with care and attention; he can quote scraps of
Italian and Latin, and he is evidently familiar with Leibniz and
Geulincx, whose images on occasion he remembers. He is in fact
a self-confessed former student of many varied disciplines: 'my
head was a store-house of useful knowledge'. As to his moral
character, he combines nobility with sadistic violence (noble in
general adversity, brutal when crossed by individuals); and he
can often horrify the reader with his gross indifference to major
human preoccupations, such as the will to live and the impulse to
procreate, both of which provoke his pithiest ironies. For he has
no Camusian attitude of dignity in the face of 'the only really
serious philosophical problem', suicide, but is merely disappointed
that he persistently fails to commit it. Moreover he steals silver-
ware from Lousse without a qualm and shows no shame in telling
us so, and the act that provoked a scornful giggle even in Wylie
despite his enthusiasm for it, is for Molloy nothing more than a
'mug's game . . . and tiring on top of that'.

Moran, at least at first, shows no such amoral indifference to the
things that are supposed to matter. Entirely different from Molloy,
he is fussy and self-important, insisting on punctuality, disliking
interruption, and is immensely conceited: he prides himself 'on
being a sensible man', on 'reining back his thoughts within the
limits of the calculable so great is his horror of fancy', and on
being 'short of sins' in the confessional. He is of course very
scrupulous in religion, assiduous in his attendance at mass and
troubled if he misses his weekly communion. He has brought up
his son in the faith, and raised him with great firmness and little
love, insisting on respect but doing little to deserve it, hoping
often to trap his son into an act of deceit less serious than his own
that provokes it. At one point he wonders, but without drawing
the obvious conclusions, why his son is so silent with him and yet
so loquacious with his companions. Jacques naturally appears
through his father's narrative as dull, slow and unco-operative,
but this seems to be Moran's fault rather than his own. *Sollst
entbehren* is the declared principle which Moran seeks to inculcate
into his son, by continually denying the latter his wishes.

Moran is sensitive to dress and possesses for instance a large
collection of hats, from which he selects for his journey only an
old straw boater, which he wears with a pepper-and-salt shooting

suit, plus-fours and black boots, in order to look as strange as possible, for 'conspicuousness is the A B C of my profession'. About Moran's height we are told nothing, but it seems he is on the short side, since his son aged about thirteen is nearly as tall as he. His turn of mind is towards a dry, rather humourless sort of irony, whereas Molloy's equally sardonic asides are usually much funnier. As he is presented at the beginning of Part II, Moran is thus a petty-minded, precise individual, given to a refined and sadistic cruelty towards his son, whereas Molloy, for all his moral failings, is more humane and sympathetic altogether. It is important for a right comprehension of this novel to thus understand their different characters, without forgetting of course that Moran changes as the book progresses whereas Molloy's personality remains static.

*   *   *

Stylistically, this novel is one of the more complex that Beckett has written. The nucleus of the book is nonetheless a simple story, very like one of the *Nouvelles*: namely the chronicle of Molloy's wanderings and of his decline. It seems probable that it was from this nucleus that the rest grew, a conclusion borne out by the fact that Part I shows several points of resemblance to the *nouvelles* which preceded it. In matters of detail, in fact, it often echoes these stories: both Molloy and the hero of the latter possess a sucking-stone and a hat fixed to their buttonhole with string or shoelace; both wander aimlessly from town to country, clash with policemen, suffer eviction and expulsion, meet with shepherds or goatherds, run dogs or old ladies down, and not knowing where they are, enquire of strangers the name of their town. These events form as integral a part of the French hero's life as the gags do in a clown's act. The comparison is not in fact far-fetched: the various episodes occurring in his history constitute the Beckettian clown's performance, each incident having become an unchanging item in his repertoire. One therefore expects, with the same assured anticipation with which one greets a clown, the Beckettian hero, in every tale, to execute certain ritual gestures, to submit to certain regular happenings.

Connections more direct, however, than these common features can be perceived between Part I of *Molloy* and the short story closest to it in tone, *La Fin*. The heroes of both, on one occasion, show their anger by knocking the furniture about; both find themselves, on another, in a refuge littered with human excrement; both spend a period of their lives at the seaside, and both have diseased scalps. At one point, indeed, Molloy makes it clear that he is a reincarnation of the hero who dreamed that he drifted out to sea and sank slowly in an oarless boat: for Molloy, speaking of the sea that adjoined his region, adds

and I too once went forth on it, in a sort of oarless skiff, but I paddled with an old bit of driftwood. And I sometimes wonder if I ever came back, from that voyage. For I see myself putting to sea, and the long hours without landfall, I do not see the return . . . and I do not hear the frail keel grating on the shore.

There is thus some evidence to show that *Molloy* was first conceived in terms of the *Nouvelles*, that Part I was written in much the same vein as they were. Part II, on the other hand, follows more closely from *Mercier et Camier*: Moran's essential possessions are the same as those of the 'pseudocouple', namely haversack, umbrella, raincoat and bicycle, and just like Camier, of course, Moran is a kind of private detective who abandons the profession. Interesting also is the fact that Moran and his son are the twin heroes of Part II, like the two men of the earlier novel.

The two parts of *Molloy* seem therefore to derive from two different experiments in French fiction, *Mercier et Camier* and the *Nouvelles*, which were the occasion of an early working-out of the leading themes of the novel that followed. In fact when *Molloy* was written it was not clearly conceived as the first novel of a trilogy: *Malone Dies* almost certainly existed already in embryo, as is shown by the fact that its beginning follows neatly from the terminal situation of *Molloy*, with the hero bedridden, writing in a room; but *The Unnamable* seems not yet to have been foreseen: the French sentence in *Molloy* implying this reads: *cette fois-ci, puis encore une je pense, puis c'en sera fini je pense, de ce monde-là*, whereas the English is as follows (my italics):

This time, then once more I think, *then perhaps a last time*, then I think it'll be over, with that world too.

Much as *Molloy* owes, however, to its predecessors, it is fully original in that it surpasses them in the complexity and breadth of its conception. It is moreover the first of Beckett's novels to be specifically a writer's book, that is to say the first which is written down by a hero obliged to record his experiences and transcribe his mental processes. Molloy, Moran, Malone, the Unnamable, all are compelled to write in this way, all tell us they are so compelled, and then offer us what they write. They are examples of what Wayne C. Booth has called the 'self-conscious narrator', who 'intrudes into his novel to comment on himself as writer, and on his book, not simply as a series of events with moral implications, but as a created literary product'. No longer therefore does an external narrator, nameless or else dubbed 'Mr. Beckett' and 'Sam', tell the story of the heroes, but Molloy himself writes down his own tale, and tells us all the while that it is he writing it and that it is a tedious task fraught with difficulty:

It was he told me I'd begun all wrong, that I should have begun differently. He must be right. I began at the beginning, like an old ballocks, can you imagine that?

In Moran's case, it is a task that calls for all his grit and defiance:

. . . if I once made up my mind not to keep the hangman waiting, the bloody flux itself would not stop me, I would get there on all fours shitting out my entrails and chanting maledictions,

and he determines to carry it through 'even though the whole world, through the channel of its innumerable authorities speaking with one accord, should enjoin upon me this or that, under pain of unspeakable punishments'.

Molloy has furthermore to keep reminding himself that he is only telling a tale, and has to be careful to remember what he represents in the story, so much so that he asks the reader to correct any lapses he may make:

I cannot stoop, neither can I kneel, because of my infirmity, and if ever I stoop, forgetting who I am [French *oublieux de mon personnage*] make no mistake, it will not be me, but another.

His lapses in fact are frequent: 'I had forgotten who I was (excusably) and spoken of myself as I would have of another'; and he adds 'excusably' because 'from time to time I shall recall my present existence compared to which this is a nursery tale', namely his existence in his mother's bed. It is the man writing in a bed what he describes as 'only a diary', who continually stands, much in the manner of Tristram Shandy, behind the man whose actions are recorded, interrupting the narrative with his own comments and reminding himself that he must tell his tale as it took place at the time and not as it would happen to him now. This technique is pushed to an extreme of artifice in the next two novels; no wonder Molloy says 'I weary of these inventions and others beckon to me'. In fact some narrated incidents in *Molloy* exist already, as Malone says, merely as a 'pretext for not coming to the point' – told less for any intrinsic interest they may have than for the fact that they help Molloy 'to blacken a few more pages'. The obsessive element, the need to say and the nothing to say, in *The Unnamable*, is thus already foreshadowed in *Molloy* and helps constitute the essential unity of the trilogy.

Much of the stylistic interest of *Molloy* arises from its division into two chapters, which as P. Bowles has said, stand in counterpoint to each other. This counterpoint is achieved by an elaborate system of parallels and echoes from part to part which must have necessitated careful planning, more even than that required by the intricate structures of *Murphy* and *Watt*. The success of this double plot attests both to Beckett's painstaking care and to his formal skill. Let us now proceed to a closer examination of the duality of *Molloy*.

Very few events or items from Part I are repeated in Part II with no alteration: usually they are, as it were, refracted, and it is when their superficial difference gives way under analysis to a realization of their fundamental similarity that Beckett's best effects are obtained, and we feel that two men of very different character are fulfilling a similar destiny. (Beckett's handling of literary quotations in *More Pricks than Kicks* is, we saw, much the same: he rarely quotes accurately but usually parodies and transforms familiar quotations.) The parallels are introduced with considerable subtlety and only a close reading can reveal them all. Molloy speaks, for instance, of the possibility of his having a son somewhere, and then mentions that the visitor who collects his pages every Sunday is always thirsty: similarly Moran tells us of his own son soon before mentioning the arrival of Gaber, who also comes on Sunday and is also thirsty; when, moreover, Gaber reappears at the end it is apparently once again Sunday and his thirst is, if anything, worse. Gaber is therefore not only Youdi's emissary to Moran but also, it is strongly hinted, the man who calls on Molloy in his mother's room: the hints lie in the repetition of details that can easily pass unnoticed.

Many such details are repeated: both Molloy and Moran say they confuse two things when they are nearly identical, such as legs or bicycle wheels; both are troubled by their testicles which 'hang a little low'; both inform us of their ignorance of botany; both carry clasp-knives, and both attach their hats by means of elastic or shoelace, and ram them hard down on their heads when the attachment breaks; both meet shepherds, and Molloy's exclamation at this (*quel pays rural, mon Dieu*) differs little from Moran's *quel pays pastoral, mon Dieu* in the same circumstances; and finally, both are unsettled by the question 'what are you doing?' and both inform us of the pleasure they would derive from describing their bicycles at length.

More important than such minor occurrences are the parallels carefully established between the journeys of Molloy and of Moran, with the significant difference, however, that Moran's pilgrimage leaves him in the same state of decay which is Molloy's at the outset, since the latter starts with one stiff leg and crutches and Moran ends up that way; and Moran's clothing at the end of his journey has been reduced to Molloy's simple trousers, coat and boots, his socks and underclothing having been discarded in tatters *en route*. But both men spend a whole winter in the woods without, apparently, feeling the cold; both are reduced to living on berries and roots and both inform us that they find it convenient to rest their stiff legs to dislodge the clots. Both men terminate their journeys in spring, and both at one point or another ride a bicycle, although Moran possesses an autocycle which on this occasion he does not use.

By such means (similar to those employed in the two acts of *En attendant Godot*) the two chapters of *Molloy* together form an asymmetrical diptych which can be compared to *Pilgrim's Progress*, a book which Beckett must have meditated upon more than once in his life: 'there is no need to despair', says Molloy thinking of St. Augustine and Bunyan at the same time, 'you may scrabble on the right door, in the right way, in the end'; indeed, *Molloy* can be seen as Beckett's resetting of Bunyan's theme, with the difference that his 'progress' is not towards eternal glory, but only towards some obscure awareness of oneself as one is. There is nonetheless in both books an insistence on the necessity of going, for Christian to the wicket-gate, for Molloy to his mother, for Moran to Molloy: and Gaber is, *quantum mutatus*, the Evangelist of Beckett's version. Bunyan's Christian is promised fatigue, pain, hunger, nakedness and darkness on his way: these are the lot also of Molloy and Moran; and, like Christian, Moran is so troubled by his burden that he cannot take pleasure in his family as heretofore. The fight with Apollyon in *Pilgrim's Progress* is paralleled by Moran's killing of the man in the wood; and Molloy's arrest reminds us of the pilgrims' seizure at Vanity Fair. From Bunyan Beckett almost certainly took the conception of two parts: Christiana follows in her husband's footsteps, more or less, in Part II of *Pilgrim's Progress*, just as Moran follows in Molloy's. But whereas Bunyan, in rewriting his homily in slightly different terms, was simply working once more a vein which had proved a rich one, Beckett's second part is an integral development of his first, an indispensable gloss on it, essential to the artistic completeness of the whole. Nevertheless that he who has said he was brought up 'almost a Quaker', owes much to this forerunner, is hardly open to doubt; a fact which need not surprise us, since Swift, so close to Beckett in inspiration, was also an admirer of Bunyan's masterpiece.

It is by these means of the added dimension provided by the self-conscious narrator, and of the Bunyanesque doubling of parts, that the simple story that constitutes the basis of *Molloy* attains its complexity. The translation from French into English was carried out by Patrick Bowles in collaboration with the author. The task took as long as eighteen months to complete, because Beckett checked Bowles' work minutely and painstakingly. He had already translated a fragment of *Molloy* himself for *Transition Fifty*, but hoped to save time by entrusting the rest to someone else; finding that this was not the case, however, he decided to translate alone thereafter, except for the *Nouvelles* which Richard Seaver has translated under his supervision. Perhaps as a result of this collaboration, the English version of *Molloy* is far closer to the original than is the English version of *Malone meurt* or of *En attendant Godot*. On the other hand it is inevitably less 'creative': the English *Malone Dies* and *The Unnamable* add considerably to their originals, are even an essential commentary on them, so much so that no student can afford to be monoglot if he would know Beckett thoroughly. There are, in consequence, fewer deletions here from the original than in *Malone Dies*, although naturally enough Moran's remark *nous avions essayé de nous tutoyer* is omitted, and a few French puns are rendered only inadequately: it is hard to reproduce well in English Molloy's remark on the subject of anal birth, *premier emmerdement*, or Moran's bilingual joke *Condom est arrosé par la Baïse* (but why not, instead of 'Condom is on the Baïse', 'Condom is watered by the Baïse'?). Other verbal jokes are however quite adequately translated: *je n'étais pas dans mon assiette. Elle est profonde, mon assiette, une assiette à soupe, et il est rare que je n'y sois pas* becomes 'I was out of sorts. They are deep, my sorts, a deep ditch, and I am not often out of them'. In the translation we even find English puns, whether deliberate or accidental it is hard to say, which do not occur in the French: the English, for instance, has 'as to her address, I was in the dark, but knew how to get there, even in the dark', whereas the French merely reads: *pour ce qui était de [son] adresse, je l'ignorais, mais savais très bien m'y rendre, même dans l'obscurité*. Then, as Ruby Cohn has remarked, the English is sometimes more sardonic than the original (Ruth *n'était pas une femme pratique* for paying Molloy to make love to her, but in English: 'she was an idealist') and uses a garbled Keatsian quotation to good effect: Youdi's words, quoted above, about life being 'a thing of beauty ... and a joy for ever' is in French merely *la vie est une bien belle chose ... une chose inouïe*. On the other hand, the occasional pithy slang of the original is rarely fully rendered: *quelle galerie de crevés* pales to 'gallery of moribunds' and *j'avais intérêt à me planquer* to 'I had the better chance of skulking with success'.

When we turn to either text we notice that periods are slightly longer than in the *Nouvelles*, but are broken up by a device that becomes, from *Molloy* onwards, fully characteristic of Beckett's prose: the wide-ranging, versatile comma, which replaces the smile, the breath-pause, the ironic stress of speech, and the colons and semi-colons of standard prose. (The words in *Watt*, 'How hideous is the semicolon', at once come to mind.) In Beckett's last English novel, the comma served to emphasize the painstaking nature of that book; the French comma, on the other hand, has subtler uses, especially in determining the pace and the rhythm of the narrative: so, in *The Unnamable*, the commas draw closer together and the phrases become consequently shorter as the novel progresses, and in *Molloy*, to a lesser degree, the same feature can be remarked towards the end of Part I and of Part II. The paragraphing is as carefully studied as the punctuation: Molloy's story consists of only two paragraphs, the first of about five hundred words, the second of forty thousand, whereas Moran's report, as befits the man, remains normally divided throughout. Variation of speed in narration is as important as rhythm: events can either take an unconscionable time to relate in all their details, or they can be hurriedly summarized in a few words: 'nevertheless I covered several miles and found myself under the ramparts' – the curtness of this sentence in the midst of Molloy's discursive second paragraph takes the reader by surprise. Beckett's two narrators digress with great frequency, not to say alacrity, but they always manage to return to their original point, with some such recalling phrase as 'that moon, then . . .'. Only a superficial reading leads one to think that *Molloy* is a rambling monologue leading nowhere in particular; only such a reading can have given rise to the unhelpful but often-proffered opinion that this is a stream-of-consciousness novel. (We blunt our terms by thus misusing them: *Molloy* is no more a stream-of-consciousness novel than is Mauriac's *Nœud de vipères*; in both cases we are confronted with a hard, clear, uncompromisingly honest self-description. A book needs more than a first-person narrator talking to and for himself before it can be bracketed with the last episode of *Ulysses*.) In *Molloy*, in fact, the monologue is firmly anchored to certain submerged reefs, or to change the metaphor, revolves on certain pivot-events, as it is hoped the synopsis above will have shown. Thus every digression ends with a return to its point of departure before the narrator passes on to the next subject. This firmness of structure provides the canvas for such typically Beckettian incidental embroidery as deliberate repetition and the use of the ejaculation 'oh', now common in his work: 'the room smelt of ammonia, oh not merely of ammonia, but of ammonia, ammonia'.

Such arabesques are now part of the repertoire, as are all the instances of the narrator's jibes at the expense of his own activity, which usually take the form of asides to himself ('no, that doesn't work', 'no, that's not it') or to the reader:

I apologise for these details, in a moment we'll go faster, much faster. And then perhaps relapse again into a wealth of filthy circumstance. But which in its turn again will give way to vast frescoes, dashed off with loathing.

Sometimes the narrator will humorously lay the blame for his obscenities elsewhere: 'I apologise for having to revert to this lewd orifice, 'tis my muse will have it so,' and sometimes he arraigns the whole literary act as a mere matter of 'complying with the convention that demands you either lie or hold your peace'. This jesting springs from a profound conviction of the impotence of language to convey anything of importance: so much so that we occasionally come across the tongue-tied collapse into silence of the prose sentence (as elaborated by artists such as Proust) for which Beckett in 1931 had only words of praise ('the clarity of the phrase is cumulative and explosive') but which in *Molloy* simply peters into nothing:

For it [the old bad leg] was shortening, don't forget, whereas the other, though stiffening, was not yet shortening, or so far behind its fellow that to all intents and purposes, intents and purposes, I'm lost, no matter.

We find, too, Molloy launched on the explanation that will finally explain everything, but simply unable to go on:

I should add, before I get down to the facts, you'd swear they were facts, of that distant summer afternoon, that with this deaf, blind, impotent, mad old woman, who called me Dan and whom I called Mag, and with her alone, I – no, I can't say it.

He expresses this lack of faith in any form of expression most forcibly in the often-quoted words 'not to want to say, not to know what you want to say, not to be able to say what you think you want to say, and never to stop saying ... that is the thing to keep in mind, even in the heat of composition', which clearly recall what Beckett said unambiguously in the Duthuit dialogues (1949):

I speak of an art . . . weary of pretending to be able, of being able, of doing a little better the same old thing, of going a little further along a dreary road . . . [and preferring] the expression that there is nothing to express, nothing with which to express, nothing from which to express, together with the obligation to express.

Beckett applies this general theory specifically to Bram van Velde, who 'is obliged to paint', and when Duthuit asks 'why is he obliged to paint?' Beckett simply replies 'I don't know'. Molloy's answer to a similar question would be much the same: 'you must choose between the things not worth mentioning and those even less so'. For Moran, similarly, writing is a 'penance', with tiresome conventions of chronology that lend a stifling artificiality to the literary act, with which he feels impelled to express his impatience in the words that close his part of the story, words which destroy the grandiose opening that he had originally chosen for its literary effect (for now, less inclined to show off to himself, he prefers truth to an impressive style):

I went back into the house and wrote, It is midnight. The rain is beating on the windows. It was not midnight. It was not raining.

Molloy however does not care for such scruples: 'truly it little matters what I say . . . saying is inventing', so long as 'the whole ghastly business looks like what it is, senseless, speechless, issueless misery'.

This monumental disdain for 'literature' (which can, paradoxically, give rise to good writing) does not preclude ironic witticisms of the following kind, indulged in largely for their own sake:

Yes, the confusion of my ideas on the subject of death was such that I sometimes wondered, believe me or not, if it wasn't a state of being even worse than life.

Remarks like this are found throughout the book, which moreover relates a number of comic incidents, such as Molloy's clash with the policeman ('your papers! he cried. Ah my papers. Now the only papers I carry with me are bits of newspaper, to wipe myself, you understand, when I have a stool'), his running over of

Lousse's dog, and Moran's secret torment, during his anxious interview with Father Ambrose, on the subject of the eucharist: 'would I be granted the body of Christ after a pint of Wallensstein?' This humour has a disrespectful vigour which is one of the the most attractive features of the novel. Not many books, in fact, seek to attain such a pitch of dry, cruel comedy, with the obvious exception of the works of Swift, whose spirit, as M. Nadeau was the first to point out, breathes in the whole of Beckett's trilogy. Molloy has in fact, together with Malone as we shall see later, completely mastered the great Dean's ironical technique:

> If I have always behaved like a pig, the fault lies not with me but with my superiors, who corrected me only on points of detail instead of showing me the essence of the system, after the manner of the great English schools, and the guiding principles of good manners. . . . On this subject I had only negative and empirical notions, which means that I was in the dark, most of the time. . . .

Swift's presence is nowhere more apparent than in the longer passages in which his methods of bland and sustained irony can be adopted with greatest effect: where else, apart from in the *Modest Proposal*, is irony employed more extensively and with a straighter face and calmer self-assurance than in the passage in which Molloy tells of his first (and last) major sexual experience?

> She went by the peaceful name of Ruth, I think . . . [I knew] it was love, for she had told me so. She bent over the couch, because of her rheumatism . . . It was the only position she could bear . . . It seemed all right to me, for I had seen dogs. . . . Perhaps after all she put me in her rectum. . . . But . . . have I never known *true love* after all? That's what bothers me sometimes. . . . What I do know for certain is that I never sought to repeat the experience, having I suppose the *intuition* that it had been *unique and perfect*, of its kind, *achieved and inimitable*, and that it *behoved* me to *preserve its memory*, *pure of all pastiche*, *in my heart*, even if it meant my resorting from time to time to the alleged joys of so-called self-abuse.

In this last quotation those words are italicized which, by conveying the opposite of their apparent meaning, act as the ironical pivots of the passage, and lead directly to the trap which, as Dr. Leavis says in connection with Swift, is sprung only in the last few words. How similar Swift's technique is can be seen from the following passage, where there occurs the same patient accumulation of words suggesting the opposite of what they state, until the final lash that follows the throwing-off of the mask:

I am very sensible what a *weakness* and *presumption* it is, to reason against the general humour and disposition of the world. . . . However, I know not how, whether from *affectation of singularity*, or the *perverseness* of human nature, but so it *unhappily* falls out, that I cannot be entirely of this opinion. . . . I do not yet see the *absolute necessity* of extirpating the Christian religion from among us. . . . [The Turks would be] scandalised at our infidelity. . . . For they are not only strict observers of religious worship, but, what is *worse*, believe a God; which is more than is required of us, even while we preserve the name of Christians. (From *An Argument against abolishing Christianity* (my italics).)

Greatly shortened as, for reasons of space, these extracts must be, they should show that Swift's ironical techniques foreshadow some of Beckett's most characteristic literary methods.

*   *   *

Not only is *Molloy* an interesting formal achievement, it is also one of the clearest statements of the leading Beckettian preoccupations, the most persistent of which is the problem of exile. In *Molloy*, the hero is not only as fully alienated as the *Nouvelles* hero, he is also just as completely indifferent to his situation. Molloy realizes full well the reaction he is liable to provoke in a stranger: 'what is it I want? Ah that tone I know, compounded of pity, of fear, of disgust'. Being an outcast, he can freely indulge in irony at the expense of his persecutors: '[he] began to interrogate me in a tone which, from the point of view of civility, left increasingly to be desired, in my opinion'. Molloy's destiny is isolation and loneliness: 'I asked the man to help me, to have pity on me. He didn't understand'; even a shepherd to whom he puts a question does not reply. He only has to kill a dog for 'a blood-thirsty mob of both sexes and all ages' to prepare to tear him to pieces; and so

morning is the time to hide. They wake up, hale and hearty, their tongues hanging out for order, beauty and justice, baying for their due. Yes, from eight to nine till noon is the dangerous time. But towards noon things quiet down, the most implacable are sated . . . each man counts his rats. . . . The night purge is in the hands of technicians, for the most part. They do nothing else. . . . Day is the time for lynching, for sleep is sacred.

When at last he hears the voice promising help at the end, Molloy ironically remarks 'well, I suppose you have to try everything once, succour included, to get a complete picture of the resources of their planet'.

Moran's exile, like Mercier's and Camier's, is more a self-imposed alienation: 'I don't like men,' he says, 'and I don't like animals.' Moran's love is devoted entirely to his piece of land, 'my trees, my bushes, my flower-beds, my tiny lawns' and he is terrified at the prospect of the 'long anguish of vagrancy and freedom' that he will have to endure away from them: 'I am too old to lose all this, and begin again, I am too old!' But once he has returned from his unsuccessful search for Molloy, he rejects his last links with humanity ('I have been a man long enough, . . . I shall not try any more') and takes to living in his garden alone with his fowls:

They were wild birds. And yet quite trusting. I recognised them and they seemed to recognise me . . . I tried to understand their language better. Without having recourse to mine. They were the longest, loveliest days of all the year.

Molloy is not however only a further statement of this now familiar theme, it also takes up again the issue of dualism. The body and mind are once more firmly separated: as Hugh Kenner suggests, the bicycle represents an ideal body that the Beckettian hero seeks (in vain) to annex to himself, since his own is in full-scale decay. The brain, it is unambiguously stated, is by far the most reliable part of the body:

. . . there were days when my legs were the best part of me, with the exception of the brain capable of forming such a judgement.

But the brain, as Descartes pointed out, is not synonymous with the mind, which in Beckett's work ever since Belacqua has been yearning, as has been seen, for the reprieve of 'ceasing to be an annex of the restless body', and ever since Murphy functions 'not as an instrument but as a place'. By *Molloy* it has become in fact

a place with neither plan nor bounds and of which I understand nothing, not even of what it is made, still less into what. . . . It is not the kind of place where you go, but where you find yourself . . . and which you cannot leave at will . . . .I listen and the voice is of a world collapsing endlessly, a frozen world, under a faint untroubled sky, enough to see by. . . . What possible end to these wastes where true light never was, nor any upright thing, nor any true foundation, but only these leaning things, forever lapsing and crumbling away, beneath a sky without memory of morning or hope of night.

How clearly this reminds us of Belacqua's mind as adumbrated in *Dream of Fair to Middling Women* there is no need to point out: the seeds of the entire Beckettian concept of mind were first sown in that book, the hero of which, however, refused the opportunity (so precious to Moran) of 'wandering in his mind'. Moran in fact takes a sensuous pleasure in this, 'noting every detail of the labyrinth, its paths as familiar as those of my garden and yet ever new . . . . Unfathomable mind, now beacon, now sea'. Here, like Murphy, he retires

far from the world, its clamours, frenzies, bitterness and dingy light, [to] pass judgement on it. . . . All is dark, but with that simple darkness that follows like a balm upon the great dismemberings. From their places masses move, stark as laws. . . . There somewhere man is too, vast conglomerate of all of nature's kingdoms, as lonely and as bound.

It is in Moran's mind ('where all I need is to be found') that his quarry also lies hidden:

And in that block the prey is lodged and thinks himself a being apart. . . . I am paid to seek. I arrive, he comes away. His life has been nothing but a waiting for this. . . .

Such a mind, self-sufficient, is quite detached from its accompanying body. Molloy sees his hand on his knee as an indistinguishable part of the external physical world, a foreign object 'which my knee felt tremble and of which my eyes saw the wrist only, the heavily veined back, the pallid rows of knuckles'; and like a truly Cartesian machine, the body only works when instructions are sent from the brain: 'my feet . . . never took me to my mother unless they received a definite order to do so'.

This body decays steadily as the story proceeds, in the case both of Moran and of Molloy: the latter has a stiff leg when Part I begins, and like Belacqua a tendency to cramp in the toes. When it ends, both legs are stiff and 'very sore', and the toes of the right foot have gone; he is reduced therefore to crawling along:

> Flat on my belly, using my crutches like grapnels, I plunged them ahead of me into the undergrowth, and when I felt they had a hold, I pulled myself forward, with an effort of the wrists.

And finally, of course, he ends up completely bedridden. Moran, on the other hand, if he begins in good health, soon feels the pain that announces the stiffening of his leg, which obliges him to adopt crutches. Moreover he gets weaker and weaker and (also like Belacqua) suffers from pains in the stomach during his painful homeward journey.

This useless body and its functions are exposed to severe ridicule. Physical disgust first becomes a Beckettian constant in *Watt*, in the revolting description of Mary the gluttonous housemaid; in *Molloy* disgust centres on Molloy's mother, 'veiled with hair, wrinkles, filth, slobber', and it is unnecessary to add that sex is derided savagely in the episode of the love-affair with Ruth. What Moran calls 'that most fruitful of dispositions, horror of the body and its functions', pervades and informs Beckett's work from this book onwards, just as it inspired much in the later writings of Swift. The dualistic obsession which accounts for this horror explains also the extraordinary contrast we remark between a body in full decay and a mind ratiocinating on, as agile as ever it was (using language of surprising formality, such as: 'judge then of my relief when I saw ahead of me, the familiar ramparts loom'), a mind principally taken up with the perplexities of epistemology, which are as pressing a concern here as they are in *Watt*.

The chief reason for difficulties of knowing is that the hero is to a large extent isolated from the world of sensibilia, immured in himself, sealed off: 'for some time past', says Molloy at the end, 'I had not opened my eyes, or seldom', which is hardly surprising, since on his side of his sense organs there is a whole world: 'behind my closed lids the little night and its little lights'; and when he does 'perceive' something, that is to say when something recognizable to him can be induced from disordered phenomena, it is always after a time-lapse. As for Moran, he 'drown[s] in the spray of phenomena', since 'each pin-point of skin screams a different message'; ensconced, then, within the castle of his mind, the Beckettian hero is with difficulty made aware of events around him, and since his memory too is uncertain (Molloy cannot even remember the name of his town), he is liable to confuse 'several different occasions'. Molloy suffers in particular from this isolation, and the slowness of his reactions to sensory stimuli gives rise to humorous incidents, especially at the police-station. His hearing is generally good, for 'sounds unencumbered by precise meaning' he registers as well as anybody, but conversation is 'unspeakably painful' to him because the understanding of the *meaning* of the words takes place some time after the registering of the *sounds* of the words. In the same way he finds it hard to name what is mirrored in his eye, 'often quite distinctly', and he usually smells and tastes things 'without knowing exactly what'.

And even my sense of identity was wrapped in a namelessness often hard to penetrate . . . already all was fading, waves and particles, there could be no things but nameless things, no names but thingless names.

Under such circumstances, where language ceases to function, no wonder that one's 'knowledge of men is scanty and the meaning of being beyond [one]', that space slips into relativity ('the confines of my room, of my bed, of my body, are as remote from me as were those of my region') and that duration loses its reality ('what had happened to those fourteen days . . . and where had they flown?'). Only matters of derisory importance, such as the fact that small windows are lavatory lights, 'from time to time . . . impose themselves on the understanding with the force of axioms'; and so it is better not to care: 'to know you are beyond knowing anything, that is when peace enters in', and Molloy's monumental contempt for ratiocination, especially mathematical computation, is shown by a sardonic comment on 'how mathematics help you to know yourself', by the fact also that, having expended a few thousand words on the problem of the sucking-rota of his sixteen sucking-stones distributed through four pockets, he dismisses the whole calculation in one sentence:

> And the solution to which I rallied in the end was to throw away all the stones but one, which I kept now in one pocket, now in another, and which of course I soon lost. . . .

Connected with these problems of knowledge is the tendency of the self to collapse into a wider self: 'on myself too I pored', says Moran, 'on me so changed from what I was' –

> And I seemed to see myself ageing as swiftly as a day-fly. But the idea of ageing was not exactly the one which offered itself to me. And what I saw was more like a crumbling, a frenzied collapsing of all that had always protected me from all I was condemned to be. . . . But what words can describe this sensation at first all darkness and bulk, with a noise like the grinding of stones, then suddenly as soft as water flowing.

The old terror of Belacqua that 'stones and thickets would flood over him . . . a nightmare strom of timber and leaves and tendrils and bergs of stone', constitutes for Molloy the mystical possibility of nirvana, when the self will expand to infinity:

> There were times when I forgot not only who I was, but that I was, forgot to be. Then I was no longer that sealed jar to which I owed my being so well preserved, but a wall gave way and I filled with roots and tame stems for example, stakes long since dead and ready for burning, the recess of night and the imminence of dawn, and then the labour of the planet rolling eager into winter . . . of that winter I was the precarious calm.

*   *   *

In this fictional universe of the imprecision of the self and the uncertainty of knowledge, the only constant is the tyrant, the mysterious overlord who, from Mr. Knott onwards, haunts, even governs, the destiny of the Beckettian hero. His existence, like Godot's, is never certain, because he never appears in person: he is only supposed by the heroes to exist and is frequently referred to by them. Both Molloy and Moran speak of a power, more malevolent than benevolent, which plays with their lives. Molloy refers to this power as 'they', but their only representative whom he sees is Gaber:

What I'd like now is to speak of the things that are left, say my good-byes, finish dying. They don't want that. Yes, there is more than one, apparently. But it's always the same one that comes. You'll do that later, he says.

'They' pay him for writing his story, or alternatively scold him, through Gaber, when he fails to do so. At one point therefore Molloy directly addresses these overlords:

I no longer know what I'm doing, nor why, those are things I under-stand less and less, I don't deny it, for why deny it, and to whom, to you to whom nothing is denied?

During his journey he has the impression that if he stays in the forest at the end he will be 'going against an imperative':

For I have greatly sinned, at all times, greatly sinned against my prompters. And if I cannot decently be proud of this I see no reason either to be sorry. But imperatives are a little different, and I have always been inclined to submit to them, I don't know why.

Likewise he feels uneasy whenever he lies down 'in defiance of the rules'. He moreover apologises to his overlords for describing his painful progress blasphemously as a 'veritable calvary', by adding the words 'saving your presence'.

Molloy is undergoing what he calls 'the immemorial expiation' in which all men are his 'fellow-convicts'; not, as Beckett said in *Proust*,

the miserable expiation of a codified breach of a local arrangement, organised by the knaves for the fools . . . [but] the expiation of original sin, of the original and eternal sin . . . the sin of having been born.

Birth, being a sin, is therefore a calamity for the person born: Molloy's mother failed to dislodge him during her pregnancy because 'fate had earmarked me for less compassionate sewers'. 'I forgive her', he remarks generously, 'for having jostled me a little in the first months and spoiled the only endurable, just endurable, period of my enormous history,' because at least she did her best to prevent his birth, 'except of course the one thing';

'and I also give her credit', he adds, 'for not having done it again, thanks to me'.

More precise information than this about the sentence they are serving the heroes do not obtain. 'It's my fault . . . but what fault?' asks Molloy, and 'crave forgiveness, forgiveness for what?' asks Moran. The latter has a more specific assignment from his tyrant, Youdi, than Molloy has from his nameless overseers, but he nevertheless speaks of it as 'a cause which . . . was in its essence anonymous, and would subsist . . . when its miserable artisans should be no more'. Moran frequently gives way to feelings of insubordination:

I wondered, suddenly rebellious, what compelled me to accept this commission. But I had already accepted it, I had given my word. Too late. Honour. It did not take me long to gild my impotence.

At another point he 'boils with anger' at Youdi for saddling him with his son, and harbours 'hatred . . . and scorn' in his heart:

At the thought of the punishments Youdi might inflict upon me I was seized by such a mighty fit of laughter that I shook, with mighty silent laughter, and my features composed in their wonted sadness and calm.

But he does not always show this courage: 'Youdi will take care of me', he whimpers, 'he will not let me be punished' for the murder in the wood; why should Youdi not protect him, since even Molloy is described as his protégé?

Grimly, doggedly, Moran writes out his pensum, accomplishes 'this paltry scrivening that is not of my province': 'he asked for a report, he'll get his report'; the real reason is not that he is afraid of Youdi, but that his inner voice, such an important organ now for the Beckettian hero, tells him to do so:

And the voice I listen to needs no Gaber to make it heard. For it is within me and exhorts me to continue to the end the faithful servant I have always been, of a cause that is not mine.

Moran feels that he will henceforward follow this voice faithfully, and at the end it is his only hope:

I have spoken of a voice telling me things. I was getting to know it better now, to understand what it wanted. . . . It told me to write the

146

report. Does this mean I am freer now than I was? I do not know. I shall learn.

Molloy's voice gives him practical instructions of the sort 'get out of here, Molloy' when he is at Lousse's, and reassures him at the edge of the forest, but he insists that this is not an ordinary voice, but rather 'a kind of consciousness', or 'something gone wrong with the silence'.

Whereas the voice is personal and friendly, the 'innumerable spirits of darkness' of which Molloy also speaks are impersonal and usually hostile. The hero is caught between the two, yielding now to one, now to the other, poised precariously and unstably between two magnetic poles of indeterminate strength. He is therefore a flimsy creature crushed by powerful forces and crippled in his body by disease, in his mind by uncertainty. He longs for a state of being like death – 'to be literally incapable of motion at last, that must be something!' – even though he has not the courage or ability to seek death itself, perhaps because death is no solution to the really desperate.

The philosopher who remotely but insistently broods over this novel is not Geulincx (whose theory of free will is however once referred to) but rather Leibniz: Molloy speaks of the 'pre-established harmony, which makes so sweet a music', of C acting in a certain way at a 'pre-established moment', and of Lousse, who 'must have thought she had left nothing to chance, so far as the safety of her dog was concerned, whereas in reality she was setting the whole system of nature at naught'.

The presence of a metaphysician like Leibniz need cause no surprise in a work that is to a large extent a meditation on the circumstances of human existence. Where *Watt* explores the epistemological poverty in which we live, *Molloy* deals rather with the issue of personal regeneration and spiritual renewal, through the medium of a fable, or of a myth, which tells of a man who went in search of another and found no one.

There is no point in trying to assign precise meaning to the details of this fable, even though each element seems artistically inevitable. I have tried to show that it is fairly certain that Molloy and Moran are victims of the same power. Youdi (from the Arabic *yahudi*) is the colloquial French word for Jew, from which it is only a step to Yahweh, the Old Testament God. Gaber, of course, suggests Gabriel, God's emissary to Zacharias, to Mary the virgin, and to Daniel. Gabriel 'stand[s] in the presence of God', and that Gaber lives in the same close dependence on Youdi is shown by the fact that his recall is so sudden after he has visited Moran that he forgets the second glass of beer he had asked for. Moran, having been sent on his journey, meets and kills a man who not only looks like himself but acts in a similarly brusque, impolite way. After this incident he slowly changes into a man much more like Molloy than like his own original self, and the latter seems, in fact, to have been his double all along:

I knew then about Molloy, without however knowing much about him. . . . He panted, he had only to rise up within me for me to be filled with panting. . . . He swayed to and fro, like a bear. . . . He was massive and hulking . . . forever on the move. I had never seen him at rest. . . . This was how he came to me, at long intervals. Then I was nothing but uproar, bulk, rage, suffocation, effort unceasing, frenzied and vain. . . . And when I saw him disappear, his whole body a vociferation, I was almost sorry.

His 'prey is lodged', as we saw above, in his own lower depths. Punctual and practising at the outset, he is indifferent to religion, as well as to time, at the end; at the beginning he 'found it painful not to understand', but not so any longer at the end. The prey seems therefore to have risen to the surface and taken possession of the man: but drastic as Moran knows his changes to have been, he nevertheless feels he is still the same person:

Physically speaking it seemed to me I was now becoming rapidly unrecognisable. . . . And yet . . . to tell the truth I not only knew who I was, but I had a sharper and clearer sense of my identity than ever before, in spite of its deep lesions and the wounds with which it was covered.

Molloy feels that 'all my life, I think I have been going to my mother . . . when I appeared to give up and to busy myself with something else . . . in reality I was hatching my plans and seeking the way to her house'. At the end of his story, however, he hears in Latin the ominous warning *nimis sero*, 'perhaps it is already too late'; and so, just as Moran only finds Molloy in the sense that and in so far as he becomes Molloy, the latter only reaches his mother by taking her place in the bed, unaware of what has become of her.

⌐ *Molloy* can therefore be interpreted as an epic of the search for one's real self: Moran, having succoured the bearded man whom Molloy designated as C and destroyed the man who looked like himself with a club like C's, returns, in a way, a healthier, a more genuine person, reconciled with the bear-like man he knew in his subconscious mind (the man who, he formerly said, was 'just the opposite of me, in fact'), reconciled with Molloy, in a word, with the hated, abandoned, courageous, recalcitrant outcast that he was commanded to hunt down. It is a psychological triumph, but if it represents salvation, the salvation is a negative one: not an expansion but a contraction, into oneself and into a more barren, if truer, existence. ⌐Beckett is too much of a pessimist to believe in any new and better dawns: our only chance lies in a retreat towards *un néant qui serait réalité la plus certaine de l'homme* (Nadeau), a retreat such as all his major heroes seek, even long, to effect. Belacqua, Murphy and Watt all fail in different ways to do so, as we have seen: if Moran alone seems to succeed, his success is sterile, condemning him to the terrible liberty, the eternal solitude of Malone and the Unnamable⌐ Against the latter situation the Beckettian hero has now only the weapons of his wit and the resources of his mind: his field of operations has moreover shifted, for the battle is no longer so much with the world of men as with the dark forces that would tyrannize over him in a twilight netherworld of his own imagining.⌐It is into this netherworld that we now follow Malone. We only emerge from it at the end of a journey through one of the most painful tracts of mental suffering mapped in literature.

* * *

'*Molloy*', said B. Pingaud in 1951, 'appears as a monstrous, disquieting myth, of mysterious origins', and Georges Bataille went even further in emphasizing Molloy's mythical nature:

This horrible shape, swaying painfully on its crutches, is the truth with which we are diseased and which dogs us no less relentlessly than our own shadow does: it is our dread of this shape that dictates our gestures, our straightforward attitudes and our distinct sentences. . . . It is the ineluctable abyss that will lure and then engulf our human display: it is oblivion and impotence.

Because of this quality, because too of the symmetry of its symbolism and the skill of its construction, *Molloy* seems Beckett's most sustained achievement, one that almost summarizes his whole work: it is certainly the most forceful statement of his fundamental preoccupations, and one of his best narratives. Professor Mayoux calls it *une œuvre de transition imparfaitement réussie*; but it would seem rather that, far from being a merely transitional novel, *Molloy* stands apart from the rest of Beckett's *œuvre*, a book which can, in terms of scope and power, be considered a great novel.

Chapter 6

MALONE

'Minds dismembered by their sexual part', Balthazar had said once,
'never find peace until old age and failing powers persuade them
that silence and quietness are not hostile'.

L. DURRELL, *Justine*

IT is easy to pass over the second novel of the trilogy, *Malone Dies*, as lightweight in comparison with the two heavy works that accompany it, and perhaps this initial misunderstanding accounts for the fact that it has received relatively little critical attention. On closer examination, however, it appears as a cleverly written book, a perfect *andantino* heard between the *andante* of *Molloy* and the *allegro assai* of *The Unnamable*.

The pattern of *Malone Dies* is quite straightforward. Malone, like Molloy, is slowly dying in a room, and he writes as he dies. What he writes, free from all explanation or addition, is what we read. Unlike *Molloy*, however, this is not a circular novel: Malone just starts writing at a given moment and stops only when death holds his hand. It is soon made clear under what conditions he is working: 'I could die today, if I wished, merely by making a little effort. But it is just as well to let myself die, quietly, without rushing things.' We recall that Molloy was not allowed to die, although he wanted to; Malone shows that he is a reincarnation of Molloy in the following words:

Something must have changed. I will not weigh upon the balance any more, one way or the other. I shall be neutral and inert. . . . I shall die tepid, without enthusiasm.

His 'old debtor', Death, is now almost ready to repay him after his long and dolorous existence.

While waiting for this settlement, he decides to tell himself stories, but stories not, as hitherto, characterized by ugliness, beauty or frenzy (perhaps he thereby refers to Molloy, to Celia and to Watt respectively). Nonetheless his old violence flares up

151

briefly once again in the execration: 'I forgive nobody. I wish them all an atrocious life and then the fires and ice of hell.' In fact, Malone's vaunted new-found calm constitutes an unstable virtue: he eventually succumbs during a mounting paroxysm of frenzy as his Lemuel slays some of the creatures of the tales.

Malone insists, with all the desperation of fear (for he does not in fact really wish to die with quite the eagerness he claims), 'it is no longer the ancient night, the recent night. Now it is a game, I am going to play'. This is not, however, the first time he has tried to play: 'people and things ask nothing better than to play . . . but it was not long before I found myself alone, in the dark. That is why I gave up trying to play and took to myself for ever shapelessness and speechlessness, . . . darkness, long stumbling with outstretched arms, hiding'.

Throughout what then follows Malone continues wrestling with these things, for his troubles are not nearly over yet. His bouts of story-telling are constantly being interrupted by precisely these periods of sombre introspection, when he slips back into the 'dead world, airless, waterless' that he aims to avoid by virtue of his new scheme 'to live, and cause to live, at last, to play at last and die alive'. This is what gives the novel its straightforward pattern: a fragment of fiction is followed by a fragment of self-examination, and vice-versa, to the end; and an important theme is the very ambiguity of what constitutes the fiction and what does not.

His programme is clear enough: first the stories (of a man and woman, of a thing and of an animal) and then an inventory of his possessions (when he will 'draw the line and make the tot'); if after that any time remains 'I shall take the necessary steps to ensure my not having made a mistake'. Needless to say, this programme is not satisfactorily carried out. We are told nothing either about the thing or the animal, and the inventory, intended for the end, creeps in at various odd moments: for Malone has a veritable mania about his possessions and cannot leave the subject alone. Molloy, too, had threatened to draw up 'the inventory of his goods', although in both cases it is quite evident that these are distinguished only by their extreme banality and paucity: an old boot, the bowl of a pipe, a small packet tied up in yellowed newspaper, and perhaps an old love-letter or two.

His present situation, too, is simple enough: he lives in an ordinary house, not a hospital; when he is not too deaf he hears sounds that are quite normal, and he can see from his window roofs and sky, as well as into a room of the house opposite, where a couple lives. The six planes of his own room seem often, however, to become the outer wall of a skull inside which he roams, listening to 'the faint sound of aerial surf that is my silence': the Unnamable, too, speaks of 'the inside of my distant skull where once I wandered . . . straining against the walls', recalling a theme that dates back to the *Echo's Bones* cycle of poems, where we read of the vulture 'dragging his hunger through the sky/of my skull shell of sky and earth', and find 'in my skull the wind going fetid'. The vulture flapping its heavy wings inside the brain seems to be an obsessional symbol of mental torment by no means limited to Beckett:

> Lady, three white leopards sat under a juniper-tree
> In the cool of the day, having fed to satiety
> On my legs my heart my liver and that which had been contained
> In the hollow round of my skull.
>
> (T. S. ELIOT, *Ash-Wednesday*)

In the corner of Malone's skull-room are his possessions: he has a long stick which he employs both to rummage among them, and to draw to himself the little table on which his daily soup and clean chamber-pot are placed by the withered hand of an old woman, whom he has not seen properly for some time. Although totally bedridden and always alone, he seems quite contented, since he lacks nothing essential: 'dish and pot, dish and pot, these are the poles'. The events that occur as he dies are few in number but serious in purport: first, the old woman unexpectedly stops renewing his soup and emptying his pots, thus ensuring that he will die of inanition; next, his stick, with which he has been trying to manœuvre his bed out of the room, slips from his grasp, leaving him marooned in his bed; and lastly, he receives the visit of a mysterious stranger whom he takes at first to be the undertaker's man come too soon. This person strikes him on the head to rouse him, then watches over him for a long time ('I think we gazed at each other literally for hours . . . he probably imagined he could stare me down'), rummages in his possessions and even speaks to him, that is 'his mouth opened, his lips worked, but I heard nothing'. These three occurrences apart, Malone is free to tell his stories in which figure a boy called Saposcat, Sapo for short, who later becomes an old man named Macmann, and an old woman called Moll who takes Macmann as her lover.

Sapo, the great hope and 'eldest child of poor and sickly parents', is a self-willed dunce, due cruelly to disappoint the expectations placed in him. For instead of working at his examinations in order, with the least possible delay, to be in a position to help provide for his younger brothers and sisters, he broods upon himself, struggling with the 'babel raging in his head', and wondering 'how he was going to live, and live vanquished, blindly, in a mad world, in the midst of strangers'. Having created 'this patient, reasonable child', Malone feels he is getting somewhere at last: nothing less like himself, he believes, can be imagined than this young person, 'avid of the least gleam, a stranger to the joys of darkness' – 'here truly', he adds, 'is the air I needed, a lively tenuous air, far from the nourishing murk that is killing me'.

During the summer holidays immediately preceding the *baccalauréat* examination, Sapo goes for long solitary walks in the country and occasionally visits the Lamberts (*les Louis*), a poverty-stricken peasant family consisting of an elderly but still active father, a young mother suffering from an unnamed but painful disease, and a son and daughter. Sapo says little to them, however, and yet regularly leaves behind him a few humble gifts in return for their hospitality. He seems to be most interested in the daughter who looks after the goats, for it is to her alone that he confides, during a tryst one moonlit night, that he is going away for ever. The prototype of Sapo was the landowner Madden of *Mercier et Camier*, who 'unsuited for intellectual exertions . . . was removed from school at the age of thirteen and boarded with neighbouring farmers', from whom he had in haste to take his leave, 'having had the misfortune to impregnate a milkmaid'. The fate of Sapo's goatherdess is not however to bear his child but rather, it is hinted, her father's, for 'incest was in the air' and Mrs. Lambert 'saw it coming with indifference'.

When Malone next runs Sapo down, to employ his expression, it is to find an aged, homeless tramp sitting on a bench 'in the heart of the town . . ., his back to the river' whose name Malone feels compelled to change to Macmann. Having lost sight of him again, he next discovers him lying prostrate on the ground, exposed 'far from shelter' to the driving rain, from which painful posture he eventually escapes by rolling away, as Molloy contemplated doing when his crawling had brought him to the edge of the forest. We are told, in parentheses, that Macmann has been as incompetent as was Madden at earning his living, for even weeding and street-cleaning have proved beyond his modest capabilities. Then we leave Macmann once again to find him later 'in a kind of asylum' which turns out to be the House of St. John of God, the private mental hospital near Dublin of which Wylie spoke in *Murphy*. He is here under the care of a 'little old woman, immoderately ill-favoured of both face and body' called Moll. Before long these two, undeterred by total impotence, begin an affair which becomes so intense that it hastens Moll's end. The latter writes 'inflammatory letters' to which Macmann replies with love-verses, but their 'dry and feeble clips' are not long to afford them 'a kind of sombre gratification', because Moll soon becomes subject to fits of vomiting of such frequency that 'half a century younger she might have been taken for pregnant', and then begins to smell and grip her stomach in pain. One morning a man called Lemuel informs Macmann that she is dead and that he has taken her place.

This Lemuel reminds one of 'Bom' Clinch, the male sister of the Magdalen Mental Mercyseat, for he is irritable, violent and not fully sane. At this point Malone's agony gathers momentum ('my voice has gone dead, the rest will follow'), his pains increase sharply ('almost unbearable, upon my soul . . . incandescent migraine'), he 'exhales with labour' and can soon turn his head no longer. Writing becomes impossibly difficult: 'try and go on . . . on . . . a last effort' and finally, in sight of the end, he announces 'I shall say I no more'. Lemuel has Macmann beaten for tearing a branch from a dead bramble, and inflicts other brutalities on the patients in his charge. One day a Lady Pedal organizes an excursion by boat to the islands for Lemuel's party, and on arrival there the male nurse's violence erupts suddenly and he slaughters the two sailors with a hatchet. After sunset, leaving Lady Pedal on the island with a broken hip, he pushes the boat off with his charges in it, and they all float into the night, 'far out on the bay'. Lemuel looks at his hatchet 'on which the blood will never dry' and with which (here Malone's sentences break up into short, often-repeated phrases) he will never touch anyone 'any more' – the two words that end the novel. Malone's pencil, of which only the lead remains, no doubt wears out at last at the moment when he dies. His hero is left, like the hero of *La Fin*, drifting at the end on the open sea.

It is left a mystery who Lemuel is and what he represents, but this is only one of many enigmas that occur in Beckett's fiction. What, for instance, did the gong signify which Molloy heard in the forest? Or the blow which Malone thinks he remembers as the last thing that happened to him before he found himself in his room? Does 'Macmann' mean 'son of man' and 'Malone' 'me alone'? – even if correct, these surmises do not enlighten us much. Beckett's novels are thus charged with matters inexplicable: therein lies part of their fascination. Their mysteries can, however, be circumscribed to some extent by a careful noting of recurrent elements, however trivial these may at first sight seem. It is therefore significant that Malone frequently hints that he is a reincarnation not only of Molloy but also of many of the other heroes; Murphy for example:

... gazing at [the stars] one night I suddenly saw myself in London. Is it possible I got as far as London?

... with the insane too I failed, by a hair's-breadth.

... there was the old butler too, in London I think, there's London again ... it seems to me he had a name.

Similarly the strange Mr. Quin, whose name Watt vociferates in *Mercier et Camier*, is twice referred to in passing:

... where have my clothes disappeared, my greatcoat, my trousers and the flannel that Mr. Quin gave me, with the remark that he did not need it any more?

... Dreamt all night of that bloody man Quin again, [the Saxon] said.

Mr. Quin, like the Yerk whom Moran speaks of in *Molloy*, does not exist as a character in the canon,[1] but the heroes seem to be

---

[1] Unless an allusion is intended by Beckett to the character called Capper Quin in *More Pricks than Kicks*: see pp. 20, 29-31 above.

acquainted with him. Only Beckett himself knows who they are –
presumably they figured in work of his, since abandoned or destroyed.[1]

Elements from the *Nouvelles* also come up for mention, such as
the donkey owned by the sandman of *La Fin*:

> My photograph. It is not a photograph of me, but I am perhaps at
> hand. It is an ass, taken from in front and close up, at the edge of the
> ocean, it is not the ocean, but for me it is the ocean.

The now familiar Beckettian collection of objects is naturally not
absent here either:

> . . . the hat . . . attached, by a string, for safety, to the topmost
> button of the coat. . . .

> . . . among my possessions I once had a little phial, unlabelled, con-
> taining pills. Laxatives? Sedatives? I forget.

This last item at once recalls *Le Calmant*, as does the fact that the
tails of Macmann's coat 'literally sweep the ground and rustle like
a train, when he walks' – this very long coat has a velvet collar
and is green in colour, just as in *Le Calmant*. Similarly, Malone
thinks he must have been driven in a cab, like the hero of
L'Expulsé, and Macmann sits by a river like the river of *La Fin*,
where the gulls 'swoop ravening about the offal'.

Most frequently of all, Malone refers to his immediate predecessor: like him, he must have arrived 'in an ambulance perhaps,
a vehicle of some kind certainly' – familiar words, but more is to
follow: 'perhaps I expired in the forest . . . yes now that I speak of
a forest I vaguely remember a forest'. 'How great is my debt to
sticks,' he adds, 'so great that I almost forget the blows they have
transferred to me.' His possessions are those one would expect a
reincarnation of Molloy to have: a sucking-stone, 'a little silver
knife-rest' (the one Molloy stole from Lousse), a club 'stained
with blood', the 'cap of my bicycle-bell' and a 'half-crutch', the
remains of those he once used to walk with.

Much as he owes to Molloy, Malone is nonetheless a distinct
character in his own right. Physically he is of great age (between

---

[1] Mr. Beckett says not. He claims not to know who they are.

eighty and a hundred) and at an advanced stage of decay: 'my body is what is called, unadvisedly perhaps, impotent'; it can do hardly anything, except that 'my arms, once they are in position, can exert a certain force'. For all contact with objects beyond the reach of these arms, of course, he relies on his stick. His sight and hearing are very poor; he is toothless but very hairy; his clothes vanished long ago, so he lies naked between the blankets. ('I don't wash, but I don't get dirty,' he explains.) The Beckettian hero has by now been robbed of almost every use of his body, and his remaining rags of clothes have also been stripped from him. Just as Malone continues Molloy in this respect, so too, it will be seen, the Unnamable continues Malone.

Malone has a plucky and resilient character. The stopping of his soup he accepts philosophically as merely fixing a date for a demise he has long been awaiting; the loss of his stick is a 'disaster' which he treats with irony. His complete solitude does not cause him any feelings of loneliness, and the visitor who gazes at him 'in anger and disgust' does not unduly perturb him. Being an intellectual, he has the resources of his mind at his disposal: he can compare Macmann's posture on the bench to that of the 'Colossus of Memnon, dearly loved son of Dawn'; quote Lucretius aptly (*suave mari magno*); see a parallel between his window and Tiepolo's ceiling at Würzburg; and pun on the falling of his stick ('catastrophe too in the ancient sense no doubt'). A less attractive side of his character, however, is a tendency to voyeurism: he gazes on the intimate activities of the couple opposite (this provides, needless to say, another occasion for an exercise of Beckett's sustained irony on the theme of the sexual act) and he hopes one day to catch a little girl and force her to 'kiss me, fondle me, . . . undress before me. . . .'

The place where this novel is set is once more Ireland (again referred to as 'the island'), and more specifically the immediate vicinity of Dublin. There is Macmann's Stillorgan asylum; there too, in North Dublin, is the Glasnevin cemetery, whither (in the French text only) Macmann dreams love leads Moll and himself; and there (as Hugh Kenner first pointed out), in the hills west of Carrickmines, live the generations of stonecutters, the lights of whose hovels and the barking of whose dogs enchant the young Malone standing at night by his high window; and there, finally, is Dun Laoghaire 'full of steeples', the harbour from which the asylum excursionists set out. It is clear, too, that the town in which Macmann finds himself is Dublin itself – the dirty Liffey, the warehouses on its banks, and Butt Bridge all figure in this book. But although, even in the French text, Malone thinks in terms of inches, miles and pennies, and refers to the Mayor of Cork and the Bank of England, he is actually writing in France. The festivals of which he speaks are the landmarks of the French year: St. John the Baptist's day, the *quatorze juillet*, Assumption and All Saints' day with its traditional chrysanthemums. Sapo has, too, all the marks of a French schoolboy, and the peasants he visits are certainly French: Beckett told me that he took as his model a family he knew in the Vaucluse during the last war, but even without this piece of information it would have been clear where the Lamberts live. Among French peasants it is customary to fatten pigs on scraps and kill them in December or January: these are consequently 'great days' for Monsieur Louis, who is much sought after in the *pays* as a 'bleeder and disjointer of pigs':

He would set forth, hugging under his arm, in their case, the great knives so lovingly whetted before the fire the night before, and in his pocket, wrapped in paper, the apron destined to protect his Sunday suit while he worked. . . . From these expeditions he reached home late in the night, drunk and exhausted by the long road and the emotions of the day.

Louis' drunkenness tells his family that the expedition has been a success: similarly any peasant in France who returns from market sober shows clearer than words can that it has been a *mauvais marché* as far as he is concerned. Louis, moreover, rules his family, especially his wife, with an iron hand, typical of a peasant *chef de famille*, and both he and his wife, she in wondering whether a neighbour has cheated her over some lentils, he in buying his mules from the knacker and then working them to death, and in turning his goats loose at night to graze in other people's fields, show the same suspicion, shrewdness and cunning that Maupassant so well describes as the leading traits of his country folk.

159

We thus find in this novel a phenomenon remarked on before, which we shall see again in connection with *The Unnamable*, namely the harmonious blending of French and Irish elements. The substratum, as always, is Irish, and concerns only a small part of Ireland (for Beckett's years at Portora seem to have left no trace on his writing): it is to this layer of his consciousness that the author regularly plunges for his most deeply felt and significant episodes – thus it quite naturally occurs that Sapo and his world should be French, but Macmann and his territory Irish.

This book too is marked with emblems by now familiar, the mental asylum being the most obvious. After Belacqua's Portrane, Murphy's 'M.M.M.' and Watt's last refuge, comes Macmann's habitat. It is not without interest to quote Beckett's brief sketches of some of Lemuel's charges:

In the first [cell] a young man, dead young, seated in an old rocking-chair [like Murphy], his shirt rolled up and his hands on his thighs, would have seemed asleep had not his eyes been wide open. . . . The second cell . . . contained one whose only really striking features were his stature, his stiffness and his air of perpetually looking for something while at the same time wondering what that something could possibly be. . . . He was called the Saxon [in French *l'Anglais*] though he was far from being any such thing. . . . In the third a small thin man was pacing up and down, his cloak folded over his arm, an umbrella in his hand. Fine head of white flossy hair. He was asking himself questions in a low voice, reflecting, replying.

Only in *Murphy* have the insane been so patiently observed or so faithfully described. It is hard not to think of the well-known passage in *Tale of a Tub* which must surely have been in Beckett's mind when he wrote the above:

You will find [in Bedlam] a third gravely taking the dimensions of his kennel, a person of foresight and insight. . . . He walks duly in one pace, entreats your penny with due gravity and ceremony, talks much of hard times, and taxes. . . . Now, what a figure would all these acquirements amount to, if the owner were sent into the city among his brethren! Behold a fourth, in much and deep conversation with himself, biting his thumbs at proper junctures, his countenance checkered with business and design, sometimes walking very fast, with his eyes nailed to a paper that he holds in his hands. . . . What a complete system of court skill is here described in every branch of it, and all utterly lost with wrong application!

(A digression concerning madness)

But where Swift compares the insane to the sane to ridicule the antics and conceit of the latter, Beckett is interested in the insane in their own right: for him, as we had occasion to see in *Murphy*, they have a kind of honesty and innocence that those with pretensions to sanity completely lack: they are men who, living absorbed in their own world, are uncorrupted by the world of men.

Other Beckettian emblems are stamped on this novel: the Sordello of Dante's *Purgatorio*, for instance:

o anima lombarda,
come ti stavi altera e disdegnosa . . .

Sordello's lofty dignity has indeed impressed itself on Beckett's imagination as deeply as Belacqua's sceptical sloth:

. . . solo sguardando
a guisa di leon quando si posa . . .

for from *Dream of Fair to Middling Women* to *Mercier et Camier* and *Molloy*, his name keeps recurring. In *Malone Dies*, we find a young lunatic compared to him:

the youth had thrown himself down in the shade of a rock, like Sordello, but less noble, for Sordello resembled a lion at rest.

Cain, too, broods over this novel:

how is it the moon where Cain toils bowed beneath his burden never sheds its light on my face?

And, needless to add, we also find Jesus and the thieves, usually evoked with irony:

could not this song have simply been to the honour and glory of him who was the first to rise from the dead, to him who saved me, twenty centuries in advance? Did I say the first? The final bawl lends colour to this view.

For why be discouraged, one of the thieves was saved, that is a generous percentage.

And there is the jab concerning Moll's two crucifix ear-rings (the thieves) and between them her solitary tooth, 'carved, with the drill probably, to represent the celebrated sacrifice'.

*   *   *

The most fascinating stylistic questions that arise in connection with *Malone Dies* concern the translation. The phenomenon of an author writing in a foreign language and then translating his work, after a time-lapse of nearly ten years, into his mother tongue, is so rare in literature as to be of considerable interest. For not only was Beckett, as an excellent translator of the writings of others, far better placed than anyone else could be to translate his own work satisfactorily, he was also provided with a unique opportunity to alter or modify the tone of his text, as his subsequent development and feelings about the novel inclined him. As Ruby Cohn first noticed, he took advantage of this opportunity to infuse a harsher, more bitter tone into the book. Two examples will suffice to show this clearly: Lady Pedal's song *Voici la riante saison* contains the line, added in English, 'Alleluiah Christ is King' and *ne poussez pas, nom de Dieu* becomes 'what in God's name are you all pushing for for Christ sake?'

Beckett occasionally treats his original text quite cavalierly, leaving out whole sentences (in one case a whole paragraph), sometimes because they cannot easily be rendered into English, sometimes for no discernible reason. It is, however, easy to see why Mme. Louis' gesture with her hands is not translated (*elle les écartait de ses flancs, je dirais brandissait si j'ignorais encore mieux le génie de votre langue*: an interesting hint that Malone considers he is writing in a language not his own) but why omit the following, even though, admittedly, the terseness would be difficult to render:

I could die today, if I wished, merely by making a little effort, *si je pouvais vouloir, si je pouvais pousser* [the last phrases being in the French only],

and the following, surely significant?

And if I tell of me, and of that other who is my little one, *et que je mangerai comme j'ai mangé les autres*, it is as always for want of love...

Since *l'Anglais* becomes 'the Saxon' in English, two sentences which are relevant only to the former are naturally omitted in translation. There are, as if to compensate, appropriate and sometimes masterly additions:

> But what it is all about exactly I could *no more* say, at the present moment, *than take up my bed and walk* [addition in italics];

> *his front, no, his back, white with, no, front was right*, his front white with dust. . . .

In the last example, the addition gives us a vivid impression of Malone's hesitation as to the accuracy of a point of detail, and so an *aperçu pris sur le vif* of his actually writing this story down. Occasionally the French meaning is considerably *altered* to give an English of greater force: *tout autour c'est le flot des emmerdés, prenant des billets . . . éternellement là où il ne faut pas* becomes 'the stench of their harassed mobs scurrying from cradle to grave to get to the right place at the right time', and *ayant traversé un marécage à pied, on se met tout simplement à tousser et à éternuer* becomes 'having waded through a bog, you merely die of pneumonia'.

Often the translation is extraordinarily apt (*parties . . . indissolublement liées les unes aux autres, jusqu'à ce que mort s'ensuive, bien sûr* becomes 'parts . . . indissolubly bound up together, at least until death do them part') and well cadenced: 'these are flights for which Macmann was not yet fledged'. It is sometimes more deft than the original: 'chattels personal' is better than *biens matériels*, 'from the well of this unending weariness' than *du fond de cette fatigue sans fin*, and 'my sliver of sky is silvery with it yet' than *il en luit encore, mon filet de ciel*. Perhaps best of all are the Shakespearian overtones of 'his coign of maximum vantage' (merely *poste d'observation optimum* in French). On the other hand, the clever little phrase *ci-gît un pauvre con, tout lui fut aquilon* does not find an equally good rendering in 'here lies a ne'er-do-well, six feet under hell'; and *j'étais foutue comme un magot* pales to 'people would run a mile from me' and *à malin malin et demi* to 'he had not thought of that'.

Beckett is occasionally content to leave gallicisms in his translation; these are not, however, either numerous or serious. '*Regretting* his pipe' for 'missing his pipe' and '*nervousness*' (*nervosité*) for 'irritability' are the only ones worth remarking. In this connection, it is interesting to note that whereas in the French *Murphy* Beckett carefully translated 'rocking-chair' into *berceuse*, in *Malone meurt* he is content to say *un rocking-chair*, quite acceptable in French, and also that he tends to indulge in neologisms that are not always very successful, such as *défunger* for 'to die' (concocted from *défunt*) and, in *L'Innommable, déje-tons*, an amalgamation of *déjeter* and *rejetons*.

I have examined in some detail the English translation of *Malone meurt*, partly because Beckett's kind of bilingualism is pregnant with suggestion and significance for students of language, and partly to bear out what was said in Chapter 5, namely that his translations are creative, that self-translation for this author (and his plays are equally instructive on this point) amounts to a revision of his original text, to its modification in the light of his development in the interval between creation and translation. By collating French text and English version, there-fore, we gain insights into the workings of a creative mind quite as valuable as those to be sought from a study of variants between different redactions in the same language.

*　　*　　*

From a more strictly stylistic point of view, this novel is as rich as any of its predecessors. It can rise, for instance, to moments of beauty: Sapo's gazing at the flight of the hawk, *fasciné par tant de besoin, de fierté, de patience, de solitude* is a memorable image, slightly marred in translation; but the following comes over well even in English:

The water cradles already the distant fires of the sunset, orange, rose, and green, quenches them in its ruffles and then in trembling pools spreads them bright again.

Beckett's use of simile, too, is good:

They made use of the spoken word in much the same way as the guard of a train makes use of his flags, or of his lantern. . . . And their son once signalled, they wondered sadly if it was not the mark of superior minds to fail miserably at the written paper and cover them-selves with ridicule at the viva voce.

But he is not above debunking his own skill:

> So he went, limp, drifting, as though tossed by the earth. And when, after a halt, he started off again, it was like a big thistle-down plucked by the wind from the place where it had settled. There is a choice of images.

'There's a nice passage', comments Malone ironically at another point: it is hardly necessary to add that the creative act is exposed in this novel to contempt even more withering than in its predecessors. This is not a paradox, for this book is founded on an artifice (whereby a decrepit man manages to write to the last) and it is the artifice that inspires the artificer with contempt. The trick indeed is common enough: Mauriac put it to good use when in 1932 he created an old man writing his confessions (interrupted by death in mid-sentence) firstly for his wife's, then for his own edification. The following words from *Le Nœud de vipères* may well have been in Beckett's mind as he wrote the beginning of *Malone meurt*:

> I place my hand on my chest and feel my heart. I glance at the mirror-wardrobe, in a corner of which are the hypodermic syringe, the phial of amyl nitrate, everything that would be needed should a crisis arise. Would I be heard if I called? . . . Death will not creep up on me unawares; it has been prowling around me for years, I can hear it and feel its breath; it is patient with me because I do not defy it, but submit myself to its discipline. I am bringing my life to an end, clothed in a dressing-gown.

Both Malone and Mauriac's character are self-conscious narrators, although their respective intentions are naturally different. They both pause from writing to tell us how their bodies are feeling, that the light is fading, and so on. Both write in an exercise-book and Malone keeps us informed of every detail of the composition:

> My little finger glides before my pencil across the page and gives warning, falling over the edge, that the end of the line is near. . . . I hear the noise of my little finger as it glides over the paper and then that so different of the pencil following after.

Pleased with his tale of the Lamberts, Malone congratulates himself: 'how plausible all that is . . .'. Mauriac's hero has his praises sung posthumously by his son: 'there are psychological insights here and even impressions of nature which show that this orator had real literary gifts', but he himself affects not to know his own capabilities: 'were I even a professional writer, I should be hard put to it to make touching reading out of my schooldays . . .' The artifice in Mauriac's novel lies in the fact that the author lends his ostensibly unsuspecting hero his own talent: in *Malone Dies* the sleight-of-hand is more subtle: Malone *knows* that he can write, and tantalizes us with fragments of gripping narrative as well as with 'psychological insights and impressions of nature'. One is indeed reminded of Krapp, who impatiently wrenches off the machine the recorded monologue of a former self he detests just as we are becoming interested. Only a born writer can permit himself to scorn writing in this way; and yet Beckett's disdain for his own gifts is quite sincere: 'there is no use indicting words, they are no shoddier than what they peddle '. . . 'what half-truths, my God'. . . 'what truth is there in all this babble?' – the list of such self-deprecatory phrases scattered through the book could be extended indefinitely. The writer feels himself pilloried on words that betray the hopes he places in them: 'Invent. It is not the word. Neither is live. No matter.' Writing therefore becomes 'mortal tedium' and one writes frenziedly, 'in a hurry to be done'. Sometimes Malone cannot continue with the pretence of story-telling any longer: 'in his country the problem – no, I can't do it'; and elsewhere he laments to himself 'how false all this is'.

Despise one's work as one will, one is compelled to write (as van Velde to paint) for no easily stated reason: the activity merely seems obscurely necessary to life, for when we cease speaking we are extinguished, as the Unnamable is painfully aware, Madden too for that matter ('I cling to existence by talking, every day a little more, every day a little better'). The endless discourse of the Beckettian hero yields, in spite of all, its crop of wit:

I shall not finish this inventory either, a little bird tells me so, the paraclete perhaps, psittaceously named;

and of macabre:

For he knew how the dead and buried tend, contrary to what one might expect, to rise to the surface, in which they resemble the drowned;

and of paradox:

The end of a life is always vivifying;

and, of course, of irony:

To think I shall perhaps die of hunger, after all, of starvation, rather
. . . I can't believe it. There is a providence for impotent old men, to
the end.

It is a disaster. I suppose the wisest thing now is to live it over again,
meditate upon it and be edified. It is thus that man distinguishes himself from the ape and rises, from discovery to discovery, ever higher,
towards the light.

Malone's finest satire, as we might expect, is occasioned by the
amorous antics of his fellow-men. Here he indulges in a cunning
form of irony that recalls the Swift of *Tale of a Tub* rather than
the author of the *Modest Proposal*, whose manner, we saw above,
is more appropriate to *Molloy*. In *Malone Dies* we find something
very like the younger Swift's sustained *badinage:*

Given their age and scant experience of carnal love, it was only
natural they should not succeed, at the first shot, in giving each other
the impression they were made for each other. . . . But far from losing
heart they warmed to their work. . . . So that Moll exclaimed, being
(at that stage) the more expansive of the two, Oh would we had but
met sixty years ago! But on the long road to this what flutterings,
alarms and bashful fumblings!

a *badinage* which can give way to harsher strokes of sarcasm:

He had time to compose ten or twelve [rhymes] more or less in this
vein, all remarkable for their exaltation of love regarded as a kind of
lethal glue, a conception frequently to be met with in mystic texts.

But it can also give rise to clever effects of ironical pastiche, as in
this parody of a love-letter:

Ah would we had met but seventy years ago! No, all is for the best,
we shall not have time to grow to loathe each other, to see our youth
slip by, to recall with nausea the ancient rapture . . . in a word to get
to know each other.

Before we leave these questions of form, two final points should be made. Firstly, Beckett skilfully varies his rhythms according to whether Malone is speaking about himself (short, jerky sentences) or about his fictional characters (more majestic, 'narrative' pace). Furthermore, Malone's writing becomes steadily more staccato as he approaches his end, and his final words are, of course, as broken and halting as Captain Scott's last entry.

Secondly, Malone's thoughts about himself are governed by the principle of random association, whereas his tales move forward in a more rational manner: the difference is as significant as the difference of pace. He cannot be said to digress in his meditations as Molloy and Moran digress, because digression implies a return to an original point of departure; Malone jumps rather from one thing to another, if a thought comes to mind he follows it awhile like a butterfly, until another crosses his path ('I choose those [things] that seem somehow akin'), seldom returning to it again, except if it concerns his possessions. To his creatures, however, he is more faithful, for he rarely fails to take up his narrative again where he last left off, allowing of course for the time lapse in which his hero has been getting older. But as far as he himself is concerned, Malone's meditations, like the Unnamable's, are governed solely by the principle of association.

*   *   *

With *Malone Dies* the questions of identity, prefigured in *Molloy*, become the overriding preoccupation of Beckett's fiction; it can in fact safely be said that the last novels are chiefly concerned with the investigation of the pronoun 'I'.

Malone shows already a longing, very similar to that of the nameless hero of the *Textes pour rien*, to lose his own *persona* completely in someone else's; in Sartrian terms, we have here an instance of the *pour-soi* seeking metamorphosis into an *en-soi-pour-soi* that will give it permanence: what Malone calls 'the brave company I have always longed for, always searched for, and which would never have me', adding that he has sought all his life to elude himself in order truly to find himself:

While within me the wild beast of earnestness padded up and down, roaring, ravening, rending . . . gravely I struggled to be grave no more,

to live, to invent. . . . But at each fresh attempt I lost my head, fled to
my shadows as to sanctuary. . . . Of myself I could never tell, any more
than live or tell of others.

But he now dreams of a 'very pretty' end, whereby 'on the threshold of being no more I succeed in being another'. The story of
Malone Dies is simply the record of his repeated attempts to do
this ('this exercise-book is my life . . . it has taken me a long time
to resign myself to that'). He states unambiguously that he has
created Macmann in order to be able to 'slip into him . . . in the
hope of learning something'.

The complex problem of eluding one's self ('I shall never go
back into this carcass except to find out its time . . . I shall hear
myself talking, afar off, from my far mind . . . wandering . . .
among its ruins') is made yet more difficult by the fact that the
self is not easy to define; it cannot, for instance, be located by the
senses:

All my senses are trained full on me, me. Dark and silent and stale,
I am no prey for them;

nor be delimited by the body's pains:

I am far from the sounds of blood and breath, immured [*au secret* in
French]. I shall not speak of my sufferings. Cowering deep down among
them I feel nothing. It is there I die, unbeknown to my stupid flesh,
. . . my witless remains;

nor even be discerned by the intelligence:

Somewhere in this turmoil thought struggles on, it too wide of the
mark. It too seeks me, as it always has, where I am not to be found.

All that can be said of it is that it suffers strange transmutations:

to me . . . the sensation is familiar of a blind and tired hand delving
feebly in my particles and letting them trickle between its fingers . . .

and at other times 'I go liquid and become like mud', or 'I would
be lost in the eye of a needle, I am so hard and contracted'.

Posed in these terms, the problem becomes not so much a
matter of eluding the self as of pinning it down. It thus comes
about quite inevitably that one tries to fasten one's self on to

another that can be contemplated with some degree of detachment: but one's efforts are from the outset doomed to failure, for
the simple reason that when one tries to 'imagine' or 'create' a
self not one's own, all one in fact achieves is autobiography:

> I call that playing. I wonder if I am not talking yet again about
> myself. Shall I be incapable, to the end, of lying on any other subject?
> . . . I must simply be on my guard, reflecting on what I have said
> before I go on and stopping, each time disaster threatens, to look at
> myself, as I am. That is just what I wanted to avoid. But there seems
> to be no other solution. After that mud-bath I shall be better able to
> endure a world unsullied by my presence.

Malone is certainly conscientious in his precautions:

> I don't like [Sapo's] gull's eyes . . . I know it is a small thing. But I
> am easily frightened now. I know those little phrases that seem so
> innocuous . . . they rise up out of the pit and know no rest until they
> drag you down into its dark.

But, for all that, he makes his self-appointed task all the harder by
breaking off every so often to reminisce: a dangerous indulgence,
for memories are contagious and can infect one's fictions with the
virus of autobiography; at one point, for instance, Malone recalls
being with his mother and seeing 'the very first aeroplane in
flight'. He does, however, try to keep such reminiscences separate
from his stories of Sapo and Macmann, and affects to mock his
creatures, Sapo for being a 'simpleton' and Macmann for being
'of the earth earthy and ill-fitted for pure reason'; but it is more
than a little suspicious that he claims to be able to remember
nothing of his life up to the time when he found himself 'here, in
the bed', although 'I have often amused myself with trying to
invent them, those same lost events' and 'my young days . . .
come back to me, in fits and starts'. At length, indeed, he gives up
the pretence altogether:

> Yes, a little creature, I shall try and make a little creature, to hold
> in my arms, a little creature in my image, no matter what I say,

and a short while later he speaks of Macmann's 'evening life
which is like a convalescence, if my memories are mine' and of
his hero's age being nothing 'compared to the age he will reach,

as I know to my cost'. Moreover Malone possesses a bowler hat like Macmann's and says that he writes about Sapo in the same exercise book as about himself, making it thus quite clear that most of the incidents in his life previous to his arrival in the room which he supposed he had forgotten, crop up in the stories he claims he is telling about others. But some uncertainty remains as to exactly how much he invents and how much he remembers, an ambiguity which gives the novel its subtlety and helps make it an interesting reflection on the nature of fiction: what Blanchot called *l'approche pure du mouvement d'où viennent tous les livres*. What is, however, certain is that Malone is the first Beckettian hero to seek to know himself through writing fiction: Moran wrote a report, because his voice instructed him to do so, in order that he might come to understand the great psychological changes wrought in him during his search for Molloy – Malone, on the other hand, writes rather in quest of an identity that eludes him, although important secondary motives are to avoid, like the hero of *Le Calmant*, his present painful realities, and, like the Unnamable, to keep at bay the fearful 'silence of which the universe is made'.

This does not mean that Malone is any freer from tyrants than are Molloy and Moran. He depends on what he calls 'powers that be' almost as much as they, although their dealings with him are more hidden. He thinks however that it might only be by their decree that he is allowed to remain in his room. And he speaks of a protector like Youdi: 'I fled . . . to his lap who can neither live nor suffer the sight of others living.' He speaks, too, of Macmann, lying on the ground in a crucified position, feeling he is being punished for something, perhaps for 'having consented to live in his mother, then to leave her'. Malone may, like Molloy, be under an obligation to write: at any rate he receives a visit ('if that amuses them . . .' he mutters) and fears that the visitor, whom he feels he has seen somewhere before, will take his exercise-book from him, and so he hides it. The man seems 'vexed', is perhaps disguised – he wears a black suit of antiquated cut, black tie and bowler hat, has greasy black hair and a long clean-shaven face, is of medium height and build; and he holds a tightly-rolled umbrella – he may well be Moran in disguise, therefore, or perhaps another of Youdi's agents. But the truth, in this matter, is not revealed by Malone: the identity and purpose of the visitor remains an unsolved enigma.

If the tyrants do not seem to loom very large the critique of the society of men definitely does. Under the traits of Mr. and Mrs. Saposcat, the 'willing little bits of sweated labour' of our civilization are ridiculed:

He would be pensioned off, she at her last gasp. They would take a cottage in the country . . . and their children, grateful for the sacrifices made on their behalf, would come to their assistance. It was in this atmosphere of unbridled dream that these conferences usually ended. It was as though the Saposcats drew the strength to live from the prospect of their impotence.

Malone complains ironically of the effort needed 'to understand, to begin to understand, how such creatures are possible', but he finds little difficulty, in fact, in painting an unflattering picture of urbanized man's leisure activities:

At this hour then erotic craving accounts for the majority of couples . . . . Soon they come to the appointed place, at home or at some other home, or abroad, as the saying is, in a public place, or in a doorway in view of possible rain. And the first to arrive have seldom long to wait, for all hasten towards one another, knowing how short the time in which to say all the things that lie heavy on the heart and conscience and to do all the things they have to do together, things one cannot do alone. . . . Then the drowsiness, the little memorandum book with its little special pencil, the yawned goodbyes. . . .

words which irresistibly recall T. S. Eliot's, inspired by a similar disgust:

> The time is now propitious, as he guesses,
> The meal is ended, she is bored and tired,
> Endeavours to engage her in caresses
> Which still are unreproved, if undesired. . . .
> (And I Tiresias have foresuffered all
> Enacted on this same divan or bed. . . .)
> (FROM *The Fire Sermon* IN *The Waste Land*)

The Beckettian hero is glad of his 'long immunity . . . from shelter, charity and human tenderness', content in 'the black joy of

the solitary way': 'yes, those were the days, ... well beguiled with
the search for warmth and reasonably edible scraps ... those brief
years when bakers were often indulgent, at close of day'. His
attitude has changed slightly from the *Nouvelles* hero's rancour,
for all he asks is to be left alone. But too often 'the grown-ups
pursued me, the just, caught me, beat me, hounded me back
into the round, the game, the jollity'.

The hero is as much astray in the world of sensory phenomena
as he is lost to the world of men: sense-data, he tells us, take time
to travel from external things to his percipient organs. He has
furthermore lost all faculty of analysis where such data are concerned: 'the noises of nature, of mankind and even my own, were
all jumbled together in one and the same unbridled gibberish'.
No wonder he says that he has 'been nothing but a series or rather
a succession of local phenomena all my life', for the categories
with which we organize experience have, for the Beckettian hero,
broken down; his memory, in particular, is notoriously unreliable,
and time has no longer much meaning: Malone says that he sometimes sees his own corpse being carried from the room, for the
future becomes confused with the present, and the present itself
is ungaugeable ('In a flicker of my lids whole days have flown').
The difference between truth and falsehood is difficult to deter-
mine ('I should be sorry to let slip this unique occasion which
seems to offer me the possibility of something suspiciously like a
true statement at last') and everything depends on the record: on
losing his pencil for a while Malone comments 'I have spent two
unforgettable days of which nothing will ever be known,' for
what he does not note down ceases to be as decisively as the un-
observed tree in the quad. Since epistemology is such a risible
science for the Beckettian hero, it is little wonder that he contemplates the puzzles of classical philosophy with irony, and is amused
by the parrot (perhaps a tilt at the one mentioned by John Locke)
that can never progress beyond *nihil in intellectu* in the Scholastic
saw. When he does state a traditional philosophical proposition,
such as the following one (in my italics), he does so ironically:

It is my possessions have weakened me, if I start talking about them
again I shall weaken again, for *the same causes give rise to the same
effects*.

Similarly he speaks of Macmann in his long overcoat as 'a great cylinder endowed with the faculties of cognition and volition'.

Malone's dualism is as fundamental as his philosophical scepticism: perhaps justifiably, he holds his body in low esteem and does not consider it capable of much: 'I shall . . . give my body the old orders I know it cannot obey'. Without its natural extension, the stick, it is of course useless. The stick occupies a place of honour in Malone's existence analogous to that occupied in Molloy's by the bicycle, the body not being viable without some non-fleshly appendage:

I have demanded certain movements of my legs and even feet. I know them well and could feel the effort they made to obey. I have lived with them that little space of time, filled with drama, between the message received and the piteous response.

Descartes would no doubt have been surprised to see the consequences an Irish admirer was later to draw from his philosophy; how alien to the mind of the Beckettian hero his body-machine has become can be seen from the following passage, the terms of which were foreshadowed in the description of the Mr. Kelly of *Murphy*:

My feet, which even in the ordinary way are so much further from me than all the rest, from my head I mean, for that is where I am fled, my feet are leagues away. And to call them in, to be cleaned for example, would I think take me over a month, exclusive of the time required to locate them. . . . My fingers too write in other latitudes and the air that breathes through my pages turns them without my knowing.

The extinguishing of life in this body occurs at a no more definable moment than the 'death' of a felled tree: one is slowly 'born into death', a fœtus dropped 'with the help of gangrene . . . head-foremost mewling in the charnel-house'; the process of dying is described as 'the lingers of evaporation'. Malone indeed takes some time to die properly, even after his soup has been stopped.

The sexual appetites of this body are exposed in this novel to the familiar ridicule: Macmann and Moll are grotesque caricatures of people in love – 'the spectacle was then offered of Macmann trying to bundle his sex into his partner's like a pillow into a pillow-slip' – this savage humour, as fierce as Swift's if not as lubricious, was bound to come sooner or later in Beckett's writing, for it lies potentially in the less overt account of the unconsummated affair between Watt and Mrs. Gorman. Malone might well, in fact, have taken as his motto, had he known them, the words of disillusionment uttered by Durrell's Balthazar.

*   *   *

After this brief examination of *Malone Dies* as a critique of society, identity, knowledge and the body, all that remains is to note that this novel is more marked by autobiographical elements than is usual in Beckett's fiction. It is only probable, for instance, that *Watt* is set near the Leopardstown racecourse, whereas it is quite certain that much of *Malone Dies* takes place in the same area, Foxrock, the place where Beckett was born and lived as a boy. Sapo himself bears some resemblance (not, however, to be exaggerated) to the young Samuel: 'he got a bit out of hand', Mr. Beckett said to me about him, with a slight smile. Like Murphy (and, may one say, like Mr. Beckett himself) Sapo has 'gull's eyes' that remind Malone 'of an old shipwreck'; the latter reminisces, moreover, about the little boy he was, seeing the bottle-green horse-drawn cabs in the streets of Dublin and one of the first loopings-of-the-loop 'above a racecourse', and listening in his bedroom at night to

the outcry without, the leaves, the boughs, the groaning trunks, even the grasses and the house that sheltered me. Each tree had its own cry, just as no two whispered alike, when the air was still. I heard afar the iron gates clashing and dragging at their posts and the wind rushing between their bars.

Beckett obtrudes in person when he makes Malone say: 'there is so little difference between a man and a woman, between mine I mean'; and when he causes him to say, of the old butler in *Murphy*, 'I cut his throat with his razor', and when he leads him to hope that this will 'be my last journey, down the long familiar galleries, . . . if I'm lucky'. Since this is not the first time Beckett has appeared in his own novels, the foregoing need hardly surprise us; more surprising however are the words said of Lemuel as he looks at the hills near Dublin: 'it was there somewhere he was born, in a fine house, of loving parents'. Perhaps we are invited to alter the Hebraic prefix of this name and see Lemuel's murderous assault on the sailors and his subsequent pushing out to sea with Macmann and the others as the gesture of the writer abandoning the world of men and preferring the company of his own creatures, be they only mental hospital inmates.

Nevertheless, both tact and critical common sense prevent one from pursuing this theme any further; the strands of autobiography in this novel are not of great importance and a knowledge of such as there are is not necessary to an understanding of the book. But they do contribute to make *Malone Dies* the absorbing and humane work it is – humane in the broad sense of the word, for such emotive subjects as sex and death are treated in it too uncompromisingly for it to be acceptable by the feebler standards of kindliness. It remains, for that reason, as cool a look at the reality of death and extinction as *Fin de Partie:* Hamm's bravado in longing to stamp out the last vestiges of life on the planet and Malone's perseverance in writing until death stays his hand, both point in different ways the same moral – death is the last enemy, one we shall never conquer.

*　　*　　*

Malone Dies brings us to the end of a phase in the evolution of the Beckettian hero, a phase that opened with *Watt*. Beckett has travelled deep into the abyss since then: he no longer contemplates his heroes enmeshed in the antinomies of existence, but has joined them in their exile, suffering, as the inevitable price that has to be paid, his writing to be undermined by an indifference not his own: to speak of a world in ruins one has to make one's art a ruin before building upon it something new. Joining his heroes in their extremity, he sends back these painful but impressive reports for us to read. As he put it once to a French interviewer: *j'ai conçu* Molloy *et la suite le jour où j'ai pris conscience de ma bêtise. Alors je me suis mis à écrire les choses que je sens.*

Part Three

THE HERO AS VOICE

L'INNOMMABLE
About 1949

TEXTES POUR RIEN
About 1950

FROM AN ABANDONED WORK
1955

COMMENT C'EST
1959-1960

M

Chapter 7

THE UNNAMABLE

Trahissons, trahissons, la trattre pensée.
MOLLOY

Toute l'invention consiste à faire quelque chose de rien.
RACINE

THE last volume of the trilogy is not only a logical (one might almost say foreseeable) consequence of the latter but also of the whole of Beckett's fiction up to its composition. The preceding heroes, whose names are occasionally mentioned in the text, are stripped away at last, leaving only the naked voice of the being who exists, and has been existing all along, behind all of them, and who has been seeking, in vain, to invest himself in their rags for lack of any of his own.

The Unnamable is one of the most painful of Beckett's books, and it imposes its pain on the reader. It would be dishonest to pretend that its anguish did not cause discomfort in us, that its hatred, grief and misery did not make it somewhat unbearable to read. More dishonest still, however, would be to wish to ignore this novel, which is considered by some as its author's best work and which has already made an impression on younger writers, such as Harold Pinter.

It is very difficult to summarize satisfactorily. In the opening pages, however, one thing is made clear: the Unnamable is describing a place where he exists, and is telling us of his 'delegates' who have enlightened him about the world of men and their ways. One of these delegates is named Basil, although before long the hero changes his name to Mahood:

It was he told me stories about me, lived in my stead, issued forth from me, came back to me, entered back into me, heaped stories on my head. . . . It is his voice which has often, always, mingled with mine, and sometimes drowned it completely.

He then narrates, but in the first person, 'one of Mahood's stories' in which he describes how 'on his surviving leg' he circled round a small rotunda where his family were living. He took so long to complete his inward-moving spiral that all the members of his family died in the meantime of food-poisoning, and he arrived only to churn up their rotting remains with his crutches before setting off again, this time in an outward-moving spiral. When Mahood next appears, he is a limbless torso 'stuck like a sheaf of flowers in a deep jar' and serves as a living ensign to a squalid eating-house near the Vaugirard abattoirs in southern Paris. His body has been so far reduced that he cannot even turn his head, resembling in this the Unnamable himself, who again tells this story, which he claims not to be his own, in the first person. Later on still, Mahood's name is further changed, this time to Worm, a creature who not only lacks any semblance of a body but even all understanding and faculty of perception. The Unnamable tries to bring him into existence, even as a reptile or a horse, if need be:

He is nothing but a shapeless heap, without a face capable of reflecting the niceties of a torment, but the disposition of which, its greater or lesser degree of crouch and huddledness, is no doubt expressive, for specialists, and enables them to assess the chances of its suddenly making a bound, or dragging its coils faintly away, as if stricken to death. Somewhere in the heap an eye, a wild equine eye, always open. . . .

Worm, a 'tiny blur, in the depths of the pit', has one great strength: 'that he understands nothing, can't take thought'. This protects him from the tyrants, for he 'doesn't know what they want, doesn't know they are there'. The Unnamable continues trying to use him as a shield against the numbing fact that 'in my life, since we must call it so, there were three things, the inability to speak, the inability to be silent, and solitude, that's what I've had to make the best of'. It is now becoming increasingly harder to make the best of anything: he is 'too tired for niceties', his mind is breaking down as his tongue chatters on, more and more frenziedly. He first notices how truly alone he is: 'the others have vanished completely, I don't like it' – even his fictions are no longer of any help. Then he is forced to become fully aware of the threatening silence – 'nothing but this voice and the silence all around' – and of his interminable wrestling with it, hoping against hope that 'the last words, the true last' will come and release him from his pensum. But as he knows only too well, there is no reprieve conceivable in the sentence passed on him; with this thought the novel comes to a close, courageous, defiant, and sublime:

it will be the silence, for a moment, a good few moments, or it will be mine, the lasting one, that didn't last, that still lasts, it will be I, you must go on, I can't go on, you must go on, I'll go on, you must say words, as long as there are any, until they find me, until they say me, strange pain, strange sin, you must go on, perhaps it's done already, perhaps they have said me already, perhaps they have carried me to the threshold of my story, before the door that opens on my story, that would surprise me, if it opens, it will be I, it will be the silence, where I am, I don't know, I'll never know, in the silence you don't know, you must go on, I can't go on, I'll go on.

*　　　*　　　*

In the Beckettian 'gallery of moribunds', the Unnamable's is the last bust of all. He is acquainted with each of the others, and even sees some of them again:

Malone is there. Of his mortal liveliness little trace remains. He passes before me at doubtless regular intervals, unless it is I who pass before him. . . . But there will not be much on the subject of Malone, from whom there is nothing further to be hoped. . . . Sometimes I wonder if it is not Molloy. Perhaps it is Molloy, wearing Malone's hat. . . . Two shapes . . . oblong like men, entered into collision before me . . . I naturally thought of the pseudocouple Mercier-Camier.

'Am I clothed?' he wonders; 'I have often asked myself this question, then suddenly started talking about Malone's hat, or Molloy's greatcoat, or Murphy's suit', implying that he is the author of all these fictions, 'my troop of lunatics' as he elsewhere calls them. Before Mahood, he says, 'there were others, taking themselves for me, it must be a sinecure handed down from generation to generation, to judge by their family air'. But now he is determined to dissociate himself from this family of heroes:

I am neither, I needn't say, Murphy, nor Watt, nor Mercier, nor – no, I can't even bring myself to name them, nor any of the others whose very names I forget, who told me I was they, who I must have

181

tried to be, under duress, or through fear, or to avoid acknowledging me, not the slightest connection,

and he feels angry when he reflects upon 'the time I've wasted with these bran-dips, beginning with Murphy, who wasn't even the first, when I had me, on the premises, within easy reach', although he permits himself an occasional allusion to them, even to their words, such as those spoken by the hero of *La Fin* and quoted *verbatim* by the Unnamable: 'They clothed me and gave me money.' He, like Molloy, claims to have been born at Bally, and to have known his mother. He remembers Watt's rats and the piano-tuners and even Belacqua's collecting a lobster 'lepping fresh'.

It would therefore be easy to say that for the Unnamable we should read Samuel Beckett, busy making fun of himself:

I think Murphy spoke now and then, the others too perhaps, I don't remember, but it was clumsily done, you could see the ventriloquist;

but the deduction would be neither helpful nor enlightening. Beckett is, of course, concerned in this novel to sap and mine his previous novels, not, however, to reveal his own *persona* as author of them, but rather to seek the source both of Murphy and the others and of Samuel Beckett, Eire citizen resident in France, himself. This is what lends this novel universality: it is an attempt to unearth the general shadow that stands behind every individual face. *Molloy* portrayed this attempt in the dramatic terms of myth; the *Textes pour rien* pursue it to the very fragmentation of the depersonalized self itself. Far from becoming, therefore, except in points of detail, more autobiographical, Beckett's novels move instead towards the creation of a universal figure, *le portrait de tous et de personne*.

*   *   *

The netherworld inhabited by the Unnamable is hardly an actual place, merely a zone of grey half-light, although even this is not certain. 'I have been here, ever since I began to be, my appearances elsewhere having been put in by other parties . . . this place was made for me, and I for it, at the same instant.' He seems, in any case, to be at the centre of it; he occasionally sees lights and once hears 'a little cry, stifled outright', a sound as inexplicable as Molloy's gong. His body is 'incapable of the smallest movement' and his 'eyes can no longer close as they once could', when, that is, he was Malone. 'They must be as red as live coals,' and certainly weep continual tears, 'which flow all over my face, and even down along the neck'. He knows little about his body, except that it occupies a seated position, although he cannot say what he is sitting on. If he is clothed, it is only lightly; his head, though covered like other heroes' with pustules,

is a great smooth ball I carry on my shoulders, featureless, but for the eyes, of which only the sockets remain. And were it not for the distant testimony of my palms, my soles, which I have not yet been able to quash, I would gladly give myself the shape, if not the consistency, of an egg . . . for the consistency is more like that of mucilage.

Malone had said 'I do not expect to see my sex again' and the natural consequence of this is that the Unnamable lacks such a member altogether: 'why should I have a sex, who have no longer a nose? All those things have fallen, all the things that stick out, with my eyes, my hair . . . I am a big talking ball'. Beckett thus strips his heroes of their organs and members until by the *Textes pour rien* they have no body left whatsoever. Mahood, for instance, still possesses a leg at first, but he soon loses it when he enters the jar; even there, however, he still has a sex, whereas his successor Worm has nothing left at all.

The Unnamable 'seems to remember' birds, such as the cockatoo, but his knowledge of the world of men is, he insists, limited either to what his delegates have told him ('years is one of Basil's ideas') or to what he has learnt from his fictions, from 'my appearances elsewhere . . . put in by other parties'. His delegates have told him 'what I know about men and the ways they have of putting up with it' and have given him 'courses on love, on intelligence, most precious, most precious'. They also have taught him 'to count, and even to reason. Some of this rubbish has come in handy on occasions, I don't deny it', so much so that 'sometimes it seems to me I am there, among the incriminated scenes, tottering under the attributes peculiar to the lords of creation, dumb with howling to be put out of my misery'. In fact the Unnamable knows quite a lot about men, enough, anyway, to hate and despise them: 'love, there's a carrot never fails' he chuckles, before laughing at 'their capacity for work and aptitude for happiness'. He tells himself a depressing tale of human inconstancy in order, he says ironically, to know 'what love can do, well well, so that's emotion, that's love':

They love each other, marry, in order to love each other better, more conveniently, he goes to the wars, he dies at the wars, she weeps, with emotion, at having loved him, at having lost him, yep, marries again, in order to love again . . . you love as many times as necessary, as necessary in order to be happy . . . .

The similarly sardonic account of Mahood's family culminates in a paroxysm of intense loathing of life, especially of women: 'the one for ever accursed [who] ejected me into this world and the other . . . in [whom], pumping my likes, I tried to take my revenge'. 'I like to fancy,' he adds, 'that it was in mother's entrails I spent the last days of my long voyage,' wallowing in her remains.

He tells himself that the world of men 'must be terrible' because it is never dark there and never deserted, and although he compares his fate to that of Prometheus, he hastens to add that 'between me and that miscreant who mocked the gods, invented fire, denatured clay, and domesticated the horse, in a word obliged humanity, I trust there is nothing in common'. He nevertheless remembers the earth quite well, or rather two places on it, Ireland ('my island home') and Paris, for both of which he feels something akin to nostalgia. It is interesting to remark in this connection that the restaurant where Mahood was a 'jar-man' actually existed. Following up a shrewd surmise made by Rayner Heppenstall, I discovered that there was formerly an eating-house called the 'Ali-Baba' with, appropriately enough, a 'thief' outside it, fixed in a jar, supporting the menu. Beckett places it in the novel (without naming it) in the rue Brancion, facing the bust of the propagator of horse-meat, Emile Decroix; this bust is set over the eastern entrance of the Vaugirard abattoirs in the fifteenth *arrondissement*. The real Ali-Baba stood, however, in the rue de Dantzig, on the western side of the abattoirs, near a dilapidated round wooden building inhabited by artists (*La Ruche*) which may well have suggested the windowless rotunda in which Mahood's family live. The restaurant, run by an old woman, fell on hard times and had to close about ten years ago. Beckett would have known it since he lived at one time in the rue des Favorites, not far away.

* * *

'I was never anywhere but here,' says the Unnamable, in spite of these recollections. 'Here' he battles with his mysterious persecutors. Malone had at one point imagined a 'consortium' of tyrants, and it is this 'college' which manifests itself to the Unnamable: 'perhaps they are watching me from afar', he thinks, for 'to testify to them, until I die, . . . that's what they've sworn they'll bring me to'. He possesses no language of his own, for they have 'stuffed me full of these groans that choke me', and even Worm is no more than a conception of theirs: 'there's no getting rid of them without naming them and their contraptions'. Behind these subordinate tormentors stands 'the other who will not give me quittance until they have abandoned me as inutilisable', and who rules them with an iron hand: 'they know how to cause suffering, the master explained to them, Do this, do that'; he is liable to punish them, like a military commander, for every lapse of duty:

they'll go silent perhaps and go, one day, one evening, slowly, sadly, in Indian file, casting long shadows, towards their master, who will punish them, or who will spare them, what else is there, up above, for those who lose, punishment, pardon, so they say. What have you done with your material? We have left it behind.

He will have little patience with their plea that they have carried out the operation as well as might be expected:

For they may come back, long after the lights are spent, having pleaded for years in vain before the master and failed to convince him there is nothing to be done, with Worm, for Worm. Then all will start over again, obviously.

'He is there, says the master, somewhere, do as I tell you, bring him before me, he's lacking to my glory.' Since they have been given such an assignment, it is evident that there can be no end to the Unnamable's expiation:

this is my punishment, my crime is my punishment, that's what they judge me for, I expiate vilely, like a pig, dumb, uncomprehending, possessed of no utterance but theirs. They'll clap me in a dungeon, I'm in a dungeon, I've always been in a dungeon,

although he occasionally allows himself to be deluded about their intentions:

> Can it be I have a friend among them, shaking his head in sorrow and saying nothing or only, from time to time, Enough, enough.

'If I could only find a voice of my own, in all this babble, it would be the end of their troubles, and of mine.' But he is at the mercy of a 'sporting God', 'my creator, omnipresent':

> I want all to be well with you, do you hear me, that's what he keeps on dinning at me. To which I reply, in a respectful attitude, I too, your Lordship. I say that to cheer him up, he sounds so unhappy. . . . What he wants is my good. I know that, at least I say it . . . let him enlighten me, that's all I ask, so that I may at least have the satisfaction of knowing in what sense I leave to be desired.

Perhaps what the master requires are his praises 'intoned, in order to obtain his forgiveness':

> what have I done to God, what have they done to God, what has God done to us, nothing, and we've done nothing to him, you can't do anything to him, he can't do anything to us, we're innocent, he's innocent, it's nobody's fault . . . .

'Into their unfortunate Jesus', he says, they stuck thorns; for him, there is not even the unequivocal clarity of physical torture, only 'the unintelligible terms of an incomprehensible damnation', in which he listens for 'the words of my master, never spoken, Well done, my child . . . you may go, you are free, you are acquitted, you are pardoned, never spoken'. Suffering as he does for reasons he cannot understand, and at the hands of a God on whom 'I depend . . . in the last analysis', he knows his only freedom to be that imagined by the stoical Geulincx in terms which the Unnamable cannot forget:

> The galley-man bound for the Pillars of Hercules, who drops his sweep under cover of night and crawls between the thwarts, towards the rising sun, unseen by the guard, praying for storm. . . . I am he who will never be caught, never delivered, who crawls between the thwarts, towards the new day that promises to be glorious. . . .

186

The punishment inflicted on the Unnamable by the master is the eternal obligation to utter words:

Yes, I have a pensum to discharge, before I can be free, free to dribble, free to speak no more, listen no more, and I've forgotten what it is . . . I was given a pensum, at birth perhaps, as a punishment for having been born perhaps.

'Between me and the right to silence, the living rest, stretches the same old lesson' which he has never recited 'perhaps for fear of silence' – silence being literally his mortal foe: 'and yet I do not despair of one day sparing me, without going silent'. He thinks of a possible solution: 'would it not be better if I were simply to keep on saying babababa?' but has to reject it: 'it seems impossible to speak and yet say nothing, you think you have succeeded, but you always overlook something, a little yes, a little no, enough to exterminate a regiment of dragoons'. It is only 'the search for the means to put an end to things, an end to speech, [that] enables the discourse to continue'. There can be no possibility of an end to speech, for such a cessation would entail the end of existence itself. Everything, therefore, fictions and fables included, is grist to the mill:

All this business of a labour to accomplish, before I can end, of words to say, a truth to recover, in order to say it, before I can end, of an imposed task, once known, long neglected, finally forgotten, to perform, before I can be done with speaking, done with listening, I invented it all, in the hope it would console me. . . .

'I have to speak', he says, 'having nothing to say, no words but the words of others' and he is never certain even that it is with his own voice that he speaks:

this voice that speaks, knowing that it lies, indifferent to what it says . . . it issues from me, it fills me, it clamours against my walls, it is not mine, I can't stop it . . . it is not mine, I have none, I have no voice and I must speak, that's all I know.

He hopes to find the words 'it behoved to say', that can result in silence, the words 'ratified by the proper authority', sifted from 'all this noise about nothing, . . . this long sin against the silence' – not the words that choke him:

the words are everywhere, inside me, outside me. . . . I'm in words, made of words, others' words. . . . I'm all these words, all these strangers, this dust of words, with no ground for their settling, no sky for their dispersing, coming together to say, fleeing one another to say, that I am they, all of them.

He even finds himself on occasion stuck in a groove of words:

I seek, like a caged beast born of caged beasts born of caged beasts born of caged beasts born in a cage and dead in a cage. . . .

'If I could remember what I have said I could repeat it, if I could learn something by heart I'd be saved', but he is never saved: 'I can't go on, I'll go on.' The silence he yearns for (his own silence, not the surrounding silence) forever eludes him.

Condemned as he is to such infinite but futile activity, it is little wonder that he despises it and scorns its 'affirmations and negations invalidated as soon as uttered', and prefers limping to temporary halts:

The fact would seem to be, if in my situation one may speak of facts, not only that I shall have to speak of things of which I cannot speak, but also, which is even more interesting, but also that I, which is if possible even more interesting, that I shall have to, I forget, no matter.

Creation is sheer monotonous torture: 'it goes on by itself, it drags on by itself, from word to word, a labouring whirl, you are in it somewhere', and what does it all matter, anyway: 'it is some considerable time now since I last knew what I was talking about. . . . Bah, no need to worry, it can only have been one thing, the same as ever'. Literature is an insult to this hero for whom it represents slavery:

How, in such conditions, can I write, to consider only the manual aspect of that bitter folly? I don't know . . . it is I who write, who cannot raise my hand from my knee, . . . I am Matthew and I am the angel, I who came before the cross, before the sinning, came into the world, came here.

Writing is mere deceit, a hollow dribble of inadequate words only approximating to what one knows is not even reality, and snatched at great price from the grudging, encircling silence.

*   *   *

THE UNNAMABLE

One of the first remarks of the Unnamable is 'I, say I' and throughout the novel he struggles heroically to speak of himself: 'me, utter me, in the same foul breath as my creatures? Say of me that I see this, feel that, fear, hope, know and do not know? Yes, I will say it, and of me alone'. The chief threat to his selfhood comes in fact from these creatures, who seek to obliterate his distinctness either by absorbing themselves into him ('what if we were one and the same after all, as [Mahood] affirms and I deny?') or by usurping his *persona* altogether and setting up on their own account:

All these Murphys, Molloys and Malones do not fool me. They have made me waste my time, suffer for nothing, speak of them when, in order to stop speaking, I should have spoken of me and of me alone. . . . I thought I was right in enlisting these sufferers of my pains. I was wrong. They have never suffered my pains. . . . Let them be gone now, them and all the others, those I have used and those I have not used, give me back the pains I lent them and vanish, from my life . . . There, now there is no one here but me. . . .

The tyrants, of course, are scheming perpetually to effect his amalgamation with another:

Yes, more than once I almost took myself for the other, all but suffered after his fashion, the space of an instant. Then they uncorked the champagne. One of us at last! Green with anguish! A real little terrestrial! . . . Mahood himself nearly codded me more than once. I've been he an instant. . . .

and he even goes so far as to lend himself to their machinations, by telling Mahood's story as his own, although he inserts a proviso: 'still Mahood speaking', or 'Mahood dixit'. The latter is nonetheless his 'vice-exister' and he welcomes the opportunity of telling stories about him – for that represents several thousand valuable extra words. He also insists, however, that before he is allowed to be himself the tyrants require him first to be another:

It's a lot to expect of one creature, it's a lot to ask, that he should first behave as if he were not, then as if he were, before being admitted to that peace where he neither is, nor is not, and where the language dies that permits of such expressions. Two falsehoods, two trappings,

189

to be borne to the end, before I can be let loose, alone, in the unthinkable unspeakable.

For he has to speak 'first of the creature I am not, as if I were he, and then, as if I were he, of the creature I am'; he is even prepared to be Worm, and to gratify them drops the first person, but without much success: 'Mahood I couldn't die. Worm will I ever get born? It's the same problem.' So he returns to 'I', to himself that is, 'calm, passably calm', although he has been Worm 'but ill'. He is, moreover, forced into quandaries of great perplexity:

How many of us are there altogether, finally? And who is holding forth at the moment? And to whom? And about what? These are futile teasers.

The way out, the tyrants suggest with insidious insistence, is surely easy for him:

But my dear man, come, be reasonable, look, this is you, look at this photograph, and here's your file, no convictions, I assure you, come now, make an effort, at your age, to have no identity, it's a scandal . . . it's you all over, look, here's the photograph, take a look at that, dying on his feet, you'd better hurry, it's a bargain, I assure you, and so on, till I'm tempted;

but he thrusts aside the temptation with a contemptuous *vade retro*:

no, all lies, they know it well, I never understood, I haven't stirred. . . . I can't go to them, they'll have to come and get me, if they want me, Mahood won't get me out, nor Worm either.

If he has failed to acquire an identity, 'it's the fault of the pronouns', he concludes, and he leaves us with this assertion, for at the end he is still standing merely on 'the threshold of my story'; and aware as we are of what torments he has already undergone, we know that he will hover thus on the threshold for all eternity:

I never spoke, I seem to speak, that's because he says I as if he were I, I nearly believed him, do you hear him, as if he were I, I who am far, who can't move, can't be found . . . there is no name for me, no pronoun for me, all the trouble comes from that.

He is therefore properly 'unnamable', unassignable and unas-
similable to anyone or anything, lost in a netherworld where no
sense resides and where duration offers no divisions ('there are no
days here') so that he is 'incapable . . . of measuring time'. He
knows, with anguish, that *esse est percipi* and so must even doubt
his own existence:

No, as long as this point is not cleared up to my satisfaction, or as
long as I am not distinguished by some sense organs other than
Madeleine's, it will be impossible for me to believe, sufficiently to
pursue my act, the things that are told about me.

If the Unnamable seems to exist only for himself but not for
others, Worm is in the opposite predicament:

His senses tell him nothing, nothing about himself, nothing about
the rest, and this distinction is beyond him. Feeling nothing, knowing
nothing, he exists nevertheless, but not for himself, for others, others
conceive him and say, Worm is, since we conceive him.

This is not the only puzzle of classical philosophy that perplexes
the Unnamable; he also wonders whether the future can be in-
ferred from the past:

From the unexceptional order which has prevailed here up to date
may I infer that such will always be the case? . . . If one day, a change
were to take place, resulting from a principle of disorder already
present, or on its way, what then?

He wonders, too, whether he has 'innate knowledge' of men and
of his mother – how else could he have learnt of them? And again:
does the wavering in the lights here result from a flickering in
the source or from 'my fitful perceiving'? It is not too much to say
that this hero raises most of the disputed issues of technical philosophy and poses them in dramatic terms. We feel the presence of
Hume doubting with no Kant at hand to comfort; Molloy had
claimed 'all I know is what the words know', but the Unnamable
cannot even claim to know that: his discourse moves like the sea,
each wave obliterating all trace of its predecessor, words destroying what words have jerry-built, speech exploding speech. In this
novel one is made to feel two things acutely: the torture of being
trapped in time ('there is no escape', Beckett had written in

Proust, 'from the hours and the days', where we are prisoners 'conscious only of two dimensions'), and the fear of the nothing-ness that haunts our *attitudes droites et phrases claires* (Bataille), that waits, sinister and menacing, behind the elements of our dis-course, behind the words which fall strangers from our lips as soon as uttered.

*   *   *

The formal principle that governs *The Unnamable* is that of accelerated forward progression. The prose slowly gathers momen-tum as the pages turn. Early on, for instance, the division into paragraphs is dropped, and the prose is unbroken from that point onward. Thereafter full-stops become less and less frequent, and the last of all is found three pages from the end, making one long sentence of the final fifteen hundred words of the novel. Where full-stops decline in number, however, commas correspondingly increase, and give a hectic, almost frenzied air to the closing sec-tions of the book; at one point one is even reminded of Lucky's desperate speech:

it has not yet been our good fortune to establish with any degree of accuracy what I am, where I am, whether I am words among words, or silence in the midst of silence, to recall only two of the hypotheses launched in this connection, though silence to tell the truth does not appear to have been very conspicuous up to now, but appearances may sometimes be deceptive, I resume, not yet our good fortune to establish, among other things, what I am, no, sorry, already mentioned, what I'm doing, how I manage, to hear. . . .

This is, incidentally, not the only echo of *Waiting for Godot*; there are others:

it's like the old jingle. A dog crawled into the kitchen and stole a crust of bread, then cook up with I've forgotten what and walloped him till he was dead, second verse, Then all the dogs came crawling and dug the dog a tomb. . . .

This novel is as rich in irony as any of the others ('they build up hypotheses that collapse on top of one another, it's human, a lob-ster couldn't do it') and humour ('when Mahood I once knew a doctor who held that scientifically speaking the latest breath could only issue from the fundament . . .'); furthermore the metaphors are well-chosen:

Ah if only this voice could stop, this meaningless voice which prevents you from being nothing, just barely prevents you from being nothing and nowhere, just enough to keep alight this little flame feebly darting from side to side, panting, as if straining to tear itself from its wick. . . .

The translation from the original French is, as Ruby Cohn has said, of 'astounding conviction and brilliance'; the novel reads indeed just as well as if it had been written in English. Beckett shows considerable ingenuity in rendering his text in a lively form and in avoiding all flatness of translation, by such means as the bold use of an English archaism ('tomorrow they must rise betimes') or the adoption of a technical term purloined from another, but ironically related, field: *tout un consortium de tyrans . . . en délibération*, becomes for example 'a whole college of tyrants . . . in conclave'. Often he chooses a more violent turn of phrase in English: 'the place . . . where the inestimable gift of life had been rammed down my gullet' for *l'endroit qui . . . m'aurait infligé le jour*; and at one point he humorously employs an Irish idiom: 'that's a darling dream I've been having' for *c'est un beau rêve que je viens de faire là*. The Protestant hymns that Mahood's family sing could not have been difficult to render, since they were literally translated from English in the first place: *Jésus amant de mon âme laisse-moi me réfugier dans ton sein* is cacophonic and unrhythmical French but 'Jesus, Lover of my soul, let me to thy bosom fly' familiar and pleasant English.

There are certain omissions in the English, with compensatory additions, and some curious changes – notably in the early pages, where the name Mahood in the French is occasionally changed to Malone, as if from a concern to link the Unnamable more firmly with his predecessor.[1]

* * *

The Unnamable is frequently hard put to it to find something to say, as we have had many an occasion to remark. He therefore

[1] In Ruby Cohn's book *The Comic Gamut* (p. 321, note 15), which I received only after completing my own, I read, however, that Mr. Beckett claims that these changes are errors, and not deliberate.

says whatever comes into his head, and, like Malone's, the sequence of his thought seems to depend solely on the principle of association. Until near the end, where he does little but mill over and over again the same meal, he returns sporadically to his fictions Mahood and Worm, by whom he is obsessed: but little other principle of order can be discerned. It is ironical that this hero, the one who hopes so earnestly to be free of chimæras, should turn, harassed by the penury of things to say, so regularly to these fantasies of his own fabrication.

*   *   *

It is well known that *The Unnamable* brought Beckett to a temporary impasse in his work. This is how he described his predicament in 1956:

The French work brought me to the point where I felt I was saying the same thing over and over again. For some authors writing gets easier the more they write. For me it gets more and more difficult. For me the area of possibilities gets smaller and smaller. . . . At the end of my work there's nothing but dust. . . . In the last book, *L'Innom-mable*, there's complete disintegration. No 'I', no 'have', no 'being'. No nominative, no accusative, no verb. There's no way to go on.

And yet he went on regardless, and produced the *Textes pour rien* (which however he considered as a failure in the attempt 'to get out of the attitude of disintegration'), the plays in English with their technical invention, and *Comment C'est*, his latest novel. How he was able, with the assistance of stylistic innovations, to wrest these works from the silence, is what must be examined in the last chapter.

Chapter 8

THE LAST HEROES

Le fond c'est mon habitat, oh pas le fin fond, quelque part entre l'écume
et la fange.

MOLLOY

the churn of stale words in the heart again/ love love love thud of
the old plunger/ pestling the unalterable/ whey of words

CASCANDO II

BECKETT'S most recent fiction seeks a way out of the impasse
with a success that seems in direct proportion to the boldness with
which, in each venture, the problem is attacked.

One should not underrate the persistence of this author in con-
tinuing to write when there seems nothing further to write
about, but rather admire the clearsightedness and determination
which have led him to refuse the obvious solutions, inadequate
because they merely avoid the issue: suicide, or silence. As he has
said: 'There are others, like Nicolas de Staël, who threw themselves out of a window – after years of struggling'; but Beckett
has preferred to go on struggling. It would be too easy to assert
that his problem is all of his own making; the matter is more
complicated than that. Beckett faces the same situation that
Sartre faces in *La Nausée* and Robbe-Grillet in *Dans le labyrinthe*:
that we appear a series of consecutive phenomena in time, fragile
and unstable, threatened in every instant by submersion in an
all-pervading nothingness. Hume's unsettling vision of the self
as a succession of events, from which he turned in dismay, has
imposed itself on some of the novelists of our age as the image of
a state of affairs which is. To adopt Beckett's own metaphor, man
seems to them a small flame, lit with difficulty to glimmer in the
universal dark, before being finally blown from the wick.

The philosophical validity of such a conception can be questioned, and since Hume it has often been questioned, but it is not
easily dismissed, and in an age of uncertainty and general scepticism it naturally takes a hold on men's imagination. Where there

195

is no God, and where the self appears indefinitely divisible into events as duration is infinitely divisible into measures of time, there seems no stability anywhere to rely on. Viewed in this light, Beckett's latest fiction becomes the dolorous saga of *l'homme absurde*, of man who will cease as totally to exist when his voice dies into silence as the *perceptum* vanishes with the departure of the *percipiens*; a sombre epic, which reflects with simplicity the numbing reality that we live in a universe where only the silence is eternal, and time not on our side.

* * *

'The artist has acquired his text: the artisan translates it' said Beckett in *Proust*, and followed this axiom with a quotation from his author: 'the duty and the task of a writer are those of a translator'. By the end of *The Unnamable*, Beckett, too, has acquired his text; he will no longer modify it in essentials. He has driven his hero, and his themes, to the end of the road; to a reduction to disembodied voice in the case of the one, to sterility and contradiction in the case of the other. From the *Textes pour rien* onwards, Beckett labours to translate his difficult text into something approaching coherent terms, whatever he can make the word 'coherent' to mean. We therefore find that in these latest fictional pieces he adds little or nothing that is new to his vision, but tries to develop, at the cost of effort and labour, the would-be ideal form to express it. It is therefore to questions of form and style that in this last chapter we have to devote most of our attention.

* * *

The title of the thirteen *Texts for Nothing* is based on the musical term *mesure pour rien*, meaning 'a bar's rest'. Thus a *texte pour rien* would be a grouping of words conveying nothing, and this is in fact, more or less, what we find: we have, in a form of fragile beauty, a content of extraordinary tenuousness, a kaleidoscope of continually changing half-meanings, and structures as brittle as thin glass, at the slightest tap flying apart.

Such content as there is can only be hinted at, and since there is no one being, human or subhuman, in these texts, but only a bodiless and self-less voice (or voices), I shall have to use the neuter pronoun 'it' in referring to this hero (or heroes).

The first text mainly evokes a remembered scene on 'the top, very flat, of a mountain . . . quag, heath up to the knees', and some family reminiscences. The second introduces a few other recollections; the third is concerned with the search for a vicarious identity. We are now beginning to lose all touch with anything stable, for in the fourth we read of a split in the hero's self itself. In the fifth, the voice figures itself as a narrator, pen in hand, hearing a trial going on inside itself about itself; in the sixth, it feels choked with words. The seventh text is set chiefly in a *Gare du Sud-Est* (Dublin's Westland Row?), the eighth in the Place de la République, the ninth near a cemetery. The tenth is wholly taken up with the voice's difficulties with speech, the eleventh centres on a urinal in the rue d'Assas, the twelfth on an old man in whose body the voice longs to be able to die, and in the last text the still disembodied, wandering voice hopes somehow to be able to go on.

It often remembers, or thinks it remembers, previous existences. It can refer to Joe Breem (or Breen), and his saga, told by a father to a little boy who later became the corpse of *Le Calmant*; verger Joly of *Molloy* is also remembered, as are Molloy and Malone themselves, envied moreover as *heureux mortels*, and Molloy's forest is nostalgically recalled. As for the sea, the voice, referring to *Malone meurt* and to *La Fin*, declares:

The sea too, I know about the sea too, it belongs to the same series, I have even drowned in it more than once, under various false appellations, don't make me laugh, if only I could laugh, all would vanish. . . .

Pozzo's name also occurs:

Why did Pozzo leave home, he had a castle and retainers. Insidious question, to make me forget I am the accused.

And, thinking of Murphy, who is not however named, the voice recalls Glasshouse Street where Neary dined, and asylums with male nurses dressed all in white; and when it has a vision of itself embodied on the Place de la République, it is wearing the domed hat and yellow boots that are almost the uniform of the Beckettian hero.

*　　*　　*

The voice exists in no readily definable world or netherworld; gone are even the Unnamable's few semi-certainties about his place. The voice has no idea whether there is any air where it is or not, but inclines to doubt this; a creator, it says, is quite out of the question, as is death also, and *comme nature c'est vague:* parhaps the ground is dry, or wet, or muddy; perhaps it is inside a head, the darkness lends support to such a hypothesis. Most likely, however, the voice exists beyond all material kingdoms: 'in the depths of this place which is not one, which is only a time for the time being endless, which is called here' – the voice is defined by only two coefficients, the present now which is an 'enormous second', and space which is 'infinite'. It exists only as an abstract, as it were mathematical entity, which seeks continually to take on concrete existence, and if the *Textes pour rien* can be said to be 'about' anything, they are the devious chronicle of these unsuccessful attempts.

The voice is however subject to nostalgia for the world it occasionally recalls and harassed by a longing to have a more than merely conceptual existence. It wanders in imagination from place to place: Paris, London and Dublin. The first text describes familiar country:

I had heard tell, I must have heard tell of the view, the distant sea in hammered lead, the so-called golden vale so often sung, the double valleys, the glacial lakes, the smoke of the city, it was all on every tongue.

In the sixth text the voice speaks of the bathroom in the childhood home (at Foxrock?):

. . . the bathroom, with a view of the sea, and the lightships at night, and the red harbour light. . . .

'I must have left my head in Ireland' affirms the voice at another point. But it is equally familiar with other sites evoking different memories: the *noble soubassement* of the Magasins Réunis at République, the Place de la Bastille and nearby Père Lachaise, not to speak of

the news, do you remember the late news, the latest news, in slow luminous letters, above Piccadilly Circus, in the fog?

and other echoes of a life spent chiefly in hiding, *rasant les murs*.

The world of men is *là-haut dans la lumière*, a place where hope, in spite of all, survives as it no longer can below:

A pity hope is dead. No. How one hoped above. At odd moments. With what diversity.

As the texts progress, the voice grows more bitter about *leur chaudepisse de lumière* and resigns itself to its own situation:

Yes, I am here for ever, with the spiders and the dead flies, dancing to the quivering of their enmeshed wings, and very glad, very glad, that it's done with. . . .

a situation in which it is free to indulge only occasionally in a *bonne bouffée de vie sur terre*, for to ask for more is to invite fiasco.

If this voice ever thinks of its former body, it does so in Cartesian terms:

I say to the body, Up you get now, and I feel it trying, like an old hack foundered in the street, trying no more, trying again, until it gives up. I say to the head, Leave it in peace, rest in peace, it stops breathing, then pants on worse than ever.

This voice is compelled to speak, there is never any question of another alternative: 'I shouldn't have begun, no, I had to begin' it laments; nothing else is possible but 'breathing and saying, with words like smoke . . . always muttering, the same thing always, the same stories, the same questions and answers'; for

as long as words keep coming nothing will be changed, there are the old words out again. Words, there is nothing else but words, a voiding of words, here as always, nothing else. But they are failing, yes, that changes everything, they are faltering, that's bad. Or it's the fear of coming to the last, of having said all, before the end, no, for that would be the end, the end of all, not sure.

Here once again is the Unnamable's fear, and his solution, namely that it matters little what one says, for *tout se vaut*. Words are a babble in one's mind, they are written down with no understanding of what they mean, or even of what they are: *avec quels mots les nommer, mes innommables mots?* asks the voice; and how can one speak when the words come 'slow, slow', when even 'the subject dies before it gets to the verb'? It seems that one's head is held from behind by two hands, as at the barber's; the forefingers close one's eyes, the middle fingers one's nostrils, the thumb one's ears, and the last four work one's jaw and tongue, all this simply *pour que je dise, pour mon bien, ce que je dois dire*, where one is not even sure what it is one is obliged to say. Everything has 'died of words' as of a disease, of words that are not the voice's words, too many words unable to say anything beyond themselves. The homeless, mouthless voice (*voix sans bouche*) has only the dust of dead words; from the very beginning, nothing but that:

il n'y a rien eu de commencé, rien eu jamais que jamais et rien . . . rien à tout jamais que mots morts,

and awaits, *pour fermer sa grande gueule morte*, the opportunity of summarizing all its drivel in a 'cadence worthy of the rest'; but the final words of the last text leave us in no doubt that such a moment can never come:

And were the voice to cease, the old flagging voice, still it would not be true, as it is not true that it speaks, it cannot speak, it cannot cease. And were there to be one day here, where there are no days, which is not a place, born of the impossible voice the uncreatable being, and a glimmer of light, still all would be silent and empty and dark, as now, as soon now, when all is done, all said, it says, it murmurs.

Since the voice is obliged to speak, it occupies itself with conjuring up images, perhaps from its own past: it 'sees again' Mme. Calvet, who used to pass every morning with her dog and old pram before the dustmen and pick over the rubbish, muttering to herself and to the dog; it 'remembers' Piers driving his plough and oxen over the plain, and thinks of M. Joly climbing his belfry on a summer Sunday to wind the great clock and ring the bells, perhaps on the same Sunday that Moran received Gaber's fateful visit. The voice's chief concern however is to annex an identity that it can make its own; the *Textes pour rien* constantly return to this desire for selfhood:

First move, there must be a body, I don't say no, I won't say no again, I'll say I have a body, a body that moves, backward and forward, upward and downward, as required, with organs and limbs in abundance, enough to live again, enough to hold out a little, I'll call that living, I'll say it's me.

Having postulated this body and adopted it as its own, the voice says to it:

I'll wait for you here, my mind at ease, at ease for you, no, I'm alone, I alone am, it's I who must go, this time it's I;

it adds this, because it suddenly realizes that if it adopts an identity, it should hold to it. Similarly the voice imagines itself as an 'aged child', with a nurse or governess who watches over it while it combs its beard in a corner, and calls it *mon Jésus*. But this fantasy soon crumbles also:

What does it matter where one says one is, what one says one is, here or elsewhere, fixed or movable, formless or oblong like man, in the dark or the light of heaven, I don't know, it seems to matter, it's not going to be easy.

'I have tried', the voice tells us, 'to make me fall from cliffs, in the street in the midst of mortals, to no avail, I gave up.' Next it adopts a friend, a former Forces acquaintance, who fought under Jellicoe while the voice was occupied attacking the enemy from behind a barrel of Guinness with an arquebus. 'Halleluiah! It's our very last winter' cries the voice, and then describes the veterans' favourite pastime – reading the daily paper, especially the racing news. 'No, twaddle', it adds, sweeping away this fiction also, but it asks itself what it can be that so indisputably prevents its slipping into a body, be the latter only a round and rolling head – and back comes the obvious answer:

I don't know, I'm here, that's all I know, and that it's still not me, it's with that I have to do the best I can. There is no flesh anywhere, nor any means of dying. Give it up, the will to give it up, all that, not knowing what is meant by that, all that, it's soon said, soon done, in vain, nothing has stirred, no one has spoken. Here, nothing will happen here, there will be no one here, for many a day. The departures, the stories, are not for tomorrow. And the voices, wherever they come from, are quite dead.

201

The voice tells stories, but not as Malone and the hero of *Le Calmant* did, to pass the time, but in a continually repeated, constantly doomed attempt to take on an identifiable existence:

And when my mouth opens again it will be, who knows, to tell a story, in the true sense of the words, of the word tell, of the word story, I don't despair, a little story, with living creatures coming and going on a habitable earth crammed with the dead, a brief story, under the shuttle of day and night, if they go that far, the words that remain, I don't despair, I swear I don't.

Je cherche à être, says the voice. Is it I, this man sitting stiff and upright on a bench on South-East Station, holding his ticket between thumb and forefinger? No, I am here, waiting for a train that will never come in nor go out. Is it I, this creature begging on a café terrace or on the steps of an underground station? No, I am here, begging in another silence, another dark, pleading for quite different alms, for the possibility of existing, or better still, of ending without ever having been. The only being, in fact, that the voice deems feasible is that of a 'ventriloquist's doll' or of a blind, deaf and dumb man, but even this form of existence is refused it. I try to situate, to place myself, it explains, in order to have the possibility, if necessary, of moving on somewhere else. The self is, however, what it calls *le même inconnu que toujours*, what Proust termed 'that stranger, oneself'. This self has furthermore an unnerving habit of dividing up into two selves:

I was my father and I was my son, I asked myself questions and I answered as best I could, I had it told to me evening after evening, the same old story. . . . And this evening again it seems to be working, I'm in my arms, I'm holding myself in my arms, without much tenderness, but faithfully, faithfully.

One part of the self may wander away, while the other stands among friends, shaking its head and wondering 'is it really he, is it possible', before leaving in the company of the same friends, abandoning its other half, like Mercier and Camier separating at the forking of the ways.

Does this voice, this *inexistant averti*, suffer from tyrants? It speaks, certainly, of 'someone' saying 'you can't stay there' when it is on the mountain-top. But am I guilty, it wonders? Judge and accused, witness and advocate and clerk of the court, the voice has all these roles to play simultaneously: the question is, on what case is this assize sitting?

But whom can I have displeased so grievously that I should undergo this incomprehensible punishment, all is incomprehensible, space and mind, false and incomprehensible, suffering and tears, and even the old paroxysmal cry, It isn't me, it can't be me.

The voice also mentions what it calls its 'guardians' – have they the right to play cards, to take a little recreation? The Unnamable asked himself the same question, to which there can be no answer. Perhaps, after all, the only tyrant is oneself:

I am not in his head, nowhere in his old body, and yet I am there, for him I am there, with him, whence all the confusion. It should be enough for him, to find me absent, but no, he wants me there, with a form of my own, a world of my own, like him, in spite of him, me who am all, like him who is nothing. And when he feels I have no existence, it's of his he would have me bereft, and vice versa, mad, mad, he's mad. The truth is he is looking for me to kill me, so that I may be dead like him, dead like the living. . . . He thinks he is at a loss for words, he thinks that by being at a loss for words he can catch my silence, go silent with my silence. . . . He would like me to be the cause of his having no history, naturally he has no history, that's no excuse for his wanting to foist one on me. . . . That's how he talks, this evening, has me talk, talks to himself, that's how I talk, there is none but me, me and my figments, this evening, here, on earth, and a voice that makes no sound, because it goes towards none.

The last text puts the matter correctly, or as correctly as may be: *nous sommes finis, qui ne fûmes jamais.*

In the dimension inhabited by the voice, nothing can be said, nothing can be named: *rien n'est nommable, rien n'est dicible.* Truth is a dirty word, so why feel ashamed of so many lies, *tant de fois le même mensonge et mensongèrement démenti*? Like Krapp sneering with a former self at an even earlier self, this voice cackles at the term *au juste*, then stops cackling, muttering that the joke was never even funny. Time converts into space (*le temps s'est fait espace*), being into nothingness, significance into non-significance, and vice versa; the pen falls from a tired hand (*je vais le décrire, non je ne peux pas*) and if you, the reader, can understand, you are more fortunate, it appears, than this voice that speaks, unaware of what it says, throwing out its words like a ball in a free-for-all, with the cynical envoi, *comprenne qui pourra!*

*   *   *

In these hard nuggets of non-sense ('not only', to quote M. Nadeau, 'has the author not desired to convey anything, he really *has* conveyed nothing') we find, paradoxically, some of the most attractive French Beckett has written. He has so far only trans-lated one or two of these texts into English, 'unsatisfactorily' as he says. It is not difficult to see why. They are almost untranslatable; stripped of the carefully developed French rhythms and intricate syntax, they tend to sound flat and empty in English. Here form is not merely indistinguishable from content, it *is* (to adapt Beckett on Joyce) content. Inside these spiders' webs of words there is nothing but pure speech, no story, characters or themes; and outside them nothing whatsoever. While we are reading these texts, they hold us and twist us as they twist, they charm us with their elegance, but they vanish once we have laid the book down. Beckett has reached in literature the limit of the rarefied. Having nothing to say, or rather trying to say the unsayable that lurks (perhaps) behind all saying, and reaching to the 'whereof one cannot speak', he gives us wall-bars of words on which to exercise our minds. These gymnastic erections are all of about the same length: not so short as to be wholly insubstantial, not so long as to weary (the morbid flux of *The Unnamable* has become a regular habit), they usually open and close on much the same words: the second starts and finishes with *là-haut*, the third with *laisse tout ça*, the fourth with *où irais-je?* and so on. The art of the short text is most difficult, but Beckett has mastered it. Each of his sentences (often quite long, they are broken up into short phrases by num-erous commas) tends to introduce a new slant; the text thus zig-zags around its main preoccupation until it returns to the word that was its point of departure, which is the signal to end. Beckett has been described as a competent amateur musician, and the information is relevant to an understanding of these texts, musi-cal in structure (we have frequently in the course of a given text modifications of theme that can be compared to changes of key in music) and musical even in sound. The French is in fact of extraordinary aural, as well as visual, beauty: not only can the language, with the most rapid of strokes, conjure up a scene, such as the flat mountain-top or the station waiting-room, it can also, and this is more significant, rise to the purely aural splendour of poetry and music:

j'y irais, à l'issue, tôt ou tard, si je la disais là, quelque part, les autres mots me viendraient, tôt ou tard, et de quoi pouvoir y aller, et y aller, et passer à travers, et voir les belles choses que porte le ciel, et revoir les étoiles.[1]

*   *   *

Having attained the hermetically sealed perfection of the *Texts for Nothing*, Beckett did not create anything of importance for some years. In 1955 he tried to start writing fiction in English again, but the attempt led to nothing. It did, however, free his pen to write the French play *Fin de partie* at the turn of the year (1955-1956); and in 1957 a piece washed up from the wreck of the English vessel appeared in the *Evergreen Review*.

This fragment covers three days in the life of the hero, who does not give himself a name, but describes himself as 'old and weak'; he was 'young then', and his mother used to hang out of the window waving goodbye to him on his departure from the house every morning. On the day he has 'hit on to begin with' ('any other would have done as well') he meets a white horse ('what I believe the Germans call a Schimmel'). On the second day he is attacked by a 'family or tribe . . . of stoats' and on the third he meets a roadman called Balfe, and then wanders into the country, crashing his way through the 'great ferns'. And that is all.

He is, like his predecessors, a vagrant: 'I have never in my life been on my way anywhere, but simply on my way.' We learn little else about him, though he seems to have had a strong affection for his mother while she was alive, and even thinks he was

---

[1] The wording of this consciously echoes the last lines of Dante's *Inferno*:

salimmo su, el primo e io secondo,
    tanto ch'i' vidi de le cose belle
    che porta 'l ciel, per un pertugio tondo:
e quindi uscimmo a riveder le stelle.

responsible for her death, perhaps because he was 'always out'. He has never married or settled down and contemplates the fact with mingled sarcasm and regret:

In a way perhaps it's a pity, a good woman might have been the making of me, I might be sprawling in the sun now sucking my pipe and patting the bottoms of the third generation, looked up to and respected, wondering what there was for dinner, instead of stravaging the same old roads in all weathers.

'No, I regret nothing,' he adds, 'all I regret is having been born, dying is such a long tiresome business I always found.' Having always talked to himself (and suffered from a sore throat in consequence) he now looks forward deliciously to the end of speech:

often now my murmur falters and dies and I weep for happiness as I go along and for love of this old earth that has carried me so long and whose uncomplainingness will soon be mine.

'I was mad of course, and still am, but harmless . . . not of course that I was really mad, just strange, a little strange.' He believes all his parents' 'blather' about an after-life (in any case, 'unhappiness like mine, there's no annihilating that') and he longs to go to hell so that he can curse them up in paradise: 'that might take some shine off their bliss'. He also however goes in some fear of tyrants, for he says that he will be able to die by drowning or by fire only 'if they don't catch me', and for him, too, composition is as futile as ever it was: 'why go on with all this, I don't know . . . . what is the sense of going on with all this, there is none'. Words (single words) have been his only loves; he delights in 'over, over, vero, oh vero' just as Krapp rejoices in 'spooool!', and hopes that his 'reward' will be the Unnamable's:

a long unbroken time without before or after, light or dark, from or towards or at, the old half knowledge of when and where gone, and of what, . . . kinds of things still, all at once, all going, until nothing, there was never anything, never can be, life and death all nothing, that kind of thing, only a voice dreaming and droning on all around. . . . the voice that once was in your mouth.

He looks forward to this situation as a release from the monotony of his present existence, which reminds us of Krapp's, as do other aspects of this fragment. Both here and in the play, for instance, the mother figures prominently and in the latter she dies; in both works an old man looks back on his youth, either in writing his memories, or in recording them on tape. Even the style of this fragment, informal and colloquial, recalls Krapp's:

Up bright and early that day, I was young then, feeling awful, and out, mother hanging out of the window in her nightdress weeping and waving. Nice fresh morning, bright too early as so often. Feeling really awful, very violent.

And as in the dramatic monologue, memories of youth (perhaps even of Beckett's own youth) play an important part:

Fortunately my father died when I was a boy, otherwise I might have been a professor, he had set his heart on it. A very fair scholar I was too, no thought, but a great memory. One day I told him about Milton's cosmology, away up in the mountains we were, resting against a huge rock looking out to sea, that impressed him greatly.

Like Krapp, this hero thinks back to his mother, who died some time after his father:

No tenacity of purpose, that was another thing I didn't like in her. One week it would be exercises, and the next prayers and bible reading, and the next gardening, and the next playing the piano and singing, that was awful, and then just lying about and resting, always changing.

This text has thus the same quality of nostalgia and regret, the same controlled pathos that makes the play so good. The technique of recall is comparable in both, although it is undeniable that the play, which exploits the dramatic possibilities of the tape-recorder, is the more powerful and impressive work of the two. One can hardly regret the abandoning of this novel, since thereby was made possible the transmutation of its best features into successful drama. There is not enough substance here for fiction, but ample for a fine one-act monologue. Guided as usual by a sure æsthetic instinct, Beckett no doubt dropped this novel in favour of *Krapp's Last Tape,* written not long after, just as he abandoned *Mercier et Camier* in favour of *En attendant Godot.*

The English here has a sensuous richness that contrasts with the more abstract beauty of the French of the *Textes pour rien,* and reveals once again what a skilled writer Beckett is in either language. The opening words, quoted above, are gusty and vivid, and the end matches up to them, despite the humorous disclaimer:

Harsh things these great ferns, like starched, very woody, terrible stalks, take the skin off your legs through your trousers, and then the holes they hide, break your leg if you're not careful, awful English this, fall and vanish from view, you could lie there for weeks and no one hear you, I often thought of that up in the mountains, no, that is a foolish thing to say, just went on, my body doing its best without me.

Euphony is everywhere a prime consideration, with sound often echoing sense:

The next thing I was up in the bracken lashing about with my stick making the drops fly and cursing, filthy language, the same words over and over, I hope nobody heard me. . . . Extraordinary still over the land, and in me too all quite still, a coincidence, why the curses were pouring out of me I do not know.

Alliteration is often exploited with effect:

. . . walking furious headlong into fire and dying burnt to bits. . . .

Well written as this fragment is, however, it evidently did not achieve what Beckett wished it to achieve, namely a new breakthrough in the field of fiction. A few more years had to elapse before a possible solution to his difficulty could present itself. Before turning to *Comment C'est*, however, we should notice how these recent fictional works are imbued with a poignancy which was hardly to be found in earlier works, *Murphy* excepted. Suppressed regrets and determination to persist are among their most striking characteristics, with humour held always in reserve to protect the mind against its own misery. In the recent plays, too, a similar tone of voice is heard; it would almost seem as if Beckett has, with age, reached a more serene resignation, or as if the rage and grief that attained their paroxysm in *The Unnamable* have now largely spent themselves. This tone of resigned regret is carried over into *Comment C'est*, where it helps to make the novel one of the more impressive the author has written, from the point of view both of the form and the interest of the themes there given powerful expression.

*   *   *

Comment C'est – How It Is – even the title is new, quite different from the bald heroes' names that serve for most of the preceding novels. Here the last three words in the book are chosen to introduce it to the reader: a small enough point in itself, but not an insignificant one. On opening the book, the next surprise we experience arises from the new form of the typography; but this is a matter to which I shall return later.

First of all a synopsis of the novel must be attempted; this is fortunately easier than in the case of the *Textes pour rien.* The nameless hero of this new work is not any longer a writer, but merely a sayer: he *utters* the 'beginning of my life latest version'. The last two words are significant; it is in them that he indicates that he is the latest incarnation of the hero whose evolution we have been studying up till now, and later in the book he substantiates this claim by relating his reminiscences of previous existences. He maintains, nonetheless, that he is merely quoting what is dictated to him, though whence or by whom is never made clear. This need not surprise nor unduly mystify us, since we are by now familiar with Beckett's voices of unexplained provenance.

The novel is in three parts of equal length. The first is mainly taken up with a description of the hero's life before he met the man whom he calls Pim; but material proper to one part tends to stray into another, as if the process of dictation temporarily suffered a minor breakdown, so in this first section we occasionally find elements proper to the second, which the hero however soon notices and corrects with the phrase 'something wrong there'.

In the first part, then, he is chiefly concerned to describe the conditions in which he finds himself; he also records certain memories, which he sees in the form of 'images' or pictures, of his life on earth (called once again *là-haut dans la lumière*).

The second section tells how he deals with Pim, his 'creature'. First he gives the latter a name, and then he adopts for himself the appellation Bom. He discovers that although they are both old men, he is the taller of the two. Surprised to find that Pim can sing, he invents a system of tortures to make Pim speak, or go silent, at will, which reminds us curiously of Molloy's programme of knocks on his mother's skull (their only available means of communication). For Pim the so-called *tableau des excitations de base* is as follows:

table of basic stimuli one sing nails in armpit two speak blade of opener in arse three stop thump of fist on skull four louder handle of opener on kidney

five not so loud index in anus six bravo slap athwart arse seven bad same as three eight again same as one or two depending

Bom, who, it appears, is quite dumb, can only 'speak' to Pim by carving words (using the Latin alphabet, he says, as in 'our civilization') on the latter's back with his very long nails, sometimes even making the blood run if Pim's comprehension is sluggish. Pim then usually turns his head and replies by speaking right into Bom's ear; their bristles intermingle, so close are lips to lobe. Bom thereby learns something of his creature's previous existence, especially of his family, and wife Pam (or Prim), who threw herself from a window and died subsequently in hospital, after which Pim took to a life of abject wandering and exile:

my life above what I did in my life above a little of everything tried everything then gave up no worse always a hole a ruin always a crust never any good at anything not made for that farrago too complicated crawl about in corners and sleep all I wanted I got it nothing left but go to heaven

In the third part, the narrator-hero extends the concept of the Bom-Pim relationship to infinity: hundreds of thousands of such couples unite and then separate, torturer and victim, hearer and heard, all similar but for their names (Bem and Pem are cited as another couple). The hero indulges in long arithmetical calculations to show that every creature will be properly occupied by his particular function at a given moment, and then, like Berkeley or Leibniz, invokes a God to oversee the smooth working (*exquisément organisé*) of the vast arrangements. We imagine that this fantasy will carry him to the end, only to find that in the last few pages he destroys systematically and with pitiless severity the entire construction of the whole book in its three parts. The scenes, the visions, the couples and processions, the overseeing God, Pim, and Bom, even the idea of tins of food to keep them alive, are swept clean away – all that subsists is the mud, the dark and the nameless voice that can never die, but whose present quotation has been brought to an end: *fin de la citation*.

* * *

In such a work, where after laborious erection all is knocked down, it is hardly possible to speak even of the existence of a netherworld. What does, however, remain unchanged even after the last fit of iconoclasm is the mud and pitch blackness in which the voice resides: it is not clear whether the body of the hero subsists at the last or not. In the first part, this body, still governed by Cartesian physiology ('I call [my hand] it doesn't come nothing ails it it won't come'), is quite unmutilated except that it lacks the thumb of the right hand, and it absorbs moisture by plunging its tongue into the warm, wet mud; it breathes the steamy, odourless air; it feeds, but only occasionally and then without appetite, on tins of tunny and other fish, which are opened and then often thrown away, covered with mildew and only half-eaten. These tins and the tin-opener are dragged around in a small jute coalsack: for the hero never walks, only crawls on the surface of the mud, into which he is never allowed to sink (despite his twenty to thirty kilos' weight) and suffocate, however much he may yearn for such a death. He is quite naked, as is Pim also, and often lies curled up with the sack held against his belly, like 'Belacqua toppled over onto his side'; he is completely alone ('I sole elect') until he invents Pim. He claims to see his 'images' in the mud, as if the latter opened up or became transparent, revealing scenes of long ago in the world of men. He states explicitly that he has no wish for any visitors, such as another Basil:

no wish for visitors in my life this time coming towards me from all sides all kinds talking to me about themselves life and death as if nothing had happened perhaps even about me in the end to help me endure then goodbye till the next time each one back the way he came

He compares himself to 'a monster of the solitudes [who] sees man for the first time and does not fly before him explorers bring home its skin among their trophies', and he determines moreover to outdo even Malone and live without the resources of fiction:

life then without visitors present version no visitors no stories but mine no sounds but mine no silence but the silence I must break when I can bear it no more it's with that I must endure

He would like a little woman as a companion, or perhaps a ewe, but there can be no question of the possibility of such a thing (there are not even any rats here):

and yet a dream I am given a dream as if I had tasted of love of a little woman within my reach and dreaming too it's in the dream too of a little man within hers I have that in my life this time on and off as I journey

or failing kindred flesh emergency dream a ewe sheep she would not come to me I would go to her huddle in her fleece but they add no mere animal here spirit is indispensable mind too a minimum of each otherwise too great an honour

Time here is quite indefinite, there exist no means of measuring it since there is no night and day, but he is at least certain that it is 'very long'. His sense of humour deteriorates, he says, but this is compensated for by the fact that he is less subject to tears. He takes no interest in the question of how he arrived, but occupies himself with the elaborate mechanics of vermicular locomotion and with the ballet danced by the four fingers of his right hand on the surface of the mud. His possessions are of course immensely important to him: his sack and tins and the precious tin-opener represent as much for him as the long stick does for Malone; and he takes great pleasure in the simplest things, as in the smell of a freshly opened tin of tunny.

Perhaps because he is so unsure of his own existence, he invokes a witness of his activities, Kram, and a transcriber of these, Krim, both of whom are swept away at the end; there is therefore little call to take them seriously. They seem to be mere survivals of the more substantial employees of the mysterious master in *Molloy* and in *The Unnamable*.

If this hero refuses to tell himself stories, he seems in his visions to indulge in a certain nostalgia for the world of men, for which he nonetheless shows nothing but contempt. His present place is only an *immesurable souille*, where millions of men-pigs wallow, and it is difficult not to see in this a symbol of our world; and yet there is a distinct nostalgia, especially for Ireland, the 'country of his childhood' – *je cherche une île home enfin* he says, and hopes to go back and die in the 'land of his birth'.

His mind is littered with flotsam and jetsam of a former intellectual's existence: being acquainted with his forbears, we do not
find this surprising. He invokes Malebranche at one moment,
Heraclitus at another, and ironically comments: *les lettres que
j'avais . . . les humanités que j'avais mon Dieu avec ça un peu de
géographie.*

Like the Unnamable he is obsessed with words ('voice once
without quaqua on all sides then in me when I stop panting now
in me tell me again finish telling me . . . snatches of an ancient
voice in me not mine') many of which are lost in dictation. He is
obliged to employ men's words (since he cannot fabricate *un
langage à ma mesure à la mesure d'ici*) and is continually surprised at them: they are imposed on him (*voilà la parole qu'on m'a
donnée*), he hears them imperfectly and therefore no doubt
repeats them incorrectly and in the wrong order. But, as for the
Unnamable, they enable him to endure (*avec ça j'ai duré un
moment*) although he is continually obliged to forage for more:
trouver autre chose pour durer encore. How is he even to know
whose voice is speaking, or who notes it down? He only knows that
without his words and 'the wild thoughts they invent' (*Textes
pour rien*) he can never end: they are an indispensable instrument, however unreliable. He seems utterly alone, 'and yet I
hear the murmur all alone in the dark the mud and yet'. The
only answer given to his eternal questions is that he can only end
when time ends (*quand les temps finiront tu finiras peut-être*) and
until then he must go on:

on ne peut continuer on continue la même chose . . . on ne peut continuer on ne peut s'arrêter. . . .

Putting questions to itself at the end, the voice learns that its
situation can never change and that the moment will never come
when it will no longer have to 'trouble the silence'.

*   *   *

In this novel, predictably, the problem of identity is especially
acute. It is difficult to be at all sure whether Pim is speaking or
Bom remembering even in the fairly straightforward second part.
When to this difficulty is added that of the 'images' in Part I, and
of the final clearing of the decks in Part III, it becomes evident

213

that we have here no valid licence to attribute any particular occurrence, vision or memory to anyone. Beckett thus convinces us skilfully of the terrifying blank to which enquiry into personal identity may lead us.

On the very first page the voice speaks of 'past moments old dreams' which come 'back again' or are 'new like those that pass'. These dreams postulate, or seem to postulate, a previous existence 'in the light':

first image someone anyone I watched him after my fashion from afar stealthily in mirrors at night through windows lighted windows first image

and said watched him and said to myself he's better than he was less foolish less cruel less dirty less old less wretched and me said to myself and me bad to worse bad to worse steadily. . . .

or said to myself I'm no worse no better no worse and was mistaken. . . .

I cut with scissors in fine shreds the wings of butterflies first one wing then the other sometimes for a change the two concurrently I set free the body in the middle never so good since

The hero even relives his own death on earth:

image a woman raises her head from her needlework and looks at me the images are all at the beginning part one I say it as I hear it I see them in the mud soon they will cease

she is ten yards from me fifteen yards she says at last to herself all is well he is working

my head lies on the table my hand trembles high wind the little clouds move fast the table slips from light to shadow shadow to light

it isn't over she stoops blindly to her work again the needle falters in the cloth and stays she draws herself up and looks at me again she has only to call me by my name come and feel me but no

my stillness she more and more uneasy suddenly leaves the house and goes to friends

He soon protests, however, that this is neither a dream nor a memory but merely 'an image the kind I sometimes see in the mud'. In another such image he sees his mother (who is perhaps the 'woman' in the image above as well):

we are on a latticed verandah tangled with verbena the perfumed sun spangles the red tiles good God

the huge head hatted with birds and flowers lowers on my pale curls the eyes burn with severe love while mine my head thrown back at the ideal angle offers her its pale upcast eyes my eyes

kneeling bolt upright on a cushion shapeless in a white nightshirt clasping my hands with all my strength I pray according to her instructions

it isn't over she drones a belief of the Apostles' Creed I look at her lips while she can't see me

she stops the eyes burn again I cast up mine in haste and repeat all wrong

but this image fades in its turn:

it's over it goes out like a lamp blown out

the space of a moment the passing moment that's my past all my past little rat on my heels the rest figments

He dismisses it and with it, in anticipation of the end of the novel, all that is yet to come:

figments that old time part one vast stretch of time when I drag myself and drag myself amazed that I can the cord sawing my neck the sack jolting at my side a hand outstretched towards the wall the ditch that never come

and Pim part two what I do to him what he says to me

figments like that dead head the hand alive still the little table tossed by the clouds the woman springing to her feet and rushing out into the wind

no matter I say no more is it me is it me I'm not that kind any more that's been done away with this time all I ever say is how endure how endure

Although we are still only at page 20, the whole book exists in bud here already. It will only put out longer shoots and fuller blossoms in the next 150. The net result of all this bourgeoning is, as we have seen, precisely nothing, but the final achievement is no less impressive for that. We are spectators at a ballet, formal and untroubled by any reality but its own, by any principle but that, inevitable and serene, of its own growth and rapid decline.

The most significant 'image' recalls a previous incarnation, namely as the hero of *La Fin* who lived in a basement and whose only companion was a flower:

it dies and I see a crocus in a pot in an area in a basement a saffron the sun crawls up the wall a hand keeps it in the sun this yellow flower with a string I see the hand long image hours long the sun goes the pot goes down lights on the ground the hand goes the wall goes

Another image forcibly recalls the ironical tone of the short story of 1934, *Fingal*, which told of Belacqua's sortie with Winnie:

suddenly we are eating sandwiches alternate bites I mine she hers and exchanging endearments my sweet girl I bite she swallows my sweet boy she bites I swallow we don't yet coo with our bills full

. . . brief black and there we are again dwindling again across the fields hand in hand arms swinging heads high towards the heights smaller and smaller out of sight first the dog then us the scene is rid of us

In Part II, Pim's divulgations about his past are evidently just another way for the hero to tell us of his own previous existence: grandfather, a father in the building trade, and wife all pass before our eyes in this way. Hugh Kenner has pointed out a striking resemblance between the sad story of Pim and the following lines in *Enueg I* (1935):

> Exeo in a spasm
> tired of my darling's red sputum
> from the Portobello Private Nursing Home. . . .

The account of their unsuccessful marriage blends the sardonic and tragic with a skill that, as I have remarked, Beckett masters fully in his recent work:

love birth of love increase decrease death efforts to resuscitate through the arse joint vain through the cunt anew vain jumped from window or fell broken column hospital marguerites lies about mistletoe forgiveness

Although there is little doubt that the hero uses Pim in this way for his own confessions, he nonetheless complains that this prevents him from being himself:

in sum more lively that's what I was getting at I've got at it I say it as I hear it more how shall I say more lively there's nothing better before Pim part one more independent I saw my images my own crawled ate thought even if you like a few dim thoughts

The problem becomes more acute as he elaborates the fantasies of Part III with their multiple *personæ*: until he explodes them all with the disturbing French obscenity which puts an end to them: *foutaises*!

Insecurity of identity is only one aspect of doubt about the whole of reality; for once again ratiocination is exposed to a mockery as resounding as any yet found in Beckett's work: *voilà la difficulté aplanie* he says in the midst of his Part III deliberations, and the ironic intention of this remark is obvious. Furthermore, a more ferocious indictment of the act of writing than those constructions, Aunt Sallys set up only to be knocked down, can with difficulty be imagined: and a heartier contempt of literary activity than 'all this should now be read back to front', words that occur in Part III, is equally hard to conceive.

The infinite system of couples is, moreover, postulated in learned mockery of Leibniz, the philosopher whose influence on Beckett is usually underestimated. In this sagely ordained universe imagined by the hero, where everything functions *dans la justice et la sauvegarde de nos activités essentielles*, Leibniz' world of monads pre-established by a benign God is heavily parodied. Beckett in fact gives the game away in the following words (my italics):

millions and millions there are millions of us and there are three *I place myself at my point of view* Bem is Bom Bom Bem let us say Bom it's better Bom then me and Pim me in the middle

The Christian God therefore quite naturally looms large in this novel, but he is always undermined by irony. The hero, who lives in eternal Limbo, laughs to himself as he says a prayer for the damned in Hell, and attributes to the divine grace his possession of a sack of tins, even going so far as to imagine *une boîte céleste*

217

sardines miraculeuses envoyées par Dieu – enough to enable him to 'vomit' God for one week more. But God's chief function is that of a *percipiens universalis*, divine ear, divine noter:

there he is then at last that not one of us there we are then at last who listens to himself and giving ear to our murmur merely gives it to a story of his own ill inspired ill told and each time so ancient so forgotten that ours may seem faithful to him that we murmur to the mud to him

But this *percipiens* also goes down with the wreck, *fou lui aussi*.

*   *   *

Impressive as this novel is as an embodiment of its author's chief preoccupations, it does not seem, as I have said, to add appreciably to them. The real advance lies in the form: in the typography, syntax and general structure.

There is evidence that Beckett originally intended to issue his text as a block of words quite unbroken by typographical punctuation marks of any kind, subject only to the breath-pauses of the reader reading it aloud – the extract from an early version published in *X* a year before he gave the final draft to M. Lindon bears this theory out. The extract translated into English, on the other hand, and published in the *Evergreen Review* a month or two before M. Lindon received the French text, is already divided into what have been called *versets*, or biblical-style verses. They vary in length from one line to ten or more, but usually contain about five. Apart from a line-gap between each, there is no other punctuation whatever, either capitals (except for proper names), commas or full-stops, throughout the book. Inside each 'verse' the breath-pause alone divides the period. Once one has grasped this elementary principle, the reading of the book is then not difficult – less difficult than that of *The Unnamable*, for instance. One feels however a certain relief that Beckett decided against a block-text before he sent in his final version, for without the verses the novel would certainly take some time to decipher.

This typographical innovation is not gratuitous. It responds to a genuine need, that of transcribing as faithfully as possible a voice that can only speak words when it stops panting. A new syntax answers to the same need: main verbs and conjunctions are suppressed here, just as they are in colloquial speech; an example, taken at random, will make this clear:

le sac [est] ma vie que jamais je ne lâche [mais] ici je le lâche [car j'ai] besoin des deux mains. . . .

In the following example, colloquial speech is followed with even greater fidelity, and all definite articles are dropped:

[Passons maintenant au] problème du dressage [, à la] solution et [à la] mise en œuvre [,] progressives [ou] simultanées [,] et parallèlement [, sur le] plan moral [, à l'] amorce [et à l'] essor des rapports proprement dits [;] mais [voici] quelques précisions d'abord [, au nombre de] deux ou trois [.]

In square brackets are a few words, which in normal literary French *might* fill out and clarify the period presented here, together with the natural punctuation marks. Thus enlarged the verse becomes a normal prose sentence; Beckett's method, therefore, consists simply in writing down the sentence as a French peasant or labourer would speak it. That his result is neither far-fetched nor unnatural can be seen from the following letter, which is quite authentic; it was sent by a French aspirant to the naval service:

Monsieur le Ministre

Je vous prie de m'écrire à Lavardac malgré que j'ai des travaux pour ma vie terrestre si les postes me trompent si les lettres ne sont pas distribuer [*sic*] ici la télégraphie sans fil à Lavardac Lot et Garonne? la prochaine lettre vous recevrez une lettre recommandé [*sic*] chose qui coute [*sic*] dur vous devez m'accepter vu que vous avez lancé à Moissac cet appel[1].

Beckett of course never sins against grammar like this volunteer, but otherwise he does transcribe faithfully the short, three- or four-word phrases which the mind employs in its thoughts, and which uninstructed people even write down. They do so because they have not been drilled in the conventions and contrivances of literary composition, the language employed therein being naturally different from that of colloquial speech: this is, of

---

[1] Quoted from the section headed *Le style des illettrés*, in André Moufflet's book *Contre le massacre de la langue française*, Toulouse et Paris, 1930, page 40.

course, the reason why tape-recorded dialogues rarely read very satisfactorily unless some editing is done after transcription. Beckett puts the familiar machinery of pedagogical instruction into reverse, strips his language of its literary props and make-weights, and thereby catches the sounds the mind makes in actually grappling with words, or rather with the elemental lumps of basic speech. His latest prose is thus in line with the rest of his work, a natural culmination, for the Unnamable's rambling utterances and the gymnastic exercises of the *Textes pour rien* appear, in retrospect, as natural forerunners to this denuded, primitive style. We should not see in this development the influence of similar experiments by practitioners of the *nouveau roman* (which, according to Mme. Serreau, Beckett in some moods holds in slight esteem), but simply the inevitable, almost predictable terminus of his own solitary journey.

If he has learnt to transcribe in this way the workings of the untutored mind, he has nonetheless retained his old skill at literary construction. The three parts are impressively symmetrical both in form and content. If each part deals in principle with a different phase, each nonetheless begins and ends on the same note: *comment c'est*. Thus the circularity that was prominent in *Molloy* is found again here, both from the opening of a part to the closing of that part, and from the beginning of the book to the end: for the novel both starts and stops with the hero quite alone. Symmetry and circularity thus have now become ends in themselves, and Beckett is concerned as much (or perhaps more) with creating an æsthetic *objet* as with writing a novel; for even as an object in one's hands, the lay-out and choice of type-face make this book a pleasure to look at and to hold. Is it too wild a deduction to suppose that this author, despairing completely of saying anything new, feels driven to making things of beauty instead? When 'literature' seems to him sham and farce, a well-produced book perhaps appears a more honourable achievement. The logical consequence of such an attitude would be to esteem the printer and binder above the writer, and this is, in fact, the sort of conclusion before which some artists of our time have shown they do not recoil.

Furthermore, this novel employs clipped and elementary syntax, not only for the reasons just mentioned, but also in an attempt to achieve something of the condensation of verse. In this connection it should be noted that the order of words is sometimes so eccentric as to resemble Latin construction rather than French:

[il] put enfin les voir un peu avant ses ongles sa mort

In colloquial French the order would be, after one had put in the commas, *il put enfin les voir, ses ongles, un peu avant sa mort.* Liberties of this kind are taken to make possible poetry of quality, as in this quotation:

quoi encore la nuit au large à la morte-eau sur la petite mer pauvre en îles. . . .

Beckett's style can throw up words or combinations of words of such beauty that one is occasionally reminded of certain lines by Saint-John Perse, such as:

. . . la terre au lointain nous raconte ses mers.

. . . les milices du vent dans les sables d'exil. . . .

And even when he twists a common expression, as in this quotation, Beckett gives it poetic resonance:

les mots vous font voir du pays avec eux d'étranges voyages

The rhythm of the sentence is intoxicating as a line of Racine, and one does not mind calling this poetry. Beckett's novel in fact is best considered as a long prose-poem, repeating words or phrases like *quelque chose là qui ne va pas* in the form of refrains, with incantatory, hypnotic effect; and the last pages, repeating *oui* continually, seem to reproduce the erotic beat of primitive dances or the ecstatic rhythms of certain liturgies.

The poetic element in the novel does not exclude humour, on the contrary. Pim at one moment, for instance, misinterprets his stimuli and provokes the following ribald comment on the part of the hero:

. . . stabbed in the arse instead of crying out he sings what a cunt this Pim damn it all confuse arse and armpit. . . .

The fact remains that this 'prose' is perhaps the best poetry Beckett has written. In doing so, he is working in line with contemporary developments in French poetry, which, freed from all conventions and metrical rules, often has the appearance of prose; Léopold Sédar Senghor has summed up these developments in the following words:

The Surrealists were not content to throw out the neat French-garden aspect of the traditional rhetoric-poem. They blasted every hinge-word away, in order to deliver naked poems that throb with the very rhythm of the soul itself. They thus rediscovered African syntax, the syntax of juxtaposition, in which words, telescoped together, burst into symbols and metaphors of flame. (*Esprit*, Nov. 1962)

* * *

This study has brought us a long way from *Dream of Fair to Middling Women*, but each step along the road has seemed necessary. From the early works, which Beckett has said he wrote with ease, to *Comment C'est* which cost him eighteen months of effort, we have followed him as he has engaged in an increasingly desperate battle with the silence. The question remains whether he has achieved in this last novel the breakthrough that seemed impossible in 1950, and only time will provide the answer to it. He must already be planning the next step; it is not likely he will let the matter rest there, for as he told Driver, 'to find a form that accommodates the mess, that is the task of the artist now'. As loyal as ever to his vocation as an artist, he will not, one feels, permit himself to neglect this crucial but difficult task.

CONCLUSION: 'The Voice Continues'

> The only fertile research is excavatory, immersive, a contraction of the spirit, a descent. The artist is active, but negatively, shrinking from the nullity of extracircumferential phenomena, drawn in to the core of the eddy.
>
> S. BECKETT, Proust

> *La marche de la pensée dans le travail solitaire de la création artistique se fait dans le sens de la profondeur, la seule direction qui ne nous soit pas fermée, où nous puissions progresser, avec plus de peine il est vrai, pour un résultat de vérité.*
>
> MARCEL PROUST

THESE two quotations can serve as the mottoes of the body of fiction we have been studying; fidelity to these texts (*in hoc signo vinces*) is what has given it strength and consistency. We must now turn to a broader discussion of the whole *œuvre*, seek to assess its importance and examine some of the background against which it was written.

'First dirty', says the Unnamable, 'then make clean'. So far I have been examining Beckett's novels chronologically, in order to set out as clearly as possible the factors that have inspired and sustained their creation. I have thereby frequently skirted what has been called 'the heresy of paraphrase'; and now that analysis, often a dubious activity, has fulfilled its function, some effort at a synthesis must be made. While viewing this body of work as a whole, however, I shall not attempt to offer any systematic conclusions here, but merely note a few of the impressions which a glance over the ground just covered suggests, in the hope that such impressions will give rise to some general considerations about the interest, relevance and significance of this canon of short stories, novels and texts.

Throughout this study, the point has continually been made that Beckett's fiction shows an overall consistency and harmony of development that is striking. At the end, it will no doubt be agreed that this has not been an exaggeration. We have witnessed the innovations of form and style going hand in hand with the gradual evolution of the hero; every step has seemed natural and justified. We can now survey an *œuvre* which has never once marked time but always moved forward to the next position. Each novel or short story has appeared the obvious successor to the one before, although on occasion, of course, one work has stood above the others in importance. It was not to be expected that all the novels in the canon should be of equal literary merit, but no item is insignificant, and in the context of the *œuvre* as a whole every element in it repays attention and contributes to our understanding of the rest.

We seem, therefore, to possess in the fiction of Samuel Beckett an example of thorough-going consistency in a progressive evolution. This rigour has been achieved not only because the author has always taken the next logical step forward, but also because he has remained faithful to certain basic themes, his literary 'obsessions', which he has developed with undeviating honesty and intrepidity. He has not shirked any of the conclusions his pen has led him into, however nonsensical, cruel or obscene they may seem. His prose is sometimes physically hard to read, his thought difficult to follow, his remarks unpalatable and his subject-matter unsavoury: *Beckett grince*, admits Mayoux, an admirer, for there is no denying the shock and pain that this author inflicts on our sensibilities. But this is the price to be paid, by writer and reader alike, for the acquisition of a body of work that goes in everything to the limit, without shame or fear.

This fidelity to the muse, even when she manifests herself in witch's rags, is one of the main reasons why we find such impressive unity in Beckett's work. Another less important reason is the adoption of an intricate pattern of cross-references. Each hero is not only reincarnated in his successor, but is also referred to by the latter and by the heroes of subsequent incarnations, until they all finally line up for inspection in *The Unnamable*, where he who is the final reduction of the Beckettian hero takes all his predecessors to task. Moreover, certain archetypes borrowed from other works are rarely forgotten for long: we continually hear of Cain, Jesus, Belacqua and Sordello. The latter first appears in *Dream of Fair to Middling Women*, where Belacqua wishes that the Smeraldina could always appear as she did when he first set eyes on her, 'rapt, like the spirit of the troubadour, casting no shade, herself shade', and only receives his last mention in

Malone Dies. This perpetual recurrence of archetypes strikes one as remarkable in itself, when one bears in mind that nearly twenty years separate the first mention from the last.

This consistency of development does not, however, mean that Beckett's novels are repetitive or at all similar; the *œuvre* grows from skilful, clever but somewhat sterile beginnings to a full and rich maturity. The first novel was written by a sensitive intellectual made disdainful by circumstance, who, feeling incapable of penning a popularly acceptable book, clothed his pain in recondite confabulation spiced with esoteric wit. The later works, while still conceding nothing to current taste, offer for the delight of all who are prepared to make an effort to penetrate them, extraordinarily invigorating and intense fictions that invite an exploration of a world which, on the face of it, seems so unpromising to literary activity, but which on examination shows itself to be one of interest and significance.

Beckett's world is both relevant and irrelevant to that of our day-to-day experience. We do not, of course, expect to learn anything from this author about Proust's Faubourg St. Germain, Forster's India or Faulkner's South; we do not read him to gain an insight into the psychology of human beings in love, as we read Mme. de La Fayette and her numberless followers; we do not believe that he will strive, like D. H. Lawrence, to change our attitude to anything, nor that he will seek, like Mauriac, to translate a religious vision into art. He is unlike other novelists, and indeed seems even deliberately to exclude from his works much of what constitutes the staple of other fiction. But although he is not interested in what attracts his colleagues' attention, he has adopted one small section of the population as his own field of study by predilection: the group that embraces the tramp, the homeless outcast and the poverty-stricken old man. 'My characters have nothing', he has said, but they manage to survive nonetheless. Their means are however totally reduced; Beckett shows what it feels like to have not even the bare necessities, and how one must therefore set about acquiring a bottle of milk and a hole to sleep in. He understands and enables us to understand the tramp's blend of rancour and cringing hopefulness, the beggar's ever-repeated humiliation in accepting contemptuous charity. He puts us inside the skin of the aged vagabond in filthy rags, evil-smelling and covered with running sores, whom bus-conductors refuse to carry and whom landladies rob and expel. He makes us feel what it is to enter an institution, to see your own clothes taken from you for incineration and to suffer the brutalities inflicted by an ill-paid staff. The old, the epileptic, the insane, the chronically jobless, the habitual criminal and those with no relatives or friends, the whole section of society that lives on its fringes, these are the people in whom Beckett is interested, in whom he places his *personæ* and whose mouths he opens to utter his voice. His attitude to them is free from sentimentality, for he lets them reveal themselves often in an unflattering light, but he treats them with compassion. The compassion lies in the plunge which the author makes with his hero, joining him in his sufferings, and then it leaps from the derelict character to man in general, of whom the hero is an archetype: not the man of cities who is blindly and unquestioningly faithful to his lusts and labours, but man reduced to the essential, *sub specie æternitatis*; man conscious of his absurdity as he dies in a fading galaxy, which being mere matter, is unaware of his presence. In taking a tramp as his archetype, Beckett indicts man and reveals his pity for him at the same time: he indicts by portraying a human outcast, perverse, selfish, foolish, wise and courageous by turns and then inducing us to see a resemblance with ourselves; he shows his pity in defending this outcast, by implication at least, and in sympathetically letting him state his case.

Beckett told Driver that he was once taken to task at a London party by an intellectual, who enquired why he (Beckett) always dealt in misery, patronizingly imputing this to an unhappy childhood. Later, in a taxi, Beckett found himself face to face with appeals for famine relief and cancer research. By way of answer to the impertinent question put to him at the party, Beckett told Driver: 'I had a very happy childhood. . . . One does not have to look for distress. It is screaming at you even in the taxis of London'.

Beckett is, of course, what is loosely termed a pessimist, but this means little more than that in company with many another artist of this century, he takes a fairly gloomy, that is to say realistic, view of our condition. He shows man's existence to be what it is: transient, and for much of the time unhappy, ended by a death that makes nonsense of hope. These are *facts* of our situation; Beckett not only states them with undeviating honesty, he also brings with him the fascination of his myths and the tonic of his knowing laughter to help us to bear them. The complaint that his writings betray cynicism or callousness or morbid despair has little or no foundation.

His reports of the small world he has chosen as his own are quite authentic; anyone who doubts whether his heroes speak in the genuine accents of the outlaw has only to open Tony Parker's book of conversations with an inveterate criminal: 'I don't want to mix at all with people who have what might be called "suburban pretensions" or respectability,' the latter says; 'I don't like them, I actively dislike them.' He resents 'the sort of patronizing you get from straight people if you're a criminal. "Fancy that" they say. "In some ways you're just like a human being!" ' and speaks of the 'black hatred' which corporal punishment inspires in those on whom it is inflicted. Transmuted into art, these words become Molloy's ironical reflections upon the police-station incident, or the hero of *La Fin's* thoughts about the landlord who evicted him to make room for a pig catching cold in the street outside.

One must not however exaggerate Beckett's debt to the everyday world; his novels would be of minor interest only if they did nothing but depict the condition of the tramp and the outcast. He uses his understanding of the human bundle of rags asleep on a *métro* grating to create works that are independent of their occasion, and which possess a significance that goes beyond it. Like several other writers, however, he refuses to explain himself, even maintains that there is nothing to explain: 'we have no elucidations to offer', he wrote to the American director Alan Schneider, 'of mysteries that are all of their [journalists'] making. My work is a matter of fundamental sounds (no joke intended) made as fully as possible, and I accept responsibility for nothing else. If people want to have headaches among the overtones, let them. And provide their own aspirin'. His unwillingness to be drawn into exegetical discussions does not spring from disdain or from the deliberate cultivation of obscurity for its own sake. He feels, rightly, that he has said all he wished and was able to say in the works themselves, and that as far as he is concerned there is nothing left to explain. His text is there to be read by all. We have seen, indeed, that his attitude is justified; that although some knowledge of the literary background of the novels and an appreciation of the rigour of their evolution are indispensable to a full understanding of them, there is no call to search for any mysterious 'key' as some critics have imagined. It is quite absurd to suppose that these works are hidden behind a veil of orphic esotericism; which does not mean of course that they do not possess, like any other works of art, their secrets and unsolved enigmas, but simply that with a certain effort their general terms can readily be grasped. Any difficulty arises rather from their denseness and variety, than from the want of an undiscovered sesame. In this *œuvre* formal beauty counts for much: it was a French critic who spoke of Beckett's *amour fou pour la beauté formelle*, and Harold Hobson, asserting of *Waiting for Godot* that its 'beauty depends on symmetry, on balance, on shape', has praised 'the exquisite ordering of its ideas, its echoes, and its associations'. Furthermore, we are presented with a diversity of styles and literary methods: we move from the involved allusiveness of the first novels, through the flat and naked prose of the *Nouvelles*, to the ironical intensity of *Molloy* and *Malone Dies*, and finally to the poetic incantation of *Comment C'est*. These works are continually enlivened by humour, irony, satire, sarcasm, pathos and grief by turns; they are enriched with the power of myth; they bestride two world languages and have a foot in both of two great literary traditions. They owe something not only to Dante, Descartes and Swift, but also to other outstanding figures such as Rabelais, Cervantes, Shakespeare, Sterne and Goncharov. The early works bear the obvious imprint of Joyce's influence, as was to be expected, and later books show parallels with Proust and Kafka which probably do not amount to influence. Professor Kermode has pointed out Beckett's 'old-fashionedness'; there is no doubt that he fits much more easily into an old tradition than into any contemporary school, new novel or existentialist (certainly not into the latter: as Beckett himself bluntly explained to d'Aubarède, who had asked about the possibility of an existentialist key to his work, 'if the subject of my novels could be expressed in philosophical terms, there would have been no reason for my writing them'). These novels are not indeed explicable or paraphrasable in terms of any theory or philosophy; the matter has been put succinctly thus: 'there is no ordinary sense in which they mean anything. Beckett acts through the novel-form, in acts of a purely linguistic nature . . . the man alone in the room makes a novel, uses words, he cannot set out to describe, transcribe or present anything except the illusion of descriptive writing, within the convention'.

The general puzzles and difficulties of Western philosophy are not however alien to this *œuvre*: quite the contrary, as we have frequently seen. Beckett owes a great deal to philosophical dualism in particular. This is not the place to attempt even a brief history of this doctrine, which under one form or another is almost as old as civilization itself. The dualist sees the universe in terms of two quite different and incompatible entities, mind and matter. It is therefore evident that much Eastern philosophy and religion is dualist; so is Plato's thought, and Plotinus'; Christianity is a dualistic religion despite its past hostility to other and more extreme forms of the doctrine, such as those put forward by the Gnostics, or by the Albigensian heretics who viewed procreation with horror as being responsible for dragging heavenly souls back once again into material (therefore evil) bodies so soon after they had managed to struggle free. (A comparison between the tenets of the Cathar heresy on the one hand and the very Beckettian phenomenon of reincarnation on the other provides food for thought; it may not in fact be a mere coincidence that in *Dream of Fair to Middling Women* Toulouse receives the enthusiastic epithet 'most beautiful', the only city mentioned in the canon to be thus honoured.) Descartes' philosophy is of course radically dualistic, following up on medieval thought; after him Malebranche, Spinoza, Geulincx and Leibniz perpetuate and modify the doctrine. It is still very much alive today, despite the efforts of behaviourists in psychology and philosophy to refute it. Professor Ryle's *Concept of Mind* (1949) is the most serious challenge offered to it in modern times, but in spite of his efforts many people remain dualists, just as despite Berkeley most people continue to attribute to a material, non-sensory cause their immaterial sensations of such things as trees. With all the logical difficulties and inconsistencies to which it is subject, it remains therefore a lively doctrine, and it is hardly too much to say that it haunts the thought of Samuel Beckett and lies behind much of his work.

In the *Phædo*, Socrates postulates that 'purification consists in separating the soul as much as possible from the body, and accustoming it to withdraw from all contact with the body and concentrate itself by itself'; Murphy would readily agree. Socrates continues:

> The soul is most like that which is divine, immortal, intelligible, uniform, indissoluble, and ever self-consistent and invariable, whereas the body is most like that which is human, mortal, multiform, unintelligible, dissoluble and never self-consistent,

and, the mysticism and optimism apart, Malone would concur with Plato here. And just as Socrates is led to reject the Pythagorean theory that our soul consists simply in the 'temperament or adjustment' of the physical extremes of hot and cold, wet and dry, so Murphy fails to apply Neary's Neo-Pythagorean technique of 'Attunement' to his own organism; he is a dualist, his body cannot be made to work in any sort of harmony with his mind, and peace only lies for him in running from the domestic acrimony altogether, for like Plotinus in Porphyry's words, he seems 'ashamed of being in a body'; and although he would reject the Plotinian doctrine of ascension to the One, he would agree that accession to whatever nirvana there is requires patience, discipline and self-purification before it can be achieved. Murphy's tragedy is that he is ultimately incapable of the necessary discipline, being too interested in Celia and too ready to fall by the wayside and seek, like Bunyan's hero, an easier byway to truth; in his case, the deceitful temptation is proffered by the insane.

Descartes, the inheritor of several elements of Scholastic philosophy, reached his extreme dualistic position by two routes: the first epistemological, in the *Méditations* (we know our minds directly and without intermediary, but not so our bodies), the second by way of his theory of the emotions, in the *Passions de l'âme*: emotion is an invasion of the mind by the body, against which the former, forewarned by philosophy, must defend itself and then take the offensive by submitting the passions to the control of reason. Descartes' 'myth', as Ryle has called it, was so persuasive as to become widely accepted and taken as axiomatic. Every person was conceived as living through two 'collateral histories'; his body's, public, his mind's, private. 'In his inner life each of us lives the life of a ghostly Robinson Crusoe . . . absolute solitude is . . . the ineluctable destiny of the soul' (Ryle). Moreover, it is impossible for the dualist, if he would be consistent, to distinguish between the sane and the insane; having no access to other minds, no one can decide with confidence whether Smith is *really* mad or merely pretending to be so, like the elder Brutus, for the public good. What strikes Ryle as an intolerable paradox, Beckett embraces wholeheartedly, even perversely: thus Murphy considers the lunatics the only truly wise members of the hospital community, and is quite unappalled at the thought of being a mental Robinson Crusoe. And what goes for Murphy applies equally well to all his successors.

Great as has been the influence of dualistic philosophy on Beckett's thought, it would be idle to pretend that he has his own consistent and systematic theory on the subject. He is quite eclectic, taking from classical philosophers what strikes a chord in his own mind and nothing else; thus the intricate and beautiful occasionalism of Malebranche and Geulincx leaves him quite unmoved; satisfied with their assertion that the mind is thought and the body extension, he is uninterested in their explanations of how the two manage to meet. In a similar way, although he is familiar with Berkeley, he only embraces the sceptical aspect of the latter's thought and rejects its indispensable constructive adjunct. This may be a cavalier way to treat philosophers, but Beckett is not a theorist, he is a novelist, haunted by an overwhelming sense of the uselessness of the body, of the horror of sex, of the imprecision of words, of the inaccuracy of sensory perception and of the indefinability of personal identity. He is therefore grateful to Descartes, Berkeley and Hume for first making him aware of the respectability and theoretical justification of some of his impressions, but there his debt ends.

His attitude to God seems to illustrate the same point. Brought up a believing Protestant, he has said that his faith 'was only irksome and I let it go. My brother and mother got no value from their religion when they died. At the moment of crisis it had no more depth than an old school tie'. And yet he returns frequently to Christian symbolism, notably in the case of Estragon's feet, one of which is blessed and the other damned: 'like the two thieves on the cross'. A case could even be made that there is religious nos-

talgia present in his work. This is going a little too far: Beckett's
heroes certainly languish for the lack of any God to save them,
and frequently give tongue to their anguish, but it would be too
much to say that, like Ingmar Bergman, Beckett is forever wishing God into existence. He seems, in fact, too much of a realist to
nourish any fleeting hope that God may, after all, not really be
dead. He told Shenker unequivocally: 'I'm not interested in any
system. I can't see any trace of any system anywhere', and he did
not (on the subject of God's existence) give Driver the impression
that he cared very much either way. If his work reveals any positive attitude towards God at all, it would seem to be one of loathing and fear, as we have seen from his indictment of the tyrants;
but the 'master' of whom he speaks may represent any sort of
despot, human, institutional or psychological, and not necessarily
a divine or quasi-divine actual being. The God of the Christians,
in whom he once believed, seems now to rouse him only to humorous irreverence: 'The bastard!' says Hamm in mock-annoyance,
'he doesn't exist!' Professor Empson, citing Beckett in *Milton's
God* as a sad example of a writer suffering from the ravages of a
Christian (Empson imagines it to have been a Roman Catholic)
upbringing, would therefore seem to have done him little justice.

*   *   *

Eclectic in its thought, freely selective in its symbolism, recog-
nizing no binding *engagement* whatsoever to any philosophical
system or religious creed, the Beckettian *œuvre* is sufficient unto
itself. The words from the Proust essay quoted above are its
motto: it prefers to plunge downwards rather than swim abroad,
to know itself more thoroughly than to explore the world about.
As Proust has it, and as Beckett would agree, the artist moves in
the only direction open to him: into himself, in search of a starker,
poorer, but more universally valid self.

Moreover, Beckett has made his own a literary realm hitherto
neglected as worthless: 'I'm working with impotence, ignorance',
he has said. 'I don't think impotence has been exploited in the
past. There seems to be a kind of æsthetic axiom that expression
is an achievement – must be an achievement. My little exploration is that whole zone of being that has always been set aside by

artists as something unusable – as something by definition incompatible with art.'

As a novelist of such revolutionary significance, Beckett cannot
be ignored, nor passed over in a sentence. He is there, looming
large and inescapable on the literary landscape; the games which
he has been playing with words for over thirty years have gradually become matters of immediate relevancy to us. His extraordinary hero roams about in our consciousness, a haunting and
troublesome shadow. The croak of Molloy's voice, his ragged
clothes, his limping gait, his festering sores, live on in our
memory. We have, in Beckett's novels, new heroes, unfamiliar
gods, a whole modern mythology. These fictions tell simply but
insistently the story of a fragile voice – a human voice – which
refuses stubbornly to die, which flickers on, somehow resisting
submersion and assimilation, repelling every assault:

Mahood is silent, that is to say his voice continues, but is no longer
renewed. Do they consider me so plastered with their rubbish that I
can never extricate myself, never make a gesture but their cast must
come to life? But within, motionless, I can live, and utter me, for no
ears but my own. . . .

(The Unnamable)

POSTSCRIPT (1970)

who may tell the tale / of the old man? / weigh absence in a
scale? / mete want with a span? / the sum assess / of the
world's woes? / nothingness / in words enclose?

WATT

SINCE I wrote this book, Beckett has published six new short texts,
and has translated into English or French a few of the remaining
single-language works in the fictional canon. Thus *From an Abandoned Work* and *Watt* have appeared in French (translated in
collaboration with Ludovic and Agnès Janvier), and *The Calmative*
and all the *Texts for Nothing* have been rendered into English by
Beckett working alone.[1] This catching-up with the backlog of translation is as fascinating as the reader of my earlier pages on Beckett's
re-creations would expect. *D'un ouvrage abandonné* reproduces
remarkably well the rhythms of the original, and the French *Watt*
manages to be close and faithful both to the sense and as far as
possible to the rhythms and forms of the English novel. Some of the
linguistic jokes have had to be dropped (the Addenda section, in
particular, has been thinned out), but renderings of other tricky
passages are impressive, such as Grehan's song to Nelly, which comes
out a shade more smutty in French. On the other side, *The Calmative*
reveals once again the idiosyncratic manner of the translator of
Malone Dies and *The Unnamable*: English syntax is nonchalantly
ignored ('Was I hungry itself?') and French idioms are rendered with
comic literalness ('pulling the devil by the tail'). Clearly Beckett, in
common with other contemporary translators, is of the opinion that
the recipient language should bend to receive the foreign text's
characteristic asperities, and not vice versa.

[1] The short story I called *The Sedative* was in the end not translated with
Richard Seaver's assistance (see p. 110 above). Furthermore, the 1945
stories have been collected, in the Grove Press volume *Stories and Texts for
Nothing*, and in *No's Knife* (Calder and Boyars). Both collections appeared in
1967 and contain the contents of the Minuit *Nouvelles et Textes pour rien*, to
which the Calder volume adds *From an Abandoned Work, Enough, Imagination
Dead Imagine* and *Ping*.

As far as original works are concerned, Beckett has succeeded in wresting a few more pieces from the silence since he completed *How It Is*. In order of composition, they are:

Imagination morte imaginez (*Imagination Dead Imagine*)
Assez (*Enough*)
Dans le cylindre
L'Issue
Bing (*Ping*)
Sans

Where the text has been translated, the English title follows the French. Of *Dans le cylindre* and *L'Issue* Mr. Beckett writes:

[They] should be regarded as rejected texts though released for limited publication. They and I think six or seven other such may be regarded as leading up to *Bing* though there is a jump from them to it which I mercifully forget. *Assez* is out of place in the series and I don't know what came over me.

All these brief texts continue the drama of voices in the mind first staged in *Texts for Nothing*, with its yes/no and I/it and silence/non-silence dichotomies. One of them, *Imagination Dead Imagine*, looks back to *The Unnamable* and the rotunda image, and another, *Sans*, is constructed like *How It Is*, that is in verses which here are broken into short sentences with few main verbs and so are less continuous in their flow.

All these texts, too, are painstakingly built (*Bing*, for instance, ran through at least ten drafts). Sometimes the principle of construction is almost mathematical, as in *Watt* and *Imagination*, the latter of which works out in careful detail the spatial relationships between the recumbent bodies of an old man and woman. In other cases the French has a strongly poetic and incantatory flavour, as in *Bing* and *Sans*, with their marked rhythms and steady beat in the diction. Everywhere the syntax is more or less elliptical and condensed, for Beckett is evolving a new kind of French for his purposes, as I implied in my discussion of *Comment C'est*; the remarks on style in Chapter 8, in fact, have been borne out by subsequent developments. Even the themes, such as they are in these diaphanous fragments, are familiar: the notion of imprisonment dominates *Imagination*, *Dans le cylindre* and *Bing*. As I said on p. 196 above, Beckett is adding little that is new to his vision; even the lyrical, *vie sentimentale* note of *Enough*[1] will not sound unfamiliar to those conversant with the latest dramatic works like *Film* and *Eh Joe:*

> We lived on flowers. So much for sustenance. He halted and without having to stoop caught up a handful of petals. Then moved munching on. They had on the whole a calming action. We were on the whole calm. More and more. All was. This notion of calm comes from him. Without him I would not have had it. Now I'll wipe out everything but the flowers. No more rain. No more mounds. Nothing but the two of us dragging through the flowers. Enough my old breasts feel his old hand.   (*No's Knife*, p. 159)

But it is hardly meaningful to speak of themes in these short fictions. They are formal exercises, exploring rhythm, repetition and circularity, rather than anything that can truly be identified as a situation; they are far from being nonsense and gibberish, but they can nonetheless only be characterized by the terms Beckett applied to Watt's experiences: 'of great formal brilliance and indeterminable purport'. They round the canon off most elegantly, but they add little to it. With characteristic modesty, Beckett admits that his Mallarmean body-clinch with words is not getting him anywhere: his 'fiascos', as he self-deprecatingly terms these latest texts, are released for the most part as exquisite bibliophilic limited editions or in *livres d'artiste* (Arikha has illustrated *L'Issue*, for example, and Deyrolle *Le Séjour*, one of the pre-*Bing* group).

*   *   *

On re-reading my book with a view to preparing this new edition, I occasionally felt that, if I were writing it now, I should alter the emphasis slightly. It might be of interest to suggest in what ways I would do so. In the first place, I think, I would lay greater stress on the humour of Beckett's writing, which I seem to be more susceptible to now than I was ten years ago. The early books, indeed, are uproariously funny, particularly when you are in a position to understand the in-jokes. It is characteristic of Beckett, for example, that as an undergraduate he should have read to the Modern Language Society

---

[1] The sex of the narrator in this piece, as an examination of the definitive text in the collection *Têtes-mortes* (Paris: Editions de Minuit, 1967) shows, is left deliberately indeterminate by the avoidance of all verbal agreements.

at Trinity a paper on 'Les Convergistes', who, he claimed, were a leading literary group in Paris. Only his friends were not taken in by the dead-pan manner of the speaker and hid their giggles at the outrageous obscenity of his title. In like manner, he cloaked a daring skit on the ban on importation of contraceptive sheaths into Eire under the guise of a philosophical dialogue which he wrote for the College newspaper. One wonders what effect the rage of the lady undergraduates, had they understood the puns, would have had on the Foundation Scholar's career. Safely away from Trinity and the Irish censor, Beckett recalled that the Abbey Theatre loo made a deafening noise when the chain was pulled; Murphy, therefore, decrees that his earthly remains shall be flushed down it 'if possible during the performance of a piece', to ensure that his last exit shall be accompanied by titters.

Today, too, I would emphasize the comedy of enumeration in *Watt*, the very real humour of the *Nouvelles* ('a comedian . . . was telling a funny story about a fiasco. Its point escaped me. He used the word snail, or slug, to the delight of all present. The women seemed even more entertained than their escorts . . .'), the stylish wit of the Trilogy and *How It Is*, and the Flaubertian echoes in *Mercier et Camier*, which must surely have been influenced by that masterpiece of donnish irony, *Bouvard et Pécuchet*. Not that I would want to play down the grief and misery which permeate so much of Beckett's work; but I would want to stress that like many other great comic novelists, Beckett makes a pessimistic vision profoundly risible – and that that, as he might himself put it, 'is a great tonic'. To be aware of one's unhappiness and yet to be able to laugh at it, therein lies Beckett's great and noble lesson for us.

Were I writing now, I should also want to explore further Beckett's recurrent symbolism: the journey, the room, the sea, the pit, the constant oscillation, in fact, between claustrophobia and agoraphobia which Kafka projects in *The Burrow*. I should try, too, to interpret some of the other novels on the lines of my more recent essays on *Molloy* and *Malone Dies*, probing, for example, the moving change of perspective that occurs from within the hero in Part I of *Molloy*, to outside him in Part II. It is this kind of shift, I am convinced, which gives Beckett's novels their power.

I would still consider *Molloy* his greatest achievement, his most profound and complex creative feat. It seems now to be generally agreed that if Beckett can be compared with Mann, Joyce, Proust and Kafka, it is on the strength, very largely, of this magnificent novel. The works preceding it seem to be sketches for the masterpiece: and since *Molloy* it cannot really be claimed that Beckett has written a book of similar weight and stature. I would, of course, continue to stress the organic nature of the entire canon, and would be less diffident than I was about stating my conviction that Beckett really does belong in the company just referred to. But since the Swedish Academy's pronouncement, one is no longer doing anything very daring in saying that Beckett is one of the greatest novelists of the century. When my book was accepted for publication, however, I was advised to tone down the dithyrambics, so it is nice to be proved right.

It is, surely, one of the paradoxes of contemporary literature that its greatest destroyer should at the same time be one of its greatest glories. Beckett is unique in his conception of fiction as something which collapses in upon itself from book to book: no other writer has pursued an issue as remorselessly as Beckett his search for the essential story and the elusive being. Having stripped away the last layers of the fictional onion, he is left, in *Bing* and *Sans*, ruefully contemplating the core. But in the act of stripping his work down he has – and this is what makes him such an important and impressive writer – produced two or three novels of the very highest quality, and one at least that ranks as a masterpiece of the genre.

*   *   *

In preparing this new edition, I have simplified the Bibliography and brought it up to date, expanded the Index, and corrected a few errors and misprints. To do more would have meant rewriting the book in very different terms, and I did not feel at liberty to undertake this. *The Novels of Samuel Beckett* seems to have become a standard work, and this prevents me from tampering with it to any great extent. I have not even brought the quotations from *Texts for Nothing* and *How It Is* into conformity with the definitive versions which appeared after my study, since as I explain in the Preface those quotations were translated by the author himself. This is not to say that I entirely approve of the work, or that I would deal with the subject in the same way if I were writing on it now. Every author has mixed feelings about his first book, and I am no exception: my affection is tempered by a slightly baffled disappointment, my mild irritation at asperities and naïveties by nostalgia for a lost fluency. Now – assuming that a costive near-silence before the terrifying complexities of fiction criticism would permit it – I should write more briefly and synthetically. But this guide, drawn up in all innocence of heart, has served, and apparently still serves, a useful purpose. So I send it forth on the second phase of its existence in the hope that it will continue to be of assistance to those making a first approach to that towering literary monument, the fiction of Samuel Beckett.

Norwich, New Year 1970

SELECT BIBLIOGRAPHY

THIS list contains a minimum of information, since fuller details can be found in Raymond Federman and John Fletcher's *Samuel Beckett: His Works and His Critics, an Essay in Bibliography* (Berkeley and Los Angeles: University of California Press, 1970). Approximate dates of composition of Beckett's works, where known and where differing considerably from dates of publication, are given in square brackets; see also ' Bibliographical Postscript ', p. 245.

A. Beckett's Published Fiction

I. English Fiction

Assumption (1929)
Sedendo et Quiescendo (1932)
Text (1932)
More Pricks than Kicks (1934)
A Case in a Thousand (1934)
Murphy (1938)
Watt ([1942–1944] 1953)
From an Abandoned Work (1956)
Jem Higgins' Love-Letter to the Alba ([1932] 1965)

II. French Translations of the English Fiction

Murphy ([1939] 1947)
D'un ouvrage abandonné (1967)
Watt (1968)

III. French Fiction

Suite (1946)
L'Expulsé (1946)
Molloy ([1947] 1951)
Malone meurt ([1948] 1951)
L'Innommable ([1949] 1953)
Nouvelles et Textes pour rien ([1945, 1950] 1955)
Comment C'est (1961)

Imagination morte imaginez (1965)
Mercier et Camier, ch. XI ([1946] 1965)
Assez (1966)
Bing (1966)
Dans le cylindre (1967)
L'Issue ([1966] 1968)
Sans (1969)

IV. English Translations of the French Fiction

Two Fragments (1950)
The End (1954)
Molloy (1955)
Malone Dies (1956)
The Unnamable (1958)
Text for Nothing I (1959)
The Expelled (1962)
How It Is (1964)
Imagination Dead Imagine (1965)
Stories and Texts for Nothing (1967)
Ping (1967)
Enough (1967)

B. Beckett's Known Unpublished Fiction

Dream of Fair to Middling Women [1932]
Les Bosquets de Bondy [1945]
Premier Amour [1946]
Mercier et Camier [1946]
Chacun son dépeupleur [1966]

Editions

Beckett's fiction is published in French by Editions de Minuit in Paris. So far this publisher has not issued any collected volume, except *Nouvelles et Textes pour rien* and *Têtes-mortes* (*D'un ouvrage abandonné*, *Assez*, *Imagination morte imaginez* and *Bing*); all the other works are published separately. They are: *Murphy*, *Molloy*, *Malone meurt*, *L'Innommable*, *Comment C'est* and *Watt*. In the next edition of *Têtes-mortes*, Mr. Beckett tells me, *Sans* (first published in

La Quinzaine Littéraire for November 1 to 15, 1969), 'will un-doubtedly appear', together, perhaps, with the 'least objectionable of the rejected texts' written recently.

In Great Britain Calder and Boyars publish *Murphy*, *Watt* and *How It Is* as separate volumes. The Trilogy (*Molloy*, *Malone Dies*, *The Unnamable*) is issued in one volume, and *No's Knife* collects the short stories of 1945 (*The Expelled*, *The Calmative*, *The End*), the thirteen *Texts for Nothing*, *From an Abandoned Work*, *Enough*, *Imagination Dead Imagine* and *Ping*.

In the United States, Grove Press issue *Murphy*, *Watt* and *How It Is* separately. The Trilogy is published as *Three Novels*, and *Stories and Texts for Nothing* contains those sixteen works.

As far as Beckett himself is concerned, the canon begins with *Murphy* and ends (at present) with *Sans*. All fiction not regularly published by Editions de Minuit, Calder and Boyars and Grove Press is considered by the author as jettisoned or rejected. The essential fiction of Samuel Beckett, therefore, is contained in the five volumes published by Calder and Boyars, to take an example.

C. Published Interviews and Other Biographical Sources Consulted

Guggenheim, P. (1946). *Out of This Century* (New York: Dial Press), pp. 194–242.

Monnier, A., J. Thomas and R. Blin (1953). *Arts*, July 3–9, p. 5.

Shenker, I. (1956). 'Moody Man of Letters'. *New York Times*, May 6, sec. 2, pp. x, 1, 3.

Gilbert, S., ed. (1957). *Letters of James Joyce* (London: Faber and Faber), pp. 280–283, 325.

Anon. (1958). 'Profile: Messenger of Gloom'. *The Observer*, November 9, p. 13.

Schneider, A. (1958). 'Waiting for Beckett: A Personal Chronicle'. *Chelsea Review*, 2 (Autumn), 3–20.

Ellmann, R. (1959). *James Joyce* (New York: Oxford University Press), *passim*.

D'Aubarède, G. (1961). 'En attendant . . . Beckett'. *Nouvelles Littéraires*, February 16, pp. 1, 7.

SELECT BIBLIOGRAPHY

Driver. T. F. (1961). 'Beckett by the Madeleine'. *Columbia University Forum*, IV (Summer), 21–25.

D. Criticism

Below are listed items quoted, drawn upon or otherwise used in the present study.

I. Books

Mayoux, J.-J. (1960). *Vivants Piliers* (Paris: Julliard), pp. 271–291.

Kenner, H. (1961). *Samuel Beckett, a Critical Study* (New York: Grove Press: London: Calder and Boyars).

II. Articles

Muir, E. (1934). Review of *More Pricks than Kicks*. *The Listener*, July 4, p. 42.

Powell, D. (1938). Review of *Murphy*. *Sunday Times*, March 13, p. 8.

Bataille, G. (1951). 'Le Silence de Molloy'. *Critique*, VII (May), 387–396.

Fouchet, M.-P. (1951). Review of *Molloy*. *Carrefour*, April 24, p. 8.

Kanters, R. (1951). Review of *Molloy*. *Age Nouveau*, 62 (June), 68–70.

Nadeau, M. (1951). 'Samuel Beckett, l'humour et le néant'. *Mercure de France*, 1056 (August), 693–697.

Pingaud, B. (1951). Review of *Molloy*. *Esprit*, XIX (September), 423–425.

Pouillon, J. (1951). Review of *Molloy*. *Temps Modernes*, 69 (July), 184–186.

Nadeau, M. (1952). 'Samuel Beckett, ou le droit au silence'. *Temps Modernes*, 75 (January), 1275–1282.

Blanchot, M. (1953). 'Où maintenant? Qui maintenant?' *Nouvelle Revue Française*, 11 (October), 678–686.

Bonnefoi, G. (1956). 'Textes pour rien?' *Lettres Nouvelles*, 36 (March), 424–430.

Hobson, H. (1956). 'Samuel Beckett, Dramatist of the Year'. *International Theatre Annual*, 1 (1956), 153–155.

Anon. (1958). Review of *Watt*. *Times Literary Supplement*, March 28, p. 168.

Bowles, P. (1958). 'How Samuel Beckett Sees the Universe'. *The Listener*, June 19, pp. 1011–1012.

Brooke-Rose, C. (1958). 'Samuel Beckett and the Anti-Novel'. *London Magazine*, V (December), 38–46.

Kern, E. (1959). 'Moran-Molloy: the Hero as Author'. *Perspective*, XI (Autumn), 183–193.

Heppenstall, R. (1960). Review of the Trilogy. *Observer*, April 10, p. 20.

Pritchett, V. S. (1960). 'An Irish Oblomov'. *New Statesman*, April 2, p. 489.

Chapsal, M. (1961). 'Le Jeune Roman'. *L'Express*, January 12, p. 51.

Cohn, R. (1961). 'Samuel Beckett, Self-Translator'. *PMLA*, LXXVI (December), 613–621.

Fletcher, J. (1961). Review of *Comment C'est*. *Lettres Nouvelles*, 13 (April), 169–171.

Luccioni, G. (1961). Review of *Comment C'est*. *Esprit*, XXIX (April), 710–713.

Mercier, V. (1961). 'Samuel Beckett and the Sheela-na-'gig'. *Kenyon Review*, XXIII (Spring), 299–324.

Fletcher, D. (1962). 'Molloy for Prime Minister'. *Left Wing*, November, pp. 22–24.

Fletcher, J. (1962). 'Samuel Beckett et Jonathan Swift: vers une étude comparée'. *Annales de la Faculté des Lettres de Toulouse: Littératures X* (1962), 81–117.

Kermode, F. (1962). Review of Kenner's *Samuel Beckett*. *New Statesman*, November 2, p. 622.

E. Some Background Materials

Below are listed a few general works which, among those that I have myself consulted with profit, are easily accessible and should prove useful to anyone studying Beckett's writings.

Dante. *Divine Comedy*, especially *Hell* and *Purgatory*.

Descartes. *Méditations* and *Passions de l'âme*.
Keeling, S. V. *Descartes* (London: Benn, 1934).
McCracken, D. J. *Thinking and Valuing* (London: Macmillan, 1950; good on Geulincx).
Ryle, G. *The Concept of Mind*, and Plato: *Phaedo*, both published by Penguin Books.

Swift. *Tale of a Tub*, *Gulliver's Travels*, *A Modest Proposal*, etc.
Ewald, W. B., Jr. *The Masks of Jonathan Swift* (Oxford: Blackwell, 1954).
Leavis, F. R. 'The Irony of Swift', in *The Common Pursuit* (Penguin Books).

Booth, W. C. *The Rhetoric of Fiction* (University of Chicago Press, 1961; for the 'self-conscious narrator', etc.)

Bibliographical Postscript

Bibliographical work is always provisional, and never more so than in the case of a living writer. As these pages go to press, Editions de Minuit announce the publication during 1970 of the hitherto discarded works *Premier Amour*, *Mercier et Camier* and *Le Dépeupleur* (see Chapter 4 and p. 241).

INDEX NOMINUM

Beckett's characters are printed in heavy type

INDEX NOMINUM

INDEX RERUM

Fictional themes are printed in heavy type